CIVIL WAR COLLECTOR'S ENCYCLOPEDIA

Volumes III, IV & V
Complete & Unabridged in
This Volume

by Francis A. Lord

BLUE & GREY PRESS

CIVIL WAR COLLECTOR'S ENCYCLOPEDIA
Volumes III, IV and IV

This edition published in 1995 by
BLUE & GREY PRESS
by permission and in conjunction with
Morningside House, Inc., under an agreement between
Morningside House and Francis A. Lord, copyright holder.

Blue & Grey Press
A division of Book Sales, Inc.
114 Northfield Avenue
Edison, New Jersey 08837

ISBN 0-7858-0468-4

Library of Congress Catalog Card Number: 63-14636

MANUFACTURED IN THE UNITED STATES OF AMERICA

VOLUME III

TO

Bill Moore of Baton Rouge, Louisiana

A real expert and
a great friend

FOREWORD

Because of the enthusiastic response to the first two volumes of the *Collector's Encyclopedia,* the author early realized that new data and previously unknown items of the 1861-1865 war **must** be preserved for posterity! Literally hundreds of letters both from home and abroad, have brought in new information. The assistance of these contributors has been substantial in preparation of this book. In several instances they have come up with important variations of items which appeared in the first two volumes of the *Encyclopedia* as, for example, some interesting types of mess kits. Of course, these variations are included in the present volume.

INTRODUCTION

I make no point in praise either to the author or to the contents of this Civil War Encyclopedia; it is my wish to be factual. Dr. Lord needs no 'yes' man to assure him, or any other, that he is presenting a service of revelation — the memorable artifacts in use by the Blue and Gray. What once were the fancies and foibles of conjecture in the contest between the North and the South are now becoming a proud excitement of historical discovery.

> "The bravest men that ever fought
> For this land of ours were boys.
> That boyhood faith may this day renew,
> Till it rivet a friendship chain
> To hold us close and keep us true
> While the last two boys remain."

This poem, written by a newspaper man in dedication to the survivors, both the Blue and the Gray, no longer can be applied to the valiant veterans who gathered for a Regimental Reunion. It can, however, score with triumph "To hold us close and keep us true" — we, the descendants of this heritage. In coordination with the 'leadership' of this Encyclopedia we are finding ourselves important contributors to the continued unearthing of our Civil War history. Yea, in the author's acknowledgements of and to those of us who "have contributed very substantially and unselfishly to this third volume", falls the gist and meaning of this work — its publication, coupled with the contributions of each historian and relic buff, has brought forth a proud excitement of discovery. Too, what we have brought to light further enhances our national heritage, giving us the degrees of eager students who are continually developing greater knowledge that brings forth delightful pleasure of fact. More importantly, perhaps, such knitting together of newly-brought-to-light memorabilia is fostering fast friendships that otherwise may not have been possible. This common ground of our deep love of the War Between — —, has brought about, and will continue to do so, a kinship of one abiding interest; history continues to grow, and friendships become more deeply cemented . . . "To hold us close and keep us true."

There is no need to expostulate on the author's handling of the items described and pictured, the contents speak for themselves. The subjects are many and varied, with no pretense attempted to glorify or romance. The articles are simply and succinctly described, giving due credit to the reader's intelligence of the item presented in a precise way — its meaning, its use, and, in many instances, its proof of soldiers ownership. Webster defines encyclopedia as . . . "General education; a work that contains information on a particular branch of knowledge, usually in articles arranged alphabetically by subject." Ah, then we have such in Dr. Lord's Civil War Collector's Encyclopedia, Volume 3! The contents run the gamut from Adjutant's Knapsack, Confederate, to Writing Kit, Yankee. Little doubt remains as to the item being factual, for manufactures material is described, dimensions are given, "where found" brings proof of battle or campsite use, as well as identification of soldiers ownership so inscribed for posterity. The author freely bows in appreciation of all contributions, giving due credit to all who combed their personal collections to aid in the continued research of Civil War knowledge.

Dr. Lord acknowledges there is "much work to be done", whether it be cleaning materials for uniforms and equipment, Confederate canteens that "are constantly turning up", or mess kits that "continue to intrigue the collector." Indeed so! If this were not true, the battle would be won with no intrigue remaining to continue the delving into fact. This, then, gives us the impetus to search more, to question further, to bring to light. Perhaps the most revealing fact is the realization that this volume, an extended and expanded search of the previous two, does even more to bring together all who express their desire for greater knowledge of this, our American Heritage through destiny.

Mayhap I do, after all, praise Dr. Lord for this presentation. For without his painstaking research, without his patience, durability and understanding of the collector's idiosyncracies, such a compilation of encyclopedic history may never have come to light. What greater knowledge to spur us on!

"Why they fought, why lost, who triumphed, who was wrong, or who was right,
Matters not; They were our brothers, and were not afraid to fight.
Let us form a noble order with sweet freedom for our shrine,
And for each enwreath a token — The Palmetto and the Pine."

In full realization of the historic 'worth' of this Encyclopedia,

I am — Jack Magune

ABOUT THE AUTHOR

Since his retirement as Professor Emeritus in History from the University of South Carolina, the author has concentrated his research on Civil War artifacts. This third volume in the series is the result of his continuing effort to utilize his extensive knowledge of Civil War memorabilia with the enthusiastic support of qualified experts, both here and abroad.

As governor of the Company of Military Historians and Associate Curator of Military History, South Carolina Museum Commission, he maintains close contact with other Civil War experts and museums. This contact is constantly expanding by his frequent appearances as guest speaker to Civil War Round Tables and similar historically oriented groups interested in the 1861-1865 struggle. By means of an extensive correspondence with collectors all over the world as well as his specialized displays of Civil War items at gun shows, Dr. Lord keeps on top of new discoveries in the field of Civil War collecting.

For over thirty years the author has contributed specialized studies on the Civil War to American and foreign journals. In addition, he has written the following:

They Fought for the Union (1960)

Civil War Collector's Encyclopedia, Volume I (1963)

Bands and Drummer Boys of the Civil War (1966)

Civil War Sutlers and Their Wares (1969)

Lincoln's Railroad Man: Herman Haupt (1969)

Uniforms of the Civil War (1970)

Civil War Collector's Encyclopedia, Volume II (1975)

Civil War Collector's Encyclopedia, Volume III (1979)

ADDITIONS AND CORRECTIONS
TO VOLUME III OF THE
CIVIL WAR COLLECTOR'S ENCYCLOPEDIA

Box Clamp (Vol. III, pp. 19-20)
This is actually a wick holder for an oil or kerosene lamp. The two bumps on the sides are to keep the wick holder from dropping all the way down into the lamp. The little punches are like gear teeth for raising or lowering the wick. (See also "Lamp Fixtures" in this volume.)

Charles S. Harris
Ooltewah, Tennessee

Fuze Wrench (Vol. III, p. 78)
The oval brass key in the center of the upper left hand illustration is actually a wrench or key to open the wooden cartridge boxes. The key came with the wooden box and fitted exactly the latch screw on the box.

Jesse Livingston
Troy, Tennessee

ACKNOWLEDGMENTS

As with the previous two volumes of the *Civil War Collector's Encyclopedia,* this third volume has been made possible by collectors' contributions. The following individuals, genuine enthusiasts in preserving Civil War memorabilia, have contributed very substantially and unselfishly to this third volume. Not only am I personally indebted to their assistance, but present and future collectors as well! Unless otherwise indicated, however, items shown are from the author's collection.

DELMER P. ANDERSON; Santa Maria, California
MARGIE BEARSS; Brandon, Mississippi
ARTHUR LEE BREWER; Durham, North Carolina
W. A. CLARK; New Egypt, New Jersey
ROBERT CORRETTE; Fitzwilliam, New Hampshire
R. V. CROFOOT; Orlando, Florida
ROGER DAVIS; Keokuk, Iowa
TOM S. DICKEY; Atlanta, Georgia
CHARLES EDELMAN; Homeland, California
W. E. ERQUITT; Atlanta, Georgia
MAURICE GARB; Baton Rouge, Louisiana
RODNEY O. GRAGG; Montreat, North Carolina
E. CANTEY HAILE, JR.; Columbia, South Carolina
DAVE HANNAH; Rexburg, Idaho
T. SHERMAN HARDING, III; Orlando, Florida
DAVE HOLDER; West Sussex, England
BILL HOWARD; Delmar, New York
JOHN HUGHES; Battle Creek, Michigan
FRANK A. HUNTSMAN; Hutchinson, Kansas
ROBERT E. JONES; Benton, Arkansas
LON WILLIAM KEIM; Coralville, Iowa
WILLIAM LANGLOIS; San Francisco, California
J. W. LEECH; Grand Junction, Colorado
RICHARD LUCAS; Rodeo, California
TOM MacDONALD; Eustis, Maine
H. MICHAEL MADAUS; Milwaukee, Wisconsin
JACK MAGUNE; Worcester, Massachusetts
CRAIG MARGISON; Riverside, California
JOHN MARGREITER; St. Louis, Missouri
JOHN A. MARKS; Memphis, Tennessee
KEN MATTERN; Wayne, Pennsylvania
JAMES M. McCAFFREY; Houston, Texas

WILLIAM C. McKENNA; Westmont, New Jersey
BILL MOORE; Baton Rouge, Louisiana
DAVID M. MORROW; Woodbridge, Virginia
CLYDE E. NOBLE; Athens, Georgia
SEWARD R. OSBORNE, JR.; Olivebridge, New York
RONN PALM; Monroeville, Pennsylvania
JEFF PEFFER; Etters, Pennsylvania
GERALD F. SAUER; Santa Rosa, California
VERNON SCOONE; Baltimore, Maryland
LOUIS G. STOCKHO: Vero Beach, Florida
A. L. TAFEL; Newark, Delaware
MIKE WOSHNER; Pittsburgh, Pennsylvania

Special thanks to RON TUNISON of Elmhurst, New York for the cover jacket.

ADJUTANT'S KNAPSACK (C.S.)

ADJUTANT'S KNAPSACK (C.S.): A very rare Confederate adjutant's knapsack. The frame is of pine wood, covered with black canvas on oil cloth material. The straps are of cotton.

Dimensions: 15 inches tall, 15 inches wide, 4¼ inches deep. Equipped with drawers of pine wood.

Markings: On one drawer, written in pencil: LT. W. E. CAMPBELL
Co. "F" 8th S.C.I.
Bratton's Brig.
Field's Division
Longstreet's Corps
    A.N.V.
General R. E. Lee Commanding
8th April 1865

ADJUTANT'S KNAPSACK (C.S.)

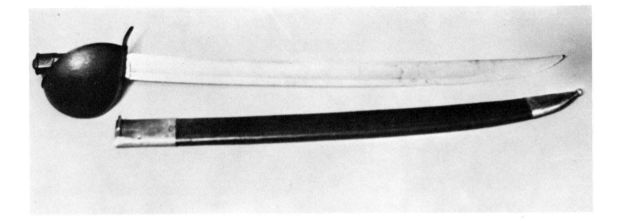

ALABAMA CUTLASS (C.S.): An undated cutlass taken off the Confederate ship **Alabama** in 1864. From the collection of the Commandant, Washington Navy Yard, Washington, D.C.

Dimensions: Length overall — 33 inches; Length of blade 26½ inches; Width of blade 1⅜ inches. Black painted hand guard; black leather scabbard with brass furniture.

ANDERSON TROOP IDENTIFICATION DISC: A rare "dog tag" worn by CALEB B. KIMBER of the Anderson Troop of Philadelphia (15th Pennsylvania Cavalry). Caleb Kimber was a member of Co. "B". [T. SHERMAN HARDING, III; Orlando, Florida]

ARTILLERY BRIDLE (U.S.): Made of heavy black leather, measuring 25½ inches from top of headstall to bottom of bit. The brass rosettes on each side of the blinders are 1½ inches in diameter and are decorated with **U.S.** in black letters. This bridle was used by a New York unit during the War.

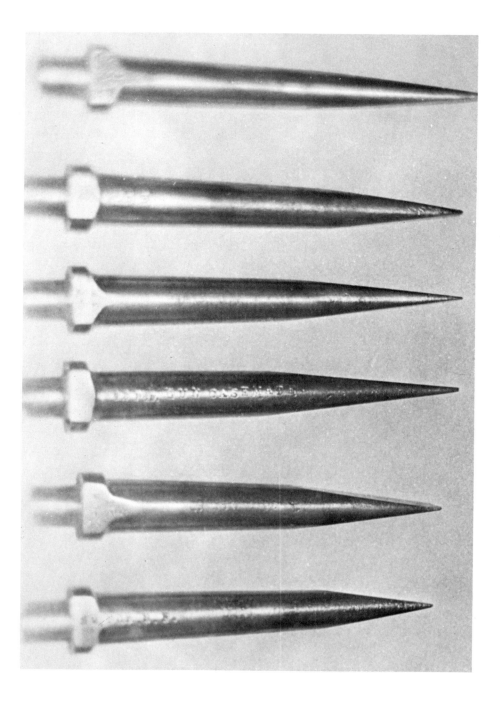

ARTILLERY GUN SIGHTS: Shown here are examples of artillery gun sights from the collection of W. E. ERQUITT of Atlanta, Georgia. These sights are for cannon ranging from howitzers up to large Parrotts and comprise only half of ERQUITT'S fine collection. Each sight is marked for its particular gun type.

AXE HEADS: Most relic seekers have found axe heads on battlefields and campsites. Shown here are eight examples. Reading left to right:

Top Row:
From C.S. breastworks at Port Hudson. **Dimensions:** 8 inches long with a 4⅞ inch blade.

From the Whitmarsh Battery, Georgia, 1862. **Dimensions:** 6¼ inches long with a 4½ inch blade. **Marked:** 8.

Bottom Row:
From the battlefield of Spotsylvania. **Dimensions:** 7⅝ inches long with a 4¼ inch blade.

From the camp of the U.S. 2nd Army Corps at Falmouth. **Dimensions:** 7¼ inches long with a 5 inch blade.

From Sherman's campsite at Edward's Station, Mississippi. **Dimensions:** 7½ inches long with a 5 inch blade.

From Stafford Heights, Fredericksburg. **Dimensions:** 7 inches long with a 5½ inch blade.

From camp of the 16th Arkansas Infantry at Port Hudson. **Dimensions:** 6¾ inches long with a 4¼ inch blade.

From Jackson's headquarters at the Yerby House, Fredericksburg. **Dimensions:** 8 inches long with a 5 inch blade.

AXE SHEATHS: Certainly axe sheaths are among the rarest of Civil War items. The two shown here are both definitely of the Civil War era; the sheath with the flap is of black leather — 9½ inches long, 4½ inches wide. **Markings:** Aug. 2, 1864.

The longer sheath is brown leather and originally had a strap and belt loops. It is 9⅝ inches long at the top, 10 inches long at the bottom and is 6 inches wide. **Markings:** Axe Sling, January 1863.

BARRACKS LAMPS

BARRACKS LAMPS: These two brass lamps were found in a collection of supplies for a U.S. barracks during the Civil War. They are typical of the non-military lamps purchased by the Federal Government for use at the permanent installations at the staging depots behind the front.

BARRACKS MATCH BOXES

BARRACKS MATCH BOXES: Barracks were generally heated by wood stoves and the match boxes shown here were nailed or screwed to the barracks' wall. These are both made of cast iron. The bottoms of each are ribbed for striking matches. Lids are decorated in an attractive manner as shown in the photograph.

Dimensions of Each: 4 inches long, 2½ inches wide, 1⅛ inches deep.

Markings: Match box on the left: SELF CLOSING FOR MATCHES
Patented Dec. 20, 1861
H. W. & Co.
New Haven

Match box on the right: Picture of a dog and
PAT'D Jan. 21, 1862

Porcelain Match Box: Dimensions: 4½ inches long, 2½ inches wide, 1¼ inches deep. Inside of cover is ribbed to permit striking of matches. **Markings:** Crossed flags on front and back. On top there is a replica of U.S. fractional currency — 25 cents, March 3, 1863.

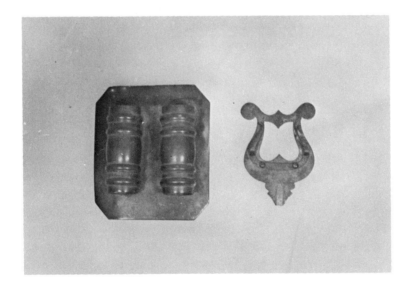

BATTLEFIELD MUSICAL INSTRUMENT ITEMS: As is well known the Civil War regiments had their own bands as well as company fifers, buglers, and drummers. Shown here are various items recovered from camp sites and battlefields. The drum stick holder came from a Rhode Island unit's picket post 4 miles out of Harper's Ferry. The music sheet holder is from the battlefield of Fisher's Hill, Virginia. The horn

BATTLEFIELD MUSICAL INSTRUMENT

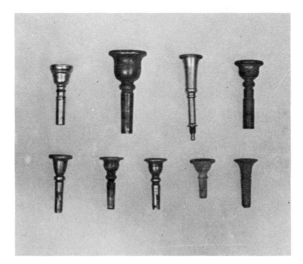

fragments are from Antietam while the mouth pieces were found on various battlefields and camp sites.

BAYONET SCABBARD TIPS: The leather bayonet scabbards were tipped with brass, pewter, steel or iron. Among the beginning collectors there is some confusion as to identification of these scabbard tips when recovered from the ground. The five shown here may be of assistance in recognizing the basic types. All came from battlefields.

Left to right:

Brass. Springfield rifle musket bayonet scabbard, 3 inches long, from the **Wilderness.**

Iron. Austrian musket bayonet scabbard, 2⅛ inches long from Champion's Hill.

Iron. Enfield short rifle bayonet scabbard, 3⅛ inches long, from Spotsylvania.

Brass. Unknown rifle or musket, sword bayonet scabbard, 3½ inches long, from LaGrange, Tennessee.

Iron. Enfield rifle musket bayonet scabbard, 4 inches long, from Vicksburg.

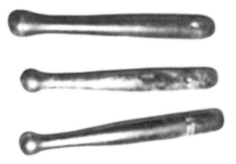

BELAYING PINS: These were used on board naval vessels to secure the ropes. (They were also useful in cracking skulls in attempts at mutiny!) Blackened with age, these pins appear to be of very stout oak. They vary in size from 12¾ to 13⅛ inches in length and about 1½ inches in diameter. No markings.

16 BINOCULARS

BINOCULARS: A typical and interesting pair of binoculars used at Fort Fisher, North Carolina.

Markings: L'ingenieur Chevallier Opt.
   Inside the top corner in ink: Gen. Terry used this glass in
                                      his reconnaissance of Fort Fisher.

   Capt. G. F. Towle
   4th New Hampshire
   Jan. 14, 1865

(Towle was captain of Co. "F" 4th N.H. Inf. He enlisted September 11, 1861 and was mustered out August 23, 1865 as major of his regiment.)

BLACKING FOR SHOES

BLACKING FOR SHOES: The Federal troops, especially in the East, were "spit and polish" soldiers. Shoes and boots had to be kept polished. Shoe blacking for this purpose was purchased from sutlers. The blacking came in tin cans with paper or stamped labels. Shown here are examples of both types. The paper label specimen was made by Mason of 138 and 140 North Front Street in Philadelphia. This can is of thin tin, 3½ inches in diameter. The other can was dug up at Falmouth, Virginia and is marked: Army & Navy
made by
F. Brown & Co.
Boston
BLACKING

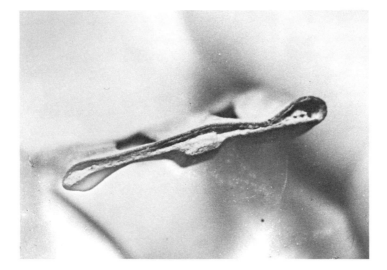

BOX CLAMP: This is a small, highly oxidized metal object found outside of Gettysburg in an area of troop movements just behind the Confederate lines. This object appears to have been used to clamp a metal band, such as a packing band around a crate or box of supplies. It is non-ferrous, probably brass, and measures 1¼ inches long, by ¾ inch wide, by 1/16 inch thick. It is double thickness of sheet metal. In making this object, two parallel ½" long by 1/16-1/8" wide slots were cut in a piece of

BOX CLAMP

sheet metal; it was then folded, the ends joined in a center seam behind the slots, flattened, and possibly crimped. It appears as though it was used to clamp a metal ½" wide band which was passed through the slots; the center and edge of this "clamp" were punched several times with a pointed punch as if to lock such a band in place. [JEFF PEFFER; Etters, Pennsylvania]

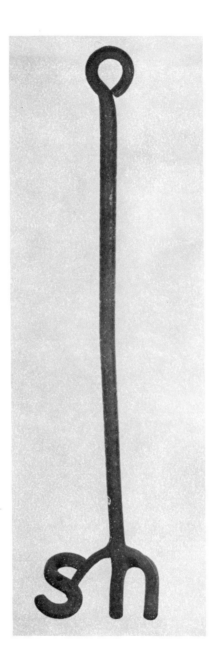

BRANDING IRON: A Federal branding iron picked up years ago on the battlefield of Shiloh, Tennessee. It is 18¼ inches long and the branding surface itself is 2½ inches wide. [TOM S. DICKEY; Atlanta, Georgia]

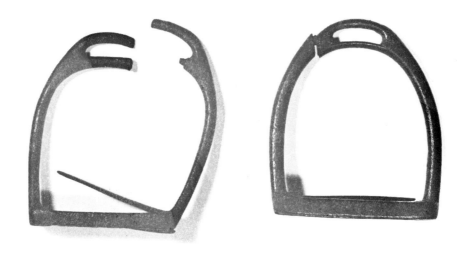

"BREAK-AWAY" STIRRUPS AND SPUR: Shown here are two variations of "break-away" stirrups, probably dating from 1861, although no information on their manufacture is known. They are not marked. The one partly opened, is from the big cavalry battle at BRANDY STATION, Virginia, June 9, 1863. The other is from CULPEPER, Virginia. These stirrups were so constructed as to open out and release the foot of the rider, thus preventing him from being dragged to his death. The spur is hinged, permitting easy attachment or detachment from the boot. [Stirrups — Collection of JACK MAGUNE]

CAMP CHAIR: Camp chairs appear fairly frequently in collections and in contemporary war photographs. This one has especial interest, not only because its original owner is known but its maker as well. Made of oak with strong carpet-like material for the seat, the chair is marked as follows:

    Trade Mark: B. J. Harrison
                     New York.

And painted on the chair are the initials H. M. G. which stand for HARLOW M. GUILD who was First Lieutenant of Co. B., 113th Pennsylvania Infantry.

    Shown also is a somewhat plainer type also used in the war. It is from the collection of ARTHUR LEE BREWER, JR.; Durham, North Carolina.

CAMP CHAIR

CAMP CHEST

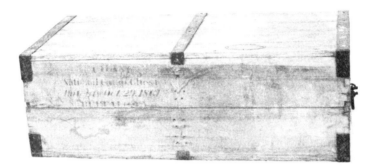

CAMP CHEST: Made of stout oak with iron bands and handles.

Dimensions: 30¼ inches long, 14 inches wide and 10 inches deep.

Markings: On an oval brass plate (3¾ inches long and 2⅛ inches wide at widest point): W. CHASE
            PATENTED
            Oct. 29th 1861
            BUFFALO, N.Y.

    Also, stencilled on front: W. CHASE
                        NATIONAL CAMP CHEST
                        PAT. Oct. 29, 1861
                        BUFFALO, N.Y.

CARBINE AMMUNITION BOX: As one would expect, all wooden ammunition boxes of the Civil War are extremely rare. Most of the wooden boxes were burned by soldiers to keep warm. (Naturally, only after removal of contents!) The box shown here is of pine wood, 17 inches long, 10½ inches wide, and 6¼ inches deep.

Markings: CARTRIDGES
SHARPS CARBINE
CAL. 52   1864

And — on one side: WATERVLIET
ARSENAL.

This box was picked up from the battlefield of Winchester, Virginia (September 19, 1864).

28 CARVED TOY CANNON

CARVED TOY CANNON: These lead cannons were found in camp sites; they were made by soldiers attempting to pass some time. The larger, is 5½ inches long, was dug at New Salem Church battlefield in front of Kennesaw Mountain. The Minie ball which the maker intended as the cannon's projectile can be seen at the end of the barrel and the vent hole can be seen near the other end.

The smaller cannon is 4 inches long and was found in a U.S. camp before Spanish Fort, Alabama. It blew up at the vent. After the soldiers made these novel toys they could not resist trying to fire them. They just did not realize that black powder explodes too violently to be contained by a lead tube. [TOM S. DICKEY; Atlanta, Georgia]

CAVALRY BELL: A horse bell used when horses were hobbled at night. The bell would be on one horse so the horses could be easily located when needed. This bell belonged to David M. Anderson, 4th Iowa Cavalry, grandfather of its present owner, Colonel Delmer P. Anderson, U.S. Army — Retired, Santa Maria, California. The 4th Iowa Cavalry served at Vicksburg and in the Georgia campaign.

The bell is rather elaborately decorated. The shield and sunburst design is repeated three times on the bell's circumference.

Dimensions: 4¼ inches tall with a diameter at bottom of 4¾ inches.

Made of good quality bronze. A sharp blow causes it to audibly ring for more than 30 seconds. [COLONEL DELMER P. ANDERSON; Santa Maria, California]

CAVALRY BELL

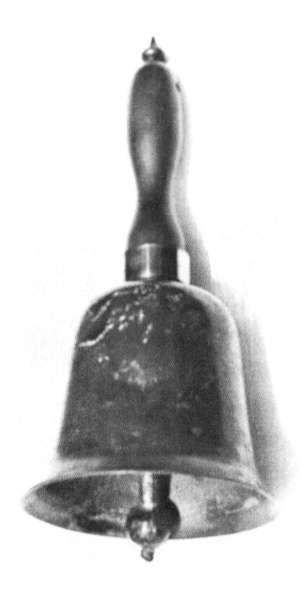

Also shown here is a cast brass bell from the camp of the 2nd Iowa Cavalry at LaGrange, Tennessee. This bell is 4½ inches tall with diameters from 5½ inches to 3⅝ inches. Since the handle, pin, and ferrule have been restored, we do not know the original carrying attachment. [JOHN A. MARKS; Memphis, Tennessee]

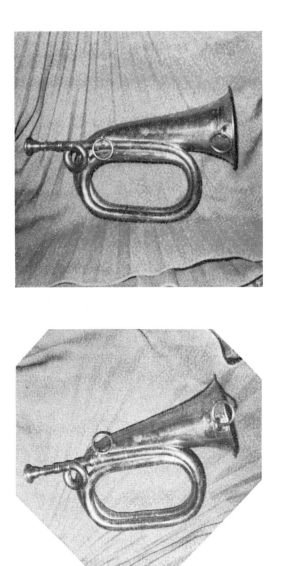

CAVALRY BUGLE: As collectors well know, Civil War cavalry bugles varied significantly in appearance and size. Many bugles were 10¼ inches long with a bell diameter of 3¾ inches. Shown here is a fine specimen of a variation on the more common types; this one is 11½ inches long with a bell diameter of 4½ inches. [DR. CLYDE E. NOBEL; Athens, Georgia]

CAVALRY HORSE BRUSH: Most Federal cavalry horse brushes were made under contract for general army use with no specific State designation. Here is an interesting exception — a brush made for Maine cavalry unit use. The hand strap is stamped: **WARRANTED ALL BRISTLES 90.** On the brush is embossed the seal of the State of Maine. This horse brush was used in the war by Lieutenant FRANK W. PRAY, Co. "I" 1st Maine Cavalry. [T. SHERMAN HARDING, II; Orlando, Florida]

CAVALRY TAR BUCKET, C.S.

CAVALRY TAR BUCKET, C.S.: Improvised from a tin coffee boiler, 5 inches tall and 4¾ inches in diameter. Some tar is still inside! Used by a C.S. cavalryman from Petersburg to care for his horse's hooves. **No markings.**

34 CAVALRYMAN'S WALLET

CAVALRYMAN'S WALLET: Brown leather, 6¾ inches long and 3⅜ inches wide. Contains locks of hair from Father and Mother of LLEWELLYN T. WING, Co. "I" 2nd Maine Cavalry (shown in photograph).

Markings: Soldier's name and home address.

Note: The picture of the cavalryman shown here is through the courtesy of RONN PALM who has the original **CARTE DE VISITE** from which the picture was made.

CHAIN FOR WHIFFLE TREE

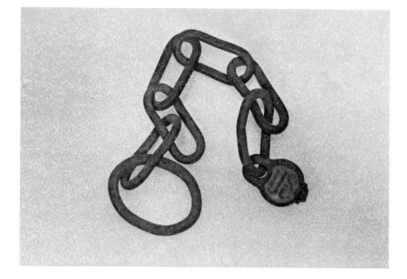

CHAIN FOR WHIFFLE TREE: Section of a whiffle tree chain used by artillery. Each link is about 2½ inches long. At one end is a circular piece of metal 1⅜ inches in diameter with the letters **U.S.** on each side. From the Battle of Winchester, Virginia, September 19, 1864.

CHEVAUX-de-FRISE: Oak tip of a Chevaux-de-frise defense at **PETERSBURG.** The section shown here is about ¾ inch in diameter. Chevaux-de-frise were logs traversed with wooden poles pointed at the end. Normally these poles were 5-6 feet long and were used to defend a position against cavalry and infantry attack. In the Civil War they were used extensively in front of intrenched positions, e.g. the siege of Petersburg.

CLEANING MATERIAL: There is still much research to be done on the cleaning materials used by the soldiers to keep their uniforms and equipment in good shape. Depicted here is the container of some type of cleaning material produced and sold by JOHONNOT & SAUNDERS of 21 Dock Square, Boston. Not shown is a round piece of beeswax, 1 inch in diameter imported from England for sale by sutlers. This beeswax cake was used to polish uniform buttons. The cake is marked: FRANCIS
ULLATHORN
LONDON

The top of the beeswax cake is decorated with the British crown.

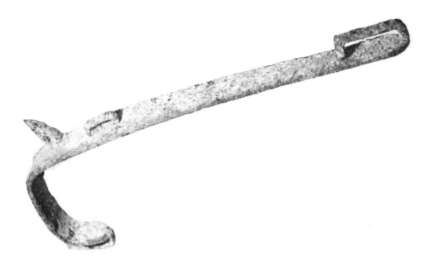

CLIMBING IRON (C.S. TELEGRAPHER): Metal climbing or leg iron used by telegraphers to climb telegraph poles in the field. The iron is 13½ inches long, 1¼ inches wide, with a pointed "spike" 1½ inches in length. Found in a C.S. camp at Front Royal, Virginia. No markings. [JACK MAGUNE; Worcester, Massachusetts]

COAT HOOK FOR BARRACKS: Interior furnishings for Civil War barracks are extremely rare. Shown here is a coat hook recovered from the site of a Confederate barracks at Fort Fisher, North Carolina. The hook is of heavy brass, 5½ inches long, with 4 holes for screwing on the wall. [RODNEY O. GRAGG; Montreat, North Carolina]

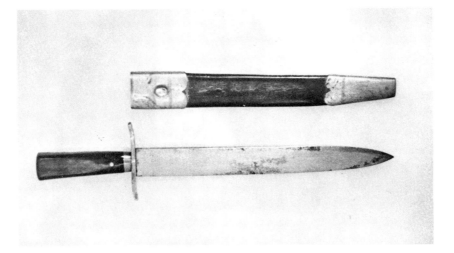

CONFEDERATE BOWIE KNIVES: Confederate bowie knives continue to interest collectors, especially because of the great variations in style and dimensions. Shown here are an individual knife and a grouping — both from separate collections. The individual C.S. bowie knife is 17 inches long with a blade 12⅜ inches in length and 1⅜ inches wide. It has a brass guard and wood grip. The blade is marked on one side:
  CONFEDERATE
SELF DEFENDER.

On the other side: YEOMAN (?)
                    CVTL - - - - -
                    C.S. (?).

It has a leather scabbard with brass furniture.

The grouping (next page) consists of 4 knives as follows:

TOP:
  Knife with a 16½ inch blade. Possibly made from a Georgia pike. Leather scabbard.

  Knife 22½ inches long, oak grip — massive D guard.

  Knife 13½ inches long. Iron D guard. Has a 2 inch wide blade with a clip point with false edge. Dug up at Alexandria, Virginia [grip is a possible replacement].

  Knife 14 inches long, with a rosewood grip and wooden scabbard.

[ARTHUR LEE BREWER, JR.; Durham, North Carolina]

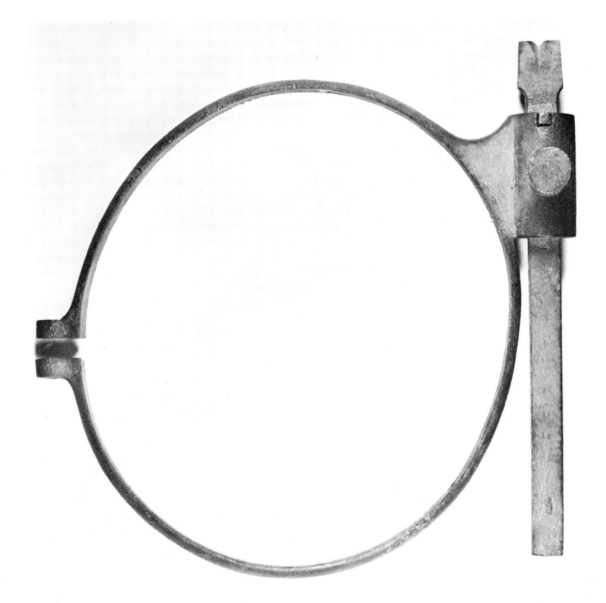

CONFEDERATE CANNON SIGHTS: Shown here are two cannon sights for British Blakeley cannon shipped to the Confederacy via the blockade runners.

The sight marked **NO. 628** is a brass muzzle sight which came off the 30-pounder Blakeley recovered from the Roanoke River in North Carolina at the site of Fort Branch.

The ring-shaped sight is a breech sight for the 3.5 Blakeley gun recovered from the sunken blockade runner GEORGIANA. [TOM S. DICKEY; Atlanta, Georgia]

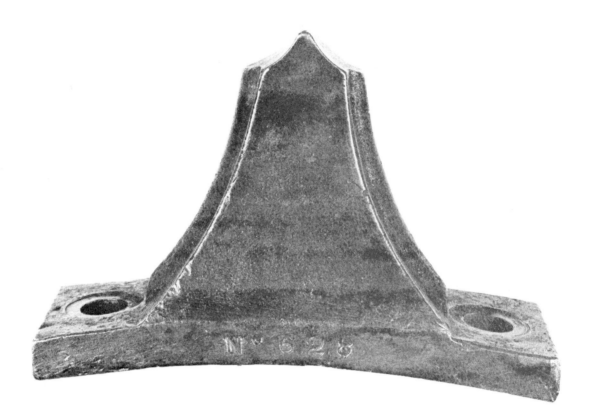

CONFEDERATE CANTEENS: Various types of C.S. canteens are constantly turning up. Depicted is a large copper canteen which is 8⅛ inches in diameter and 2⅛ inches deep at the center. This canteen holds exactly 3 pints. The markings are clearly shown in the photographs. **S & K** refers to **SCHNITZLER AND KIRSCHBAUM,** a German exporter of military supplies during the Civil War.

The two tin canteens shown here are probably typical of many used by Johnny Reb. The diameters of both are the same — 6⅛ inches. But one is 2 inches deep while the other is only 1⅝ inches. There are no markings on either specimen.

46 CONFEDERATE CAP BOX

CONFEDERATE CAP BOX: Made of black leather 3¾ inches tall and 3 inches wide. This has an unusual inside covering flap, much different from the U.S. cap boxes. There are two leather loops in back for attachment to the waist belt. No markings. From Fort Macon, North Carolina taken by a Federal soldier after the fort's surrender on April 23, 1862.

Unit Designation:

Color:

Field	Canton	Stars
three horizontal bars, red, white, and red, bound on three sides with 1¼" deep gold fringe; motto "FOR LIBERTY WE STRIVE" in gold, 2" high Roman letters in center bar.	dark blue, 40½" on the staff by 29" on the fly with 2" high white Roman letters "CSA" in its center.	ten (10), white, 5 pointed stars, each 6½" in dia., six set in a circle, 15½" in diameter and one in each corner.

Material: silk field and lettering   silk canton & letters   silk

Method of attachment to the staff not determined

61" (exclusive of fringe)

20¼"

20¼"

20½"

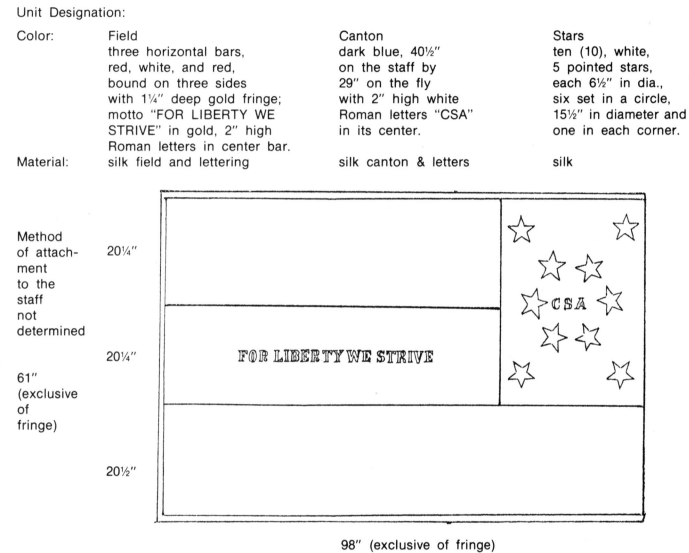

98" (exclusive of fringe)

Note: Motto is sewn to reverse bar only.

CONFEDERATE FLAG: A recently acquired C.S. flag is depicted in the sketch shown here. This flag came from a G.A.R. post and was one of the first Confederate flags captured in Virginia during the war. The capturing unit was very probably from Pennsylvania. **Very** substantial assistance in tracing this flag's history has been rendered by H. MICHAEL MADAUS, Assistant Curator of History, Milwaukee Public Museum. Mr. Madaus is a highly recognized authority on C.S. flags. "Mike" Madaus has authored some extremely fine research studies on Confederate flags.

CONFEDERATE COFFEE POT: Very rare — and used early in the war — because it is made of heavy copper. There are no markings on this coffee pot which was used by an 1861 South Carolina regiment in the Columbia, S.C. training area. **Dimensions:** 10½ inches tall at the tallest point. It has a diameter of 6⅝ inches at the bottom and 4⅝ inches at the top.

CONFEDERATE PISTOL: This "monster" was made from a caliber .69 Model 1842 Springfield smoothbore musket! Its overall length is 18 inches. The lockplate is marked with the eagle, U.S., and 1844. The cut-down barrel is 11⅛ inches long. Although the trigger guard and wood enclosing the barrel and lockplate have been retained, a pistol grip has replaced the original butt of the musket. This weapon was carried by a soldier from North Carolina.

CONFEDERATE SABERS AND SWORDS

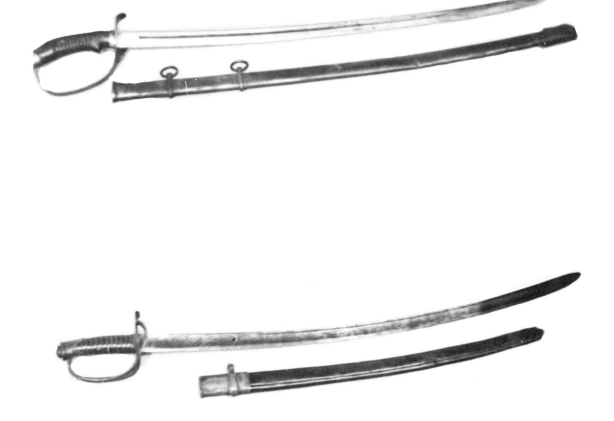

CONFEDERATE SABERS AND SWORDS: Although several excellent works on Confederate edged weapons have already been written, interesting variations still appear which merit discussion. Shown here are a C.S. saber and sword which vary in design from others previously covered in published works.

The unmarked saber from South Carolina is 40 inches in overall length, with a 31½ inch blade. It has a brass guard and an unusual grip. The scabbard is of steel.

The officer's sword was worn during the war by MAJOR HUNTER McGUIRE, 2nd Virginia Infantry, and later medical aide to "Stonewall" Jackson. This sword is 37½ inches long, with a 32 inch blade. The grip is of brass. Leather scabbard with brass furniture. No markings.

CONFEDERATE SHARPS BULLET MOLDS: The larger mold in the photograph is a C.S. Sharps bullet mold made of crude brass. Its total length is 8½ inches. This mold is marked: **STUBS(?).** To show its size it has been photographed with a steel caliber .58 mold which is 5¾ inches long.

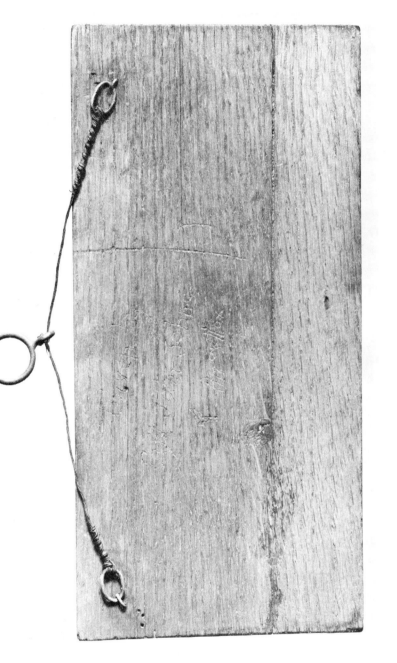

CONFEDERATE SOUVENIRS: Some Confederates were able to take home mementos of their service at the end of the war. Shown here is one such example. The Virginia belt plate and piece of battleflag were taken home after Appomattox by CAPTAIN JOHN W. JOHNS, Co. "I", "Appomattox Reserves". These relics were nailed to a piece of oak, probably part of an artillery limber seat. WILLIAM LANGLOIS; San Francisco, California]

CONFEDERATE SOUVENIRS

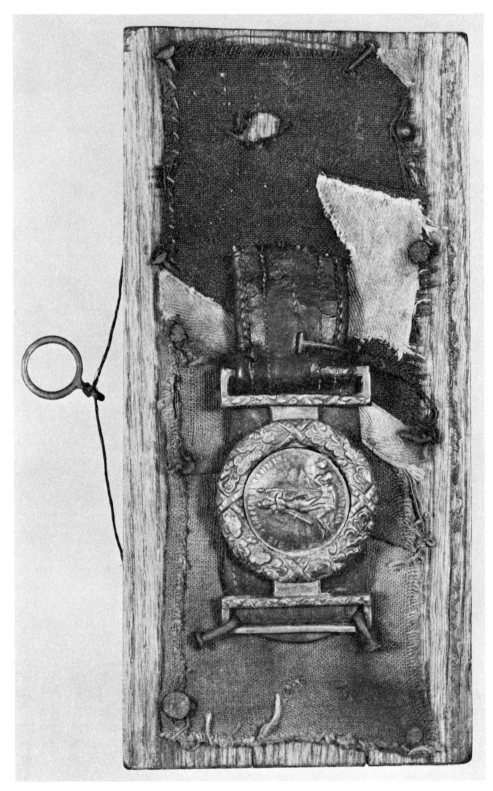

THE CONVALESCENT CAMP
at
ALEXANDRIA, VIRGINIA

Although life in Alexandria, Virginia, during the 1861-1865 period has been well described in several books, the role of the city as a "staging area" for the United States has not received its just attention. This is especially true for the vast "convalescent camp" in the city which handled thousands of soldiers during the war.

Federal troops occupied Alexandria very shortly after the outbreak of war. For more than a year the city witnessed the construction of large forts as part of the series of earthworks ringing the national captial and known as the "Defences of Washington." The regiments that manned these forts as well as thousands of other troops passing through, took whatever shelter they could find or pitched their tents in the open lots and fields surrounding the city. However, as the Federal government realized the war was to be a long one, the Capital area became one huge staging area for the thousands of volunteers and draftees coming by boat and rail, especially in late summer and early fall of 1862.

Trains arrived from the north day and night and the Federal authorities had to establish a reception area for the troops as they arrived and a dispatching area for them when they left. It soon became evident that the dispatch area would also have to handle the care and forwarding of the thousands of soldiers released from the many hospitals in the area.

Two main functions were assigned to the Washington-Alexandria staging complex because of the close connections by rail with Baltimore, Philadelphia and New York. The city of Washington thus became the reception center for the new regiments on their way to the front. The role of a forwarding center was awarded to Alexandria. This was a logical choice as not only did the latter have substantially more open land to accommodate camps, it also had an excellent port for shipping troops by sea to points south. In theory the reception and forwarding of troops should have been a reasonably smooth operation. Such was not the case, however. The war grew to such a scale never imagined by the Federal military leadership thinking in terms of 1812 or 1848, and much of the responsible leadership was unimaginative and non-innovative.

Let us examine first the conditions that confronted the young volunteers as they arrived in the Nation's capital. Then we can turn our attention to Alexandria, itself. These two cities can be likened to the forward and exit ends of a tunnel leading to the war zones. A complex of buildings in Washington was the receiving end. These buildings bore such signs as "Soldiers Retreat" and "Soldiers Rest." To the thousands of travel-weary young soldiers from Maine and other points north, the sign boards must have appeared enticing — especially after their heart-warming reception in Philadelphia with its cheering throngs. But their anticipation soon turned to disgusted disappointment.

CONVALESCENT CAMP

When one reads first-hand accounts of the abominable reception given the volunteers in the Washington area, one finds it extremely difficult to explain or excuse the Nation's capital which symbolized the United States war effort. It should have been the best administered and supplied staging area of the entire war effort. Washington was, after all, the center of the war effort; here were the headquarters of Ordnance, Quartermaster and Commissary departments. The Capital was the main reception and forwarding area for the thousands of men volunteering from the northeast United States. But Washington failed miserably in aiding these men to the front. There were only poor reception facilities as the men arrived after a long, fatiguing train ride; poor housing — often not even tents — and incredibly poor food. The effect on the recruits' physical condition and morale is obvious. A sampling of soldiers' reactions to their reception is interesting, not only as illustrative of the mismanagement but also because it has not been noted in any detail before.

As early as September 1861 the 6th Connecticut Infantry arrived at "Soldiers Retreat." Here were three long rows of tables, running the length of the building, "each piled up with chunks of half-boiled pork which looked as if they had been cut from the hog when just killed for the bristles were long enough to lift up each piece by." Also present was a quantity of stale and musty bread and some very muddy coffee. The men walked out and went to eat at nearby restaurants. A month later, another Connecticut Infantry regiment (7th) found fat maggots in their beef at the "Soldiers Rest." Some men ate at these establishments more than once, having little money of their own to spend, and therefore, could compare their reactions over a period of time. When the 122nd Pennsylvania Infantry visited "Soldiers Retreat" on August 16, 1862, it found the supper to be "very scanty." But on re-visiting the Retreat on May 9, 1863, the men were provided with a "bountiful supper of fresh bread, hot coffee and the proverbial 'salt horse' — vastly different from the [first] reception."

The reaction of most soldiers was very similar to that of Robert Tilney of the 12th New York Infantry. He and his comrades were received royally in New York and Philadelphia but met a cool reception in Baltimore and "no welcome" at all in Washington. "They let us down gradually." In Philadelphia at the Cooper Shop Refreshment rooms the tables were covered with cloths, the china was clean and homelike. Everything was neat and good and was "served in a friendly manner." At Baltimore there was some effort; the food was plain but good. But, on arrival in Washington "we were sent into a shed, with a shelf along the walls and no seats. We were given bread without butter, and something which by courtesy, was called coffee. The shelves, from frequent use and infrequent cleaning, were sloppy with spilt coffee, which was served in tin cups, while the slices of bread, two or three in number, were slapped down on the wet boards." Other regiments found similar conditions.

Soldiers found conditions bad not only on their entrance to the Washington area but also during their stay and departure. In late 1862 the flow of battle casualties to the Nation's capital had created a space crisis in the hospitals in Washington. The slaughter at Second Manassas (August 29-30) and Antietam (September 17) was filling the hospitals to overflowing. A partial solution was to remove the convalescing soldiers from the hospitals and put them elsewhere. They could be housed with the many stragglers who left their regiments after the battles, or were separated in the heat of the battles.

Accordingly, on September 15th, the General-in-Chief H. W. Halleck, ordered Major General N. P. Banks to establish a camp near the fortifications of the capital city for housing the many stragglers in the Washington area. These men were to be organized into their companies and regiments and forwarded to their units. That same day Banks responded to Halleck's order in the following General Order No. 3 of "Defences of Washington." In brief, this order directed the military governor of Alexandria to organize immediately a "camp of convalescents, stragglers, and recruits." These men were to be organized in squads according to their original division or corps. Shelter was to be provided for the officers and men, and all enlisted men without haversacks, canteens and blankets were to be re-issued these necessities. As opportunity occurred the officers and men were to be forwarded to their regiments. About a month later (October 29) Major General George B. McClellan, in General Order No. 179, directed that "all patients discharged from hospitals at Washington, Georgetown, and Alexandria, belonging to the Army of the Potomac, [would] be sent to the convalescent camp, near Alexandria."

By mid-January 1863, the camp had 1200 men with others constantly arriving. According to a report of January 14th some 60 men were being discharged each day. It was expected that the camp would house at least 5,000 men, with a possibility of being expanded to 20,000.

As the months went by there was an ever-shifting assemblage of men waiting for transportation to their regiments and often waiting for months.

The camp facilities did not improve as time went on and soon the camp acquired the significant title of "Camp Misery." Julia S. Wheelock, a "hospital agent" made several visits to the camp. According to her, "Camp Misery" was located about 1½ miles from Alexandria proper. Her comment on the camp is indicative of the aptness of the title "Camp Misery."

> Here were 10,000-15,000 soldiers — not simply the convalescent, but the sick and dying — many of them destitute, with not even a blanket or an overcoat, having little or no wood, their rations consisting of salt pork and hardtack . . . They had no fire with which to do the cooking — consequently much of the time they were obliged to eat their pork raw."

In those days the eating of raw pork was extremely dangerous and evoked the dread of painful and fatal disease.

Another observer, Captain Robert G. Carter, in his reminiscences located the camp as occupying the original "Excelsior Hospital," located on the summit of Shuter's Hill, overlooking Alexandria, and between the Little River and Leesburg turnpikes. The captain called the camp a "burning disgrace," where a show of greenbacks procured a man's discharge from the service as easy as tumbling off a log." In the early morning the "bummers and beats" exercised up the steep hills in the vicinity, just before surgeon's call, and then religiously attended the call and "with hearts thumping from a hard run, and a generous display of the filthy lucre, were pronounced badly affected with heart disease and booked for what they had long desired — a journey to 'Home Sweet Home.' It was here that red ink, or some other substitute, was skillfully used to simulate blood from the mouth and lungs, or the last stages of consumption." In order to keep the men occupied they were marched out every morning to work on the fortifications. The working party usually numbered about 400 men when it left camp but about 75 when it arrived at the fort where work was to be done. The others visited the city of Alexandria or other camps. The camp was investigated by a committee of Congress but for the greater part of its existence it "remained a perfect scourge to the army."

Primarily, of course, the camp was a camp for convalescing sick and wounded soldiers. No discussion of the camp is complete without reference to the medical facilities in operation. The first hospital ward in the camp was a converted barracks. When the regiments left the Alexandria area for the front more barracks were turned into improvised hospitals. And when these buildings had reached their capacity in beds, tent wards were set up. By the end of 1864, there were 25 hospitals in the Washington-Alexandria area. The total bed capacity of this complex was 21,426.

Assisting in the recuperation of the thousands of wounded and sick patients were such semi-military organizations as the U.S. Sanitary Commission and the U.S. Christian Commission. Realizing the need for a "home away from home," these volunteer philanthropic organizations established in various key locations a type of stopping-off place where the soldier could find rest, food, and some recreation — the embryonic U.S.O. of today. These "homes" also took the soldier in off the street and protected him from the many pickpockets and swindlers who met every train of furloughed soldiers and attempted to relieve them of their money.

The Sanitary Commission organized a "Special Relief Department" which administered a whole system of "homes" and "lodges" to care for the soldiers. The Commission members visited hospitals, worked on back pay and pensions for the soldiers, and compiled a basic "Hospital Directory." Due to very faulty records the military establishment frequently had no idea where sick or wounded soldiers were being treated. The Hospital Directory, prepared by the Commission covered hospitals all over the war area. Between October 1862 and July 1864, this Directory was expanded to a total of 700,000 names!

The main purpose for the founding of the Commission had been to aid the army medical service. Some of the most prominent Commission members were medical doctors themselves. Their contribution to military medicine was very substantial. And, as close observers of the conditions at "Camp Convalescent," they inevitably became involved in the correction of the camp's evils. The Commission certainly took a forward step when it successfully secured the appointment of the very competent William A. Hammond as Surgeon General of the Army.

The Commission was especially active in enlarging the ward facilities at the camp. The east wards of Camp Convalescent were much less attractive than the wards in the

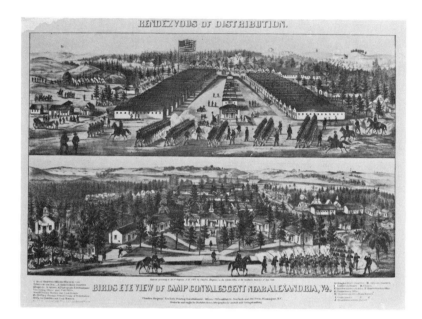

RENDEZVOUS OF DISTRIBUTION.

BIRDS EYE VIEW OF CAMP CONVALESCENT NEAR ALEXANDRIA, VA.

capital city, itself. The Alexandria camp had inferior housing for the men, the buildings were poorly ventilated, drainage of rain water was a constant problem. In rainy weather the camp would be a sea of mud. Death rate at Camp Convalescent was higher than at most hospitals and even some prisons.

After a few months of operation it was obvious that corrective measures were imperative. Barracks were built to get the men out of their sodden tents. Overall conditions were improved under the impetus of the Sanitary Commission with the unsung heroine, Amy Bradley, taking the lead. To support the Commission's activities, on January 3, 1863, the officers of the medical inspector's department of the Army Medical Corps were charged with the duty of making "regular and frequent" inspections of all military general hospitals and convalescent camps. (There were camps in operation in New York City and other places.) These inspections were for the purpose of determining which soldiers should receive discharges and which ones were ready to rejoin their regiments. The next month, March 24, 1863, the Army Paymaster General was directed to take "immediate measures" for the prompt payment of the sick and wounded soldiers in hospitals and convalescent camps. Some attempts were made to provide entertainment for the men awaiting official assignment for time passed slowly while the wheels of officialdom creaked forward. For example, a soldier of the 14th New Hampshire Infantry noted in his diary that Julia Ward Howe read her magnificent battle hymn, the "Battle Hymn of the Republic" to the convalescents in Alexandria late in 1864.

CONVALESCENT CAMP

In preparation of this study of "Camp Convalescent" the author was fortunate in having notes he took on conversations with this diarist who was in the camp in early 1865. He was Francis H. Buffum, and his observations were as follows:

There were some 2,000 men at the camp awaiting orders to be forwarded to their regiments. Each corps of the Army of the Potomac was represented in the camp by a street. Despite the construction of barracks, there were still a chronic shortage of housing and many men were quartered in the large Sibly tents. But after the heavy battles in the Shenandoah Valley, many wounded passed through hospitals and at the beginning of 1865, found themselves at this camp.

Buffum had been severely wounded at Cedar Creek, Virginia, October 19, 1864. After treatment in a hospital in Philadelphia (Chestnut Hill) he was sent by rail to Camp Convalescent. On his arrival, January 25, 1865, he found the food to be "quite poor" and the barracks "uncomfortable". As he noted in his diary on February 1st — although he disapproved of grumbling he could hardly believe that this camp was so poorly supplied with food and comfortable quarters as its position and importance would warrant. Finally, on February 22nd, Buffum and 700 other soldiers left Alexandria on the *Ericsson* for their regiments. The war ended a few weeks later.

"Camp Convalescent" is an example of how a good plan for care of convalescing soldiers was well-nigh ruined by red tape, bad management, and official indifference. In view of the camp's close proximity to Army headquarters and the essential service agencies, it is difficult to excuse the continuing failure in its operation. "Camp Misery" was no misnomer, many men died here. One might expect the bad conditions in a prison under enemy control, but hardly in the shadow of the capitol dome in Washington, D.C.

CROWS-FOOT: Made of cast iron and about 2 inches from point to point. This type of item was strewn in roads and in front of defense positions as a deterrent to cavalry attacks. The crows-foot would be scattered on the ground in large numbers to catch in the hooves of horses approaching the position. This was actually a very old type of primitive booby trap.

"CUMBERLAND" PASS BOX

"CUMBERLAND" PASS BOX: One of the very few items to survive the naval action of March 8, 1862 in which the U.S.S. CUMBERLAND (a wooden ship) was sunk by the Confederate ironclad MERRIMAC (Virginia). This pass box is of thick leather, painted orange, 15 inches tall and 7½ inches in diameter. In addition to the markings shown in the photograph the pass box has stamped on the cover — **1852.**

DAGUERROTYPE (ROUND): A charming little gutta percha case, 1⅝ inches in diameter, from Ohio. The case is in two sections which screw together. The bottom section has a picture of a young lady under a glass protection while the top section has the maltese cross in the center of floral decorations. Possibly 5th Corps but more probably the maltese cross is for decoration rather than to indicate the 5th Corps. **No markings.**

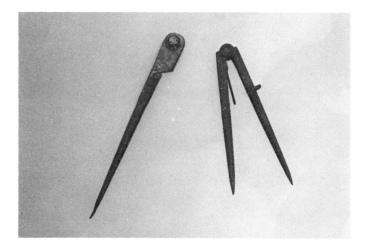

DIVIDERS: As is well known by collectors and students of the 1861-1865 war, both sides made extensive use of engineer troops. This was especially true in preparing defensive positions in the field. Many of the instruments used were very similar to those of today. The complete divider in the photograph is of iron — each "arm" is 5 inches long. Dug up at Petersburg. The incomplete specimen had "arms" 7 inches in length and was found at Spotsylvania. Recently acquired by the author is a specimen marked **U.S.** with "arms" 8 inches long. In addition to the **U.S.** this specimen is marked **8** and **P.C. TENTRAUT, NEWARK, N.J.** This divider is made of cast steel.

DRUM BEATERS

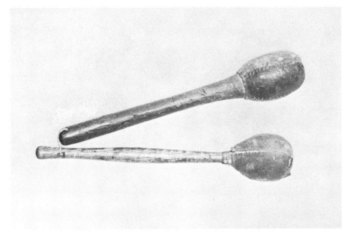

DRUM BEATERS: Rare indeed are these beaters used with the big drums of Civil War bands! These beaters are of oak with leather covering for the "beating end." Each beater is 13¾ inches long. The "beating end" is 3½ inches in length and 2¾ inches thick at its thickest point. **No markings.**

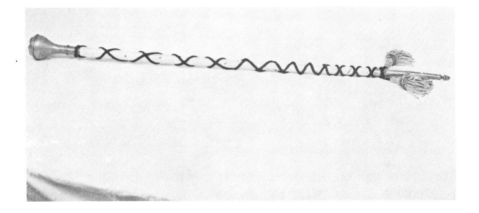

DRUM MAJOR'S BATON: A fine example of a drum major's baton carried by a Massachusetts drum major. Note the beautiful eagle which decorates the solid brass head of the baton.

ENFIELD BAYONET SCABBARD: The mystery of Enfield rifle musket accouterments has plagued collectors for a long time. Here, at least, is a beginning in determining exactly what these accouterments were as used from 1861 to 1865 in America. This scabbard and bayonet came together in a collection. The bayonet fits the scabbard perfectly. The owner's sketch is given here without any revisions. [DAVE HOLDER; West Sussex, England]

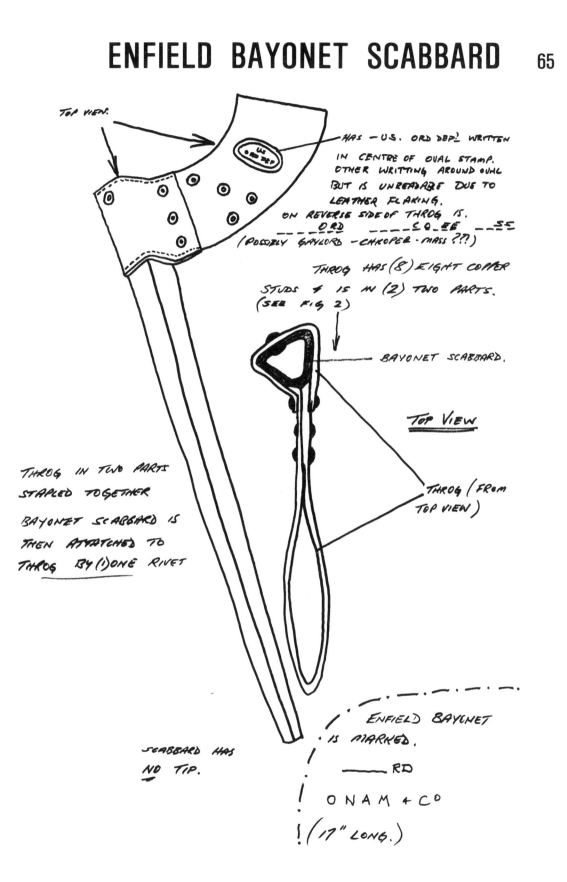

TOP VIEW:

HAS —U.S. ORD DEP⁺ WRITTEN
IN CENTRE OF OVAL STAMP.
OTHER WRITTING AROUND OVAL
BUT IS UNREADABLE DUE TO
LEATHER FLAKING.
ON REVERSE SIDE OF THROG IS.
_ _ _ _ _ _ ORD _ _ _ _ CO EE _ _ SS
(POSSIBLY GAYLORD - CHROPER - MASS ???)

THROG HAS (8) EIGHT COPPER
STUDS & IS IN (2) TWO PARTS.
(SEE FIG 2)

BAYONET SCABBARD.

TOP VIEW

THROG (FROM
TOP VIEW)

THROG IN TWO PARTS
STAPLED TOGETHER
BAYONET SCABBARD IS
THEN ATTATCHED TO
THROG BY (1) ONE RIVET

SCABBARD HAS
NO TIP.

ENFIELD BAYONET
IS MARKED.
—— RD
ONAM & Cᵒ
(17" LONG.)

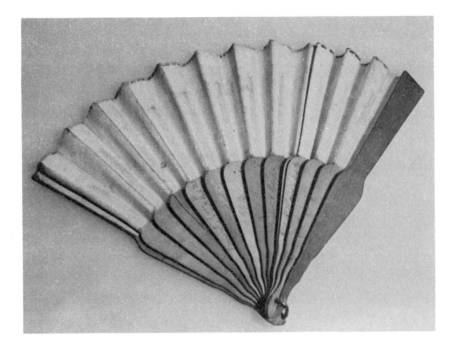

FAN: A lady's fan from a dance put on by the 44th Massachusetts Infantry. The fan is made of light wood, probably birch, with linen cloth, and has been autographed by the various regimental personnel who danced with the fair lady! This lady was Nellie Hannerde of Boston and the fan was used at a military ball at Readville, Massachusetts where the 44th was raised. The fan is about 12 inches across when fully opened.

There is a rich field for insignia collectors in U. S. shoulder straps. These are colorful, reasonably small and light, and often with interesting personal association. Descendants of Civil War officers often inherit the sword *and* the shoulder straps. All too frequently the uniform itself was eaten up by moths but the shoulder straps survived.

There is some confusion about what Civil War shoulder straps actually looked like. In researching for this article I have examined U. S. Army Regulations for 1857, 1861, and 1881. The 1881 Regulations are necessary to help us differentiate between the Civil War and Indian wars periods.

Collectors frequently ask me about Confederate shoulder straps. Here one must not dogmatically say that there were no shoulder straps worn by C. S. officers. It is true that the C. S. regulations, promulgated in May 1861, provided that "all indications of rank will be marked on collars and sleeves". There was no authorization of shoulder straps of any kind. But, as is well known, many Confederates had served in the "old Army". Many of these wore their old shoulder straps on their new Confederate uniforms after entering the C. S. service. Some even wore their old uniforms due to lack of the new Confederate gray. An excellent photograph of a Confederate officer wearing shoulder straps — *a year after the war had started* — can be seen on page 289, Volume 1 of *Photographic History of the Civil War.* The officer is Lieutenant J. B. WASHINGTON, a West Point graduate, who was captured May 31, 1862 while serving as an aide to Joe Johnston at Fair Oaks, Virginia.

In the Army of the United States the rank of officers was determined by the insignia on the epaulettes and shoulder straps. Epaulettes were quite gaudy and were worn mainly at dress affairs. Shoulder straps were worn in lieu of epaulettes, both in rear areas but almost universally at the front.

According to all three regulations studied (1857, 1861, 1881), shoulder straps were to be 1⅜ inches wide and 4 inches long, with an embroidery of gold ¼ inch wide. But, in practice, there was considerable diversity in size; lieutenants (perhaps characteristically!) were prone to wear unusually larger shoulder straps than called for by the regulations.

An officer's shoulder strap told three basic items of information to the observer. The *color* told the branch of service, metal insignia told the rank, and other metal insignia told the regiment or branch specialty.

According to both the 1857 and 1861 Regulations, rank was shown on the shoulder straps as follows:

Lieutenant General	— 3 silver stars
Major General	— 2 silver stars
Brigadier General	— 1 silver star

Captain J. Homer Edgerly

Colonel	— Silver embroidered eagle
Lieutenant Colonel	— Silver leaf
Major	— Gold leaf
Captain	— 2 silver bars
First Lieutenant	— 1 silver bar
Second Lieutenant	— Blank

These insignia were the same for all branches of the service.

The following table shows the color authorized for branches of the service as well as for the specialized branches.

Branch of Service	Color	Authorization
Infantry	Light or "Sky" Blue	1857 Regulations
Cavalry	Yellow	1857 Regulations
Artillery	Scarlet	1857 Regulations
Dragoons	Orange	1857 Regulations
Riflemen	Medium or "Emerald" Green	1857 Regulations
General Staff and Staff Corps	Dark Blue	1857 Regulations
Signal Corps	Dark Blue	General Order No. 32 Adj. Gen. Office, June 15, 1861
Chaplain	No shoulder strap authorized	General Order No. 102 Adj. Gen. Office, Nov. 25, 1861
Invalid Corps	"According to 1861 Regulations BVT worked on Dark-Blue Vel.	General Order No. 158 Adj. Gen. Office, May 29, 1863

Also, major generals were authorized dark blue for their shoulder straps, but some specimens in my collection are definitely *light* blue — and have not faded in color since the War.

The 1861 Regulations provided that the regimental number should be embroidered in gold on the shoulder strap. This, however, was done only in rare cases — probably for reasons of military security. Moreover, I have seen several specimens where the regimental numbers are of silver! The 1861 Regulations also provided for the following insignia for the specialized services!

Specialty	Insignia
Medical Department or "Service"	**MS** in old English characters
Pay Department	**PD** in old English characters
Engineers	Turreted castle (silver)
Topographical Engineers	A shield embroidered in gold and the letters **TE**
Ordnance	A shell and flame in silver embroidery

It was not until 1881 that Chaplains were authorized to wear shoulder straps. In that year the army chaplain was authorized to wear a shoulder strap of "black velvet with a shepherd's crook of frosted silver on the center of the strap".

Confederate sharpshooters always looked with great interest on Federals with shoulder straps! In fact, their interest frequently ended with abrupt finality, the individual's earthly career on whom they bestowed their special attention. Accordingly, many officers wore their rank designation as inconspicuously as possible. Grant often wore an enlisted man's coat while Sheridan avoided glamorous uniform accessories. A member of the 1st Maine Cavalry (Edward P. Tobie) who saw Sheridan very frequently "could not remember to have ever noticed any insignia of rank about him". Naturally, all officers dressed up when they were to be photographed. On one occasion a soldier of the 1st Connecticut Light Battery was approached for a piece of tobacco by a man in a private's uniform. The soldier gave the man some tobacco and while talking with him noted that he had the star of a brigadier general on his collar — the only mark of rank he was wearing.

Miniature insignia of rank were worn by some officers in lieu of the conspicuous shoulder straps. By General Order No. 286, November 22, 1864, the War Department permitted officers in the field to dispense with shoulder straps, but they had to continue to wear their rank designation. Some officers removed their shoulder straps altogether on going into combat.

A good example of an officer who has substituted the miniature bars for shoulder straps can be seen in the photograph of Captain E. A. Flint, 1st Massachusetts Cavalry (*Photographic History of the Civil War,* Vol. 4, page 53). The captain is wearing a 4-button enlisted man's blouse with no shoulder straps, only the miniature captain's bars. It is difficult to tell that he is an officer at all. Of course, this practice of being inconspicuous only makes sense; his men knew who he was, but why tell the enemy!

But, as if to prove that nothing had been learned from the Civil War experience, the 1881 Army Regulations provided that "officers serving in the field may dispense with prominent marks likely to attract the fire of sharpshooters, but all officers must wear

the prescribed shoulder-strap to indicate their rank"! Fortunately, we did learn later as attested to by the blackened rank insignia in World War I and the "subdued" insignia in more recent times.

FIELD CANDLE HOLDER: Fits in socket of bayonet which could be stuck in the ground. The author's collection has two types — one of thin brass, the other of silvered brass. Diameter is 2⅜ inches with a beaded rim encircling the candle holder proper. The holder itself is 1¼ inches deep with a "breather" hole in the bottom. Sold by sutlers in the field. **No markings.**

FIELD DESK: Made of cherry wood with a brass carrying handle. The compartments are labelled for various papers — e.g. CLOTHING INVOICES, ORDNANCE FORMS, DISCHARGE PAPERS, etc.

Dimensions: 18 inches tall, 20 inches wide, and 10¼ inches deep.

Markings: On the back of the desk: CAPT. J. H. MURRAY
Co. "M" 62 Reg Pa

Also shown here is a field desk owned by ARTHUR LEE BREWER, JR. of Durham, North Carolina. Note the different arrangement of the interior. The bottom section has been placed on top of the desk for better photographic results.

FIELD SIGNAL LANTERN: Made of japanned tin, 5 inches tall and 2¼ inches in diameter. For use in signalling the inner center is equipped with a red glass through which the candle light shows when the inner center is rotated. There are two wire loops in back for handles. These loops fold back against the lantern when not in use. No markings.

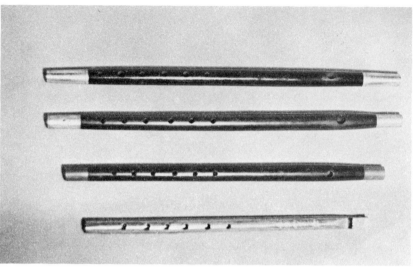

FIFES: The top fife is silver mounted, 16⅞ inches long. It is marked CROSBY.

The next fife, also silver mounted is 16⅝ inches long but with no markings. It was reportedly made under contract by William Hall & Son of 543 Broadway, N.Y. This fife was carried by Charles H. White, Co. "B" 47th Massachusetts Infantry.

The third fife from the top is brass mounted and has no markings. It came from Fort Smith, Arkansas and reportedly was used by a Confederate soldier.

The bottom specimen is a tin flute, 12⅝ inches long, decorated with **U.S.** and eagle. It is marked **ELTON** and **MADE IN U.S.A.** and reportedly was used in the Civil War.

Also shown is the rare fife mouth piece. This specimen is made of pewter. It is ⅝ inch long and ½ inch wide. There is a screw for tightening on the fife. No markings.

FISHING SINKERS: The Civil War was a "seasonal" war, i.e. there were long periods of inactivity between battles. Many soldiers just went fishing! Shown here are 3 "sinkers" made from bullets. The center one is from Fredericksburg and the other two are from Fort Fisher. [RODNEY O. GRAGG; Montreat, North Carolina]

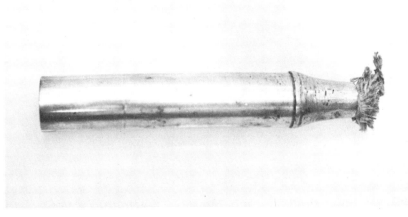

FLARE (SIGNAL?): Heavy brass flare with rope-type wick. Flare is 10¼ inches tall and 1¾ inches in diameter. A flange near the top suggests that the flare may have been inserted in a container of some sort. **No markings.**

FLEAM: The fleam (or lancet) was a surgical instrument used for making small incisions. The one shown here is of heavy brass. Total length when closed is 3¼ inches. Equipped with two steel blades; each blade is 3⅛ inches long.

Markings: On one of the steel blades — R [B?] ORWICK. Also, on the brass frame — Wm. Child 5 N.H.

William Child was appointed 2nd Assistant Surgeon in the 5th New Hampshire Infantry at age 28. Promoted to Surgeon October 28, 1864. Mustered out on June 28, 1865. [DR. GERALD F. SAUER; Santa Rosa, California]

FOOTBATH: This certainly has to be one of the most unique items in any Civil War collection! This footbath came from Fairfield, Connecticut. It is 20 inches long at the top and 13 inches long at the bottom. The width is 16½ inches at the top and is 6½ inches deep. It is painted white inside and russet red outside. The material is a composition similar to "PAPIER-MACHE". No markings.

FROG FOR SWORD BAYONET (C.S.): A good example of C.S.-manufactured leather goods. Frog for sword bayonet, 8½ inches long. It is well made — strongly stitched. Markings: B.H. & G. CO.
ALABAMA

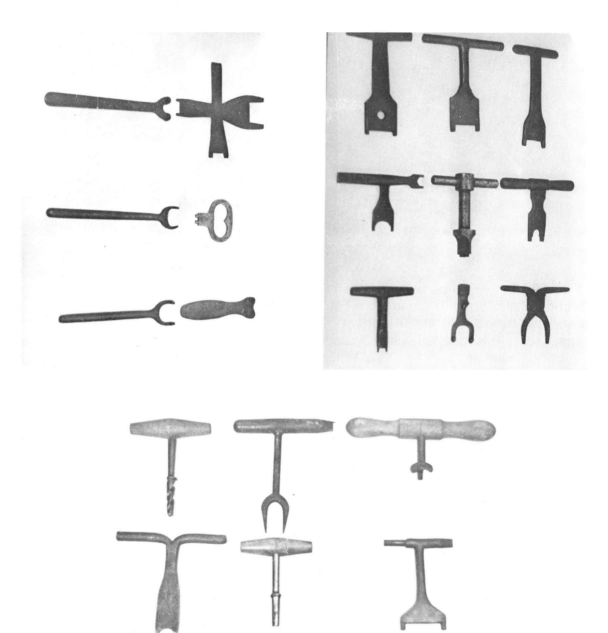

FUZE WRENCHES: The variety of these is almost endless! Shown here are some basic types but there are many more. Much work is yet to be done on these and other appendages of U.S. and C.S. artillery.

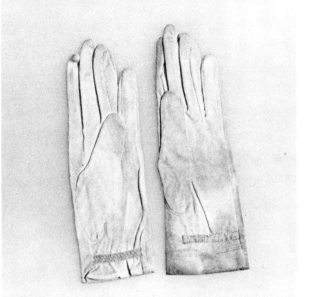

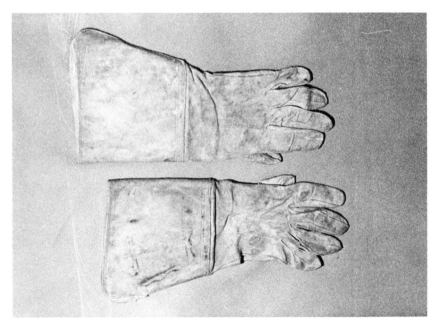

GLOVES AND GAUNTLETS: In the Army of the Potomac and on dress occasions in rear areas the Federals were required to wear white gloves. These were called "Berlin gloves" because apparently many were imported from that city. These are white cotton with a strip of elastic at the wrist. The pair shown here are 8⅝ inches long at the longest part.

Officers and some enlisted cavalrymen wore gauntlets — especially on parade. The gauntlets depicted here are buff leather, 13½ inches long at the longest point. Worn in 1861 by Captain CHARLES H. PAUL, 4th Massachusetts Infantry.

GRATER (POTATO)

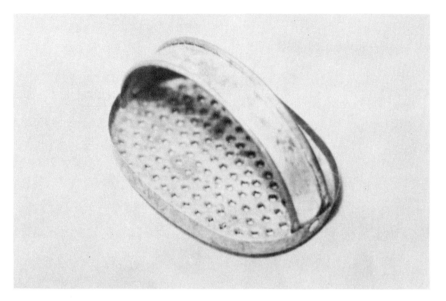

GRATER (POTATO): Tin with many perforations. 4⅛ inches long and 2⅞ inches wide at the widest part. From South Carolina. No markings.

GUN TOOLS: Often called "appendages", these are among the most baffling of Civil War items. All we can do here is show **some** of the tools known to collectors.

C.S. Spring Vise: An unusually large spring vise as can be seen with the C.S. specimen for comparison made of heavy steel — 3¾ inches tall.

Markings: 36 LA
            10   38

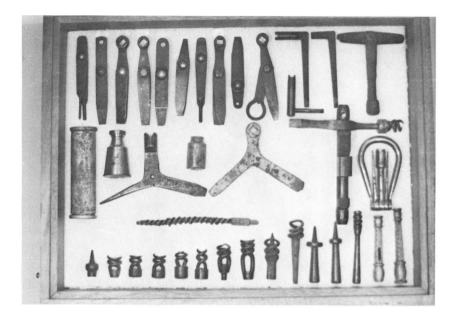

In the group picture are shown many of the more common types. They are:

Row 1 **Left to Right**
    No. 1-8 U.S.
    No. 9 Found in a Sharp's Cartridge box.
    No. 10-13 U.S.
    No. 14 C.S. from battlefield of Spotsylvania

Row 2   No. 1 Oil can and tool combination.
    No. 2 Oil can
    No. 3 Austrian gun tool
    No. 4 Oil can. The can was found on Spotsylvania battlefield; the top came from a Federal camp at LaGrange, Tennessee.
    No. 5 Gun tool from the crater at Petersburg, Virginia.
    No. 6 Musket gun tool
    No. 7 Non-regulation gun tool.

Row 3 Wire brush from Fredericksburg battlefield.

Row 4 Types of worms and bullet extractors.
    No. 9 (reading left to right) was picked up on the battlefield of Monocacy, Maryland (July 1864). Probably Confederate.

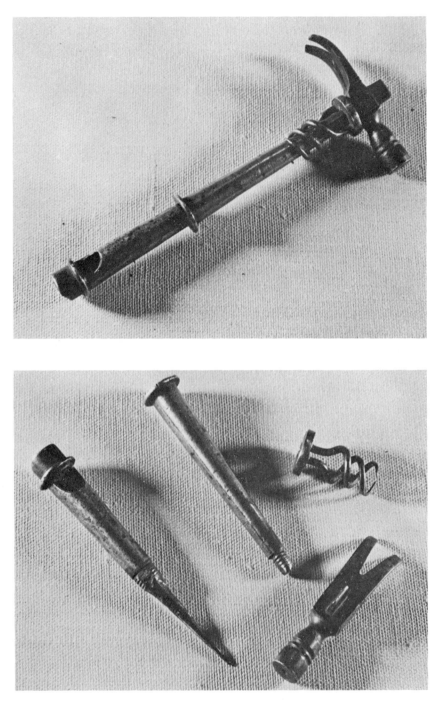

Combination Tool: Iron combination tool, probably Confederate. Each "arm" of this rare tool is approximately 2½ inches long. Rather crudely made. Photographs show tool assembled and disassembled. **No markings.** Used by Edward S. Kendall, Co. "B" 15th Massachusetts Infantry. [ROBERT CORRETTE: Fitzwilliam, New Hampshire]

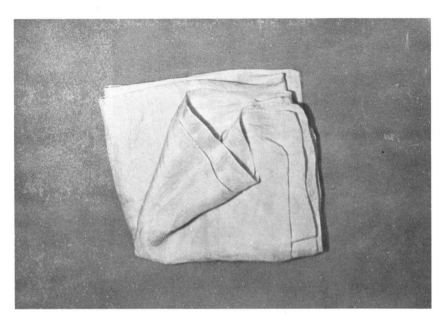

HANDKERCHIEF: Shown here is a handkerchief of the Civil War period. These handkerchiefs rank with suspenders in the high rank of **rarity.** The item shown here is of white silk, 24¾ by 27 inches. It was carried by Sergeant JOSHUA P. GRAFFAM of the 1st D.C. Cavalry.

HARMONICA: Wood is missing. Brass, 4 inches long, 1 inch wide. From camp of 7th Indiana Infantry, Fredericksburg. **No markings.**

HARMONICA BOX: Made of cardboard, 4¼ inches long and 1⅛ inches wide. Made by M. HOHNER of Philadelphia. This firm was established in 1857.

HATCHET HEADS

HATCHET HEADS: Battlefield and campsite collectors are constantly coming up with axe and hatchet heads. Naturally, the wooden handles have disappeared years ago. But here are 7 different types — and we well know there are many more!

Top Row — Left to Right
1) 5⅛ inches long with a 3¼ inch blade. Markings: **U.S.** on one side; **PLUMB** on the other. From Spotsylvania.
2) 4¾ inches long with a 2⅜ inch blade. From the Wilderness.
3) 5¾ inches long with a 3¼ inch blade. From Cold Harbor.
4) 5 inches long with a 3⅜ inch blade. From the 9th Corps area at Bethesda Church.

Bottom Row — Left to Right
1) 6½ inches long with 3½ inch blade. **Markings:** PLUMB. From the camp of 10th N.Y. Battery at Brandy Station.
2) 6⅜ inches long with a 3⅝ inch blade. The broken handle had been repaired with three nails. From Spotsylvania.
3) 6½ inches long with a 3⅞ inch blade.
   Markings: D. SIMMONS & CO
   CAST STEEL
   COHOES, N.Y.
   WARRANTED. From 5th Corps area — Wilderness.

HENRY CARTRIDGE BOX: Extremely rare — extremely interesting! The box is 7⅜ inches long, 4¾ inches tall and 3¾ inches tall on the inside.

Markings: **U.S.** on outer flap and HENRY ARMS
COMPANY
1864

HENRY CARTRIDGE BOX

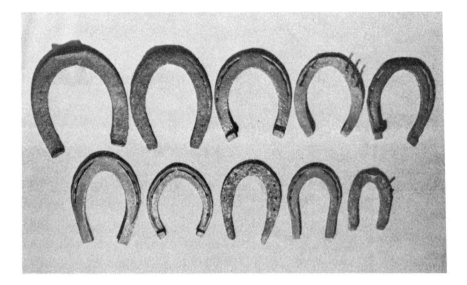

HORSESHOES: As all students and collectors well know, horses and mules were used very extensively in the campaigns by both sides. Shown here are a few of the many types and sizes of horseshoes used:

Top Row — Left to Right (All measurements are at the greatest length and width in inches.)

	Length	Width
Wilderness	7⅜	7
Alexandria, Va.	7⅛	6
LaGrange, Tenn.	6⅜	5⅝
Winchester, Va.	6	5⅛
LaGrange, Tenn. (C.S.)	6⅛	5
Bottom Row — Left to Right		
LaGrange, Tenn.	6¾	5¼
LaGrange, Tenn.	5⅝	4⅞
Corinth, Miss.	6¼	4½
LaGrange, Tenn.	5½	4
Wilderness	4½	3¼

HORSESHOE (MUD, SNOW?): An extremely odd and rare type of horseshoe from the battleground of Chattanooga. I have never seen another and do not know its original function. But it is **not** a blacksmith's creation. The shoe is 5¼ inches long, 4 inches wide, and the protuberance which extends about 3 inches below the shoe is permanently attached to the shoe in front and on both sides. **No markings.**

HOSPITAL BULLETS: The controversy still rages as to whether wounded men in the Civil War really chewed on bullets to ease their pain or not. In any event, the bullets shown in the accompanying photograph **do** have teeth marks. (Whether these are **human** teeth marks or that of animals is difficult to ascertain.) All the specimens shown are from Chattanooga except the extreme right specimen which is from Cold Harbor. [BILL HOWARD; Delmar, New York]

HOSPITAL DEPARTMENT BOTTLES

HOSPITAL DEPARTMENT BOTTLES: For some time now collectors have been finding U.S. Hospital Department bottles in campsites and — more rarely — on battlefields. Here are some of the more basic types encountered:

Left to Right

Amber — 9 inches tall, 3¾ inches in diameter.
Markings: U.S.A.
HOSP. DEPT.

Light blue — 7½ inches tall, 3 inches in diameter.
Markings: U.S.A.
HOSP. DEPT.

Light blue — 6¾ inches tall (excluding stopper), 2⅝ inches in diameter.
Markings: U.S.A.
HOSP. DEPT.

Clear — 4¾ inches tall, 1⅞ inches in diameter.
Markings: U.S.A.
HOSP. DEPT.

Clear — 3 inches tall (exclusive of stopper), 1 5/16 inches in diameter.
Markings: U.S.A.
HOSP. DEPT.

Dark blue — 2½ inches tall, 1¼ inches wide (oval).
Markings: U.S.A.
HOSP. DEPT.

HOSPITAL FLAG

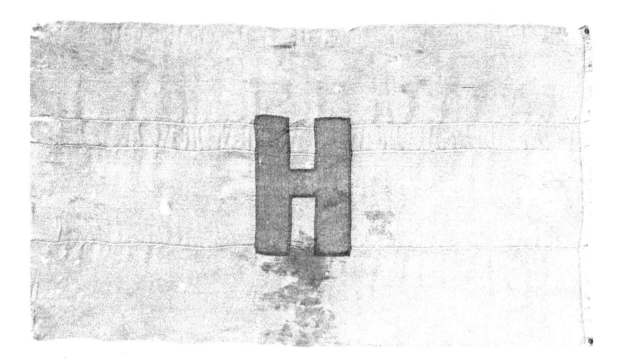

HOSPITAL FLAG: Exceedingly rare U.S. hospital flag which flew over the hospital complex at City Point, Virginia 1864-1865. Brought home by the Surgeon-in-charge, ROBERT LOUGHRAN, 20th New York State Militia. (Known also as the 80th New York Infantry.) Shown also is a contemporary picture of this hospital complex; the hospital flag is shown flying under the national flag. **Dimensions:** 110 inches long and 58 inches wide. The **H** is 17½ inches long and 24½ inches wide. The color is standard as described in the first volume of the *Collector's Encyclopedia.* [SEWARD R. OSBORNE, JR.; Oliverbridge, New York]

Post. Hospital City Point Va.

Surg'n R. Loughran 20th N.Y.S.M.
In charge.

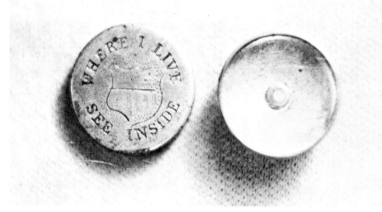

IDENTIFICATION LOCKET: Identification discs or — more popularly named — "dog tags" have been well described in previous publications. Here is a unique type of identification medium — a locket. It is of brass, about the size of a U.S. 25-cent piece, and has a screw-on cover.

INSPECTOR'S PUNCH: One of the real rarities! This inspector's punch is made of fine steel, 2½ inches long and ¼ inch wide at each end.

Markings: 62
            GDC

The letters refer to GILBERT D. GREASON who was an armory sub-inspector.

INSURANCE WATCH FOB: A unique dug relic. This brass watch fob was found with a U.S. belt buckle, cartridge box plate, and "eagle plate" all together in one spot in Spotsylvania. In addition to the insurance company seal, the fob has the following markings: THE OWNER OF THIS NUMBER IS
REGISTERED ON THE BOOKS OF
THE COMPANY.

INSURANCE IN ALL ITS BRANCHES
     894
1004 UNION BANK BLDG
     PGH
DUQUESNE UNDERWRITERS INC.

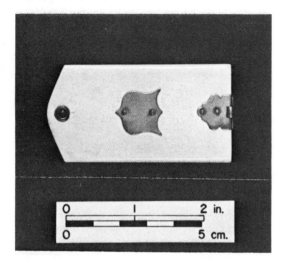

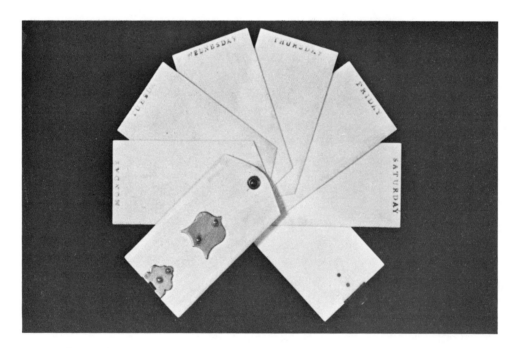

IVORY POCKET DIARY: Made entirely of ivory, cut into rectangular sheets, hinged at one end, and silver mounted with silver shield and latch. Open, the sheets fanned out allowing the owner to pencil notes on the appropriately titled page. A sheet is available and titled for every day from Monday through Saturday. When the notes were no longer needed, they were simply erased. **Dimensions:** 1 3/5 inches wide and 3 1/10 inches high. **Markings:** None. This is an exquisite little gem of a soldier's personal item and very rare.

KENTUCKY KETTLE: Made of cast iron, 7¼ inches tall and 9½ inches wide at the widest point. The cover is marked: HARE, LEAF & CO.
LOUISVILLE, KY.
PATENTED
JUNE 23, 1863

KNAPSACKS: Although in general the topic of knapsacks has been discussed in previous volumes of the *Encyclopedia,* these photographs of marked knapsacks merit attention. Both are regulation size and made of black waterproof canvas.

The New Hampshire item is stamped in red:

Co. B
13 N.H.

Stencilled on the inside: U.S.
1864

This knapsack belonged to HENRY C. WILLARD, Co. "B" 13th New Hampshire Infantry. Willard was promoted corporal and was wounded at Cold Harbor, June 1, 1864.

The Massachusetts item is stamped:

> GLP
> Co. E
> 44th M V M

On the inside flap is stencilled:

> G. L. Pulsifer
> Co. E, 44th
> REGT. MASS.

Also: MANUFACTURED BY
> JOSEPH SHORT
> SALEM, MASS.
> PATENT JAN. 28, 1862
> SOLD BY
> PALMERS & BELDERS [?]
> BOSTON, MASS.

LEGGINGS

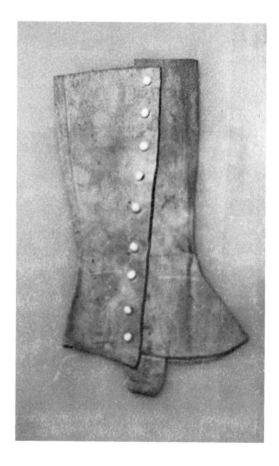

LEGGINGS: White canvas leggings, 13 inches tall, with an instep and 9 white china buttons on each. **Markings:** (On inside of each legging) NON PAREIL. The French lettering suggests that these may very well have come over with the shipment of Zouave uniforms early in the war.

LITHOGRAPH: A good example of the lithograph which was popular up through and for years after the war. Lithography vied with photography in getting the war scenes to the home front. The example here is entitled: SHERIDAN'S FINAL CHARGE AT WINCHESTER. It was put out by the American Lithographic Company after the war and depicts the battle scene fairly accurately. Many lithographs were highly inaccurate but they were produced by the thousands. Probably the best known producers were Currier and Ives; Prang, and Kurz and Allison. In a class of its own is the Chas. Magnus lithograph. Magnus produced many; his hospital scenes are especially good.

MAP READER: Brass map reader, 1⅜ inches tall (closed) and 2¼ inches tall (open). Diameter 1⅛ inches. Used by Sergeant Austin C. Stearns, Co. "K", 13th Massachusetts Infantry. **Markings:** PATENTED
MAY 24, 1864

This map magnifer or "reader" was used by topographical engineers to magnify smaller print of creeks, elevations, terrain features, etc. There are two sections with the "eyepiece" fitting snugly over the base; the "eyepiece" can be pulled up, extended, to the desired clear magnified view of the object or printing. There are two magnifying lens in this reader.

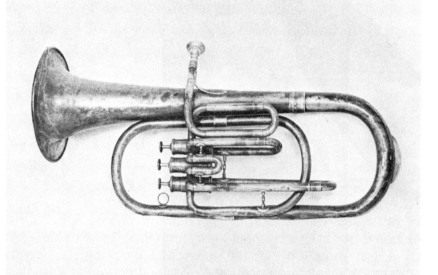

MASSACHUSETTS HORN: The brass horn shown here was carried by Warren Gilchrest, a member of the band of the 1st Massachusetts Infantry. **Dimensions:** 25¼ inches long and 8¼ inches in diameter at the "bell" of the horn.

Markings:

JOHN F. STRATTON
NEW YORK

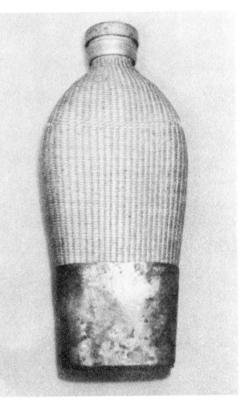

MEDICAL FLASK: Unusually large flask used by medical officers for brandy for patients undergoing surgery. Made of pewter and covered with wicker. The flask is 9½ inches tall and is equipped with a pewter cup 2½ inches tall. This flask is much larger than the pocket flasks carried during the war. From Antietam. **No markings.**

MESS KITS: The amazing variety of Civil War mess kits continues to intrigue the collector. Eventually, some dedicated, research-inclined individual will come out with a definitive treatment. Here are a few "new discoveries" since the publishing of early volumes of the *Encyclopedia*.

Mess Kit — Canteen Combinations: Consists of four tin utensils which can be assembled for carrying. The carrying apparatus is of thick black leather with a shoulder sling 4½ feet long. The utensils are:

Canteen — Height 7¼ inches; width 5 inches at bottom, tapering up to 6 inches at widest point; 2½ inches deep.

Pan — No handle. Length 7¾ inches; width 5¾ inches at bottom, tapering up to 6¼ inches at widest point; 3 inches deep.

Pan — Similar to above pan but equipped with a folding handle 5½ inches long.

Soup Pan — Equipped with two folding handles. This pan is 6⅛ inches long; 2½ inches wide, and 4 inches deep.

No markings.

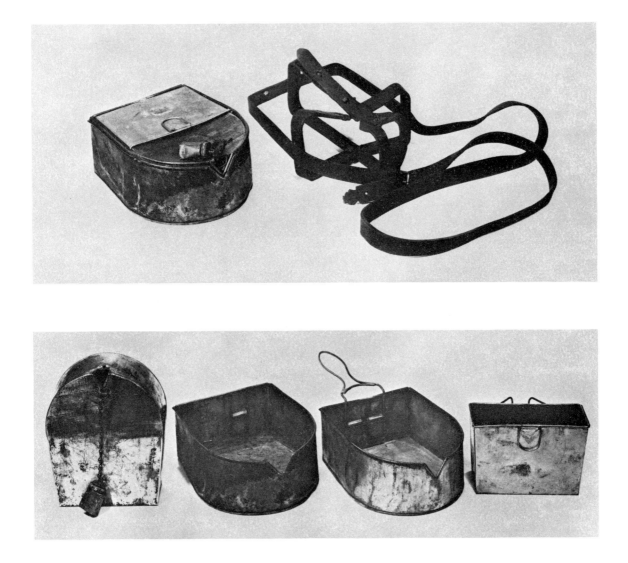

Mulligan's Patent Mess Kit: Made of tin. Height 5¼ inches. Bottom part is a mess pan 4⅝ inches in diameter and 2½ inches deep. Its cover forms a smaller pan 1⅝ inches deep over which fits a tin cup 3⅝ inches in diameter and 2½ inches deep. This cup is similar in shape and design to the "normal" Civil War tin cups. There are two metal loops on the bottom mess pan, apparently designed both as handles and to hold a strap. These loops are one inch wide. No markings.

Mess Kit of a Conn. Officer: The leather container is stencilled:
LT. WILLIAM E. PHILLIPS
Co. "K" 7th Conn. Inf.

Phillips was captured in July, 1863 at Battery Wagner. The leather top is stamped:

TOBIAS & WALL MAKERS
BOSTON

The metal lid of the pot is stamped: PAT 1861. The three half-moon containers have scratched in their tops **COFFEE, CREAM, SUGAR.** Each container shows a little evidence of the content. [T. SHERMAN HARDING, II; Orlando, Florida]

Confederate Mess Kit: Another interesting mess kit is described by VERNON SCOONE of Baltimore, Maryland. (Unfortunately, no photograph of this mess kit is available for inclusion in this book.) On one side the mess kit is marked: 27 NCT. This refers to the 27th Regiment, North Carolina Troops. The size is 9½ inches long and 4 inches high. It is oval shaped, all tin, with a leather sling and roller buckle.

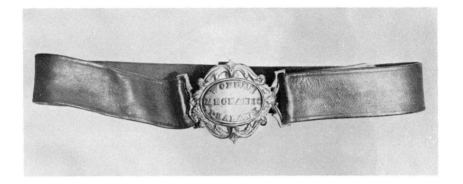

MILITIA BELT: Patent leather belt 32 inches long, 1¾ inches wide, Brass, 2-piece buckle, stamped WOBURN MECHANIC PHALANX. Worn at 1st Bull Run by Captain J. H. PARKER, 5th Massachusetts Volunteer Militia.

MILITIA BUCKLES:

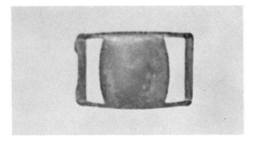

Louisiana Buckle: Made of thin brass. It is 3 inches long, 2 inches wide, and was recovered from a Louisiana regiment's position at the battle of Shiloh.

U.S. militia or non-regulation. Gold-plated, 2 inches tall and 1⅞ inches wide. A real beauty! [J. W. LEECH; Grand Junction, Colorado]

South Carolina Buckle: Made of heavy brass, 2 15/16 inches long and 2⅜ inches wide. Each of the letters **S** and **C** is ¾ of an inch high. The letters are brass but the palmetto tree decoration is silver. **Markings:** Scratched on the back of the buckle is the name: D. J. COLE. D. J. Cole first served in Captain Millet's company, 20th S.C. Militia. On August 1, 1863 he enlisted in the 4th S.C. State Troops. Reportedly he was captured and exchanged the buckle shown here with the U.S. buckle worn by his captain. [WILLIAM LANGLOIS; San Francisco, California]

SOUTH CAROLINA BUCKLE

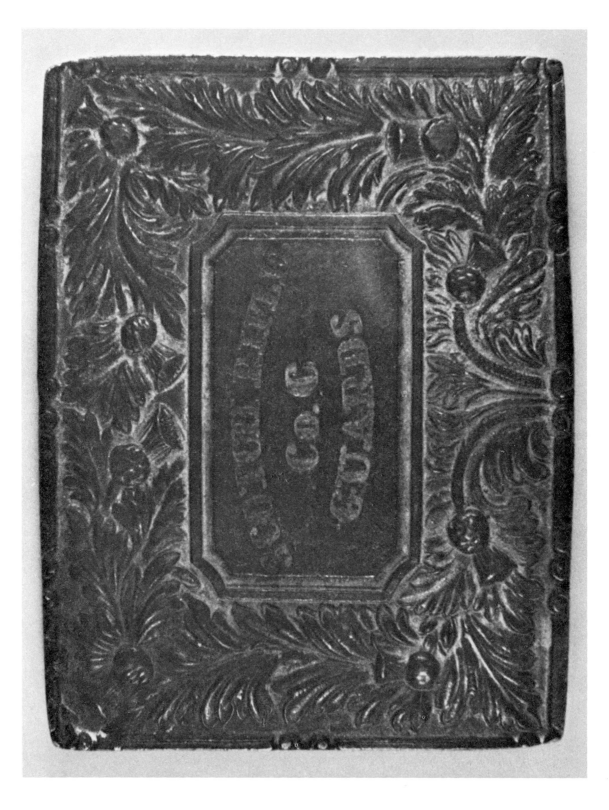

C.S. Militia Buckle: Shown here are front and rear views of a Virginia (?) militia company's buckle. The buckle was made by ROBINSON ADAMS COMPANY, Richmond, Virginia. [R. V. CROFOOT; Orlando, Florida]

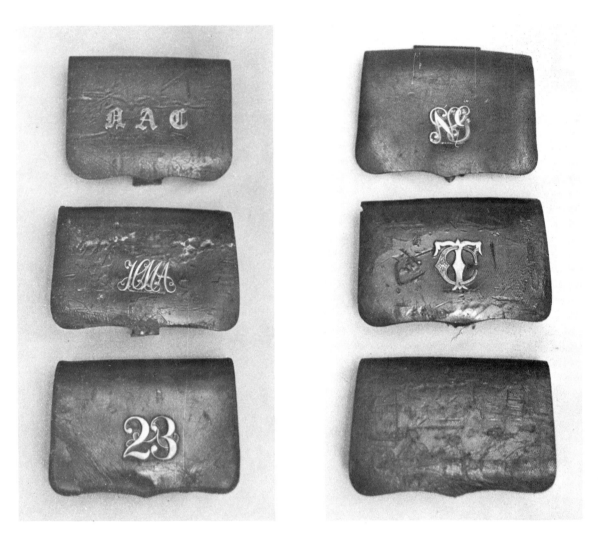

MILITIA CARTRIDGE BOXES: Here again — in this field of Civil War militia cartridge boxes — there is much to be done! Shown here are 12 such boxes. Most are of patent leather; the largest is 7¼ by 5 inches; the smallest is 6½ by 3½ inches. Most have wooden blocks holding from 16 to 18 rounds of ammunition. Three of these boxes were made by BAKER & McKENNY, NEW YORK. The others are unmarked.

Accouterment deluxe: A regulation cap box and cartridge box but with silver plates. The cartridge box and cap box plates are the same size — 2¼ by 1⅜ inches.

Markings: Cartridge Box — WATERTOWN
ARSENAL
1864

Cap Box — C. S. STORMS
MAKER N.Y.

Pennsylvania Cartridge Box: Carried by a soldier named GREIER who served in a Pennsylvania regiment at Gettysburg. (Quite possibly his unit was part of the "emergency troops".) The cartridge box contained a pen and a New Testament. **Dimensions:** 9¼ inches wide, 5½ inches high, 3¼ inches deep. **Markings:** On the flap under the cover — 1861.

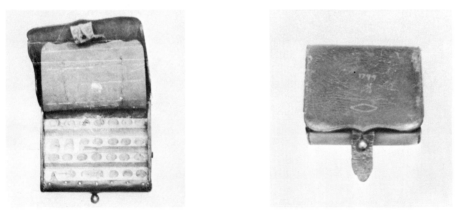

Confederate Militia (?): A black leather cartridge box, 6¼ inches wide, 5½ inches high; 2¼ inches deep. Contains a wooden block for 28 paper cartridges. Scratched on the outer flap: 1794
                            N.W. KUSS (?)

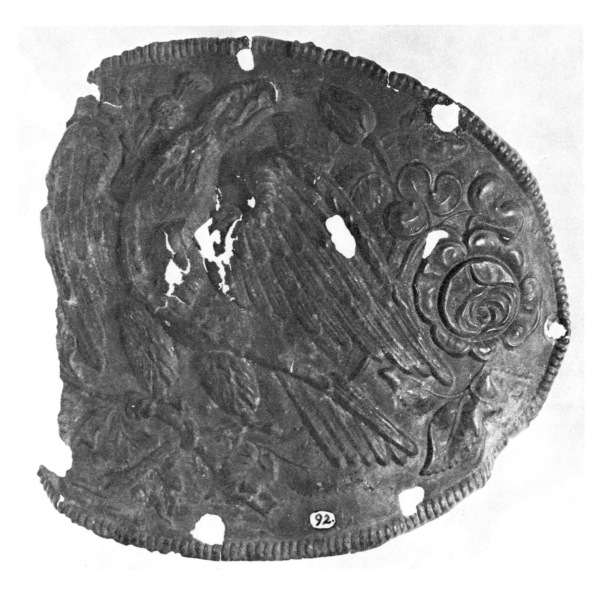

MILITIA INSIGNIA: Shown here are three examples of militia insignia.

Brass Eagle Plate: Brass eagle plate found at Fort Fisher, N.C. It is 5½ inches high and if complete, 8 inches long. Use of this plate is unknown. [TOM S. DICKEY; Atlanta, Georgia]

Hat Insignia: Gold-gilted eagle used as a hat ornament, 1¼ by 1¼ inches in size. Found in a New York regimental camp site. [DAVID M. MORROW; Woodbridge, Virginia]

South Carolina Palmetto Insignia: From the coattails of a militia uniform coat of South Carolina — possibly as early as 1835. Some of these militia uniforms were still being worn when hostilities broke out in April, 1861.

MUSKET BOX: Very few musket boxes survived the war. They were made of pine wood and made excellent kindling for camp fires! However, here are two "survivors".

Springfield Rifle Musket Box: Made of pine boards, 1-inch thick, painted grey. **Dimensions:** 5 feet 2 inches long. 17¾ inches wide and 13½ inches deep (without the lid). **Markings:**

```
        20
No  BAYONETS
SPRINGFIELD
RIFLE MUSKETS
    CAL. 58
1st CLASS
```

Trenton Rifle Musket Box: Made of pine boards 1-inch thick, unpainted. **Dimensions:** 5 feet, 1 inch long, 17¾ inches wide, and 13½ inches deep (without the lid). **Markings:**

```
          20
      RIFLE MUSKETS
         CAL. 58
     TRENTON F. A. CO.
       STAMPED N.J.
```

NAVAL CANNON LOCK: Federal naval cannon lock (hammer) recovered from the site of a U.S. Navy battery on Maryland Heights. [TOM S. DICKEY; Atlanta, Georgia]

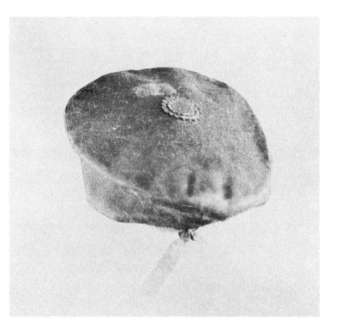

NAVAL CAP: Items of naval uniforms are rare, even for the Federal navy. Shown here is a seaman's cap of the U.S. Navy during the Civil War. Heavy blue cloth, 9¼ inches in diameter at the crown or top, and about 3½ inches deep. There is a black silk ribbon tied in a bow at the back of the cap. This ribbon is about ¾ of an inch wide. No decoration except a circular cloth design (1½ inches in diameter) is sewed in the middle of the top of the cap. **No markings.**

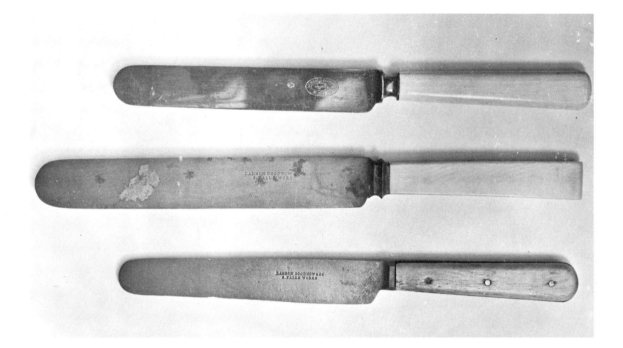

NAVAL MESS KNIFE: This knife is shown here (at top) along with two Army mess knives. All three were made by LAMSON AND GOODNOW of Shelburne Falls, Massachusetts. This famous cutlery firm was established in 1842 and by 1860 was the largest cutlery manufacturer in the United States.

The Navy specimen is 8½ inches long and has an ivory handle. It is marked in an oval with **LAMSON & GOODNOW MFG CO** and an anchor. Shown here through the courtesy of R. V. Crofoot of Orlando, Florida.

The center specimen is 9¾ inches long and also has an ivory handle. Marked LAMSON GOODNOW & CO.
    S. FALLS WORKS

The bottom specimen is 8¼ inches long with a **wood** handle. It is marked:
LAMSON GOODNOW & CO.
S. FALLS WORKS.

This knife was carried in the war by GEORGE WHITMAN, Co. "A" 27th Michigan Infantry.

NAVAL SHRAPNEL FUZE BOX

NAVAL SHRAPNEL FUZE BOX: As with so many wood containers of the Civil War period, this fuze box is excessively rare! Made of heavy pine boards and measures 10 by 10 by 10 inches. Rope handles. **Markings:**   8 INCH
SHRAPNEL
5 SEC
ORD. 1864

The markings also include the navy anchor.

NAVAL SIGNAL LIGHT (?)

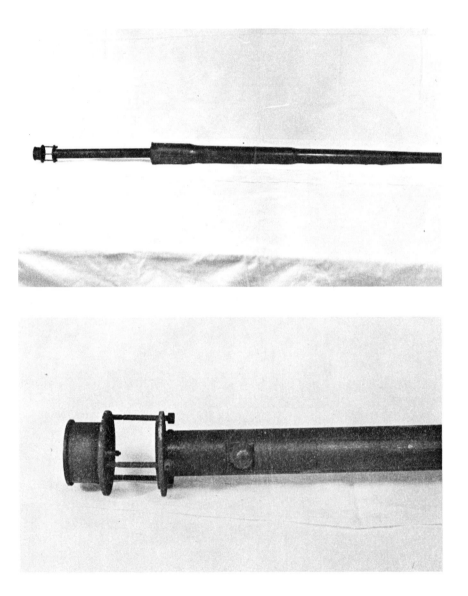

NAVAL SIGNAL LIGHT (?): This unusual light is presumed to be for naval use. It is 4 feet 7 inches tall. The bottom section is of light wood which in turn separates into 3 sections which are hinged so as to form a tripod. The "light" proper is only about 3 inches tall with the open section 1½ inches tall. The glass has been broken out. **No markings.**

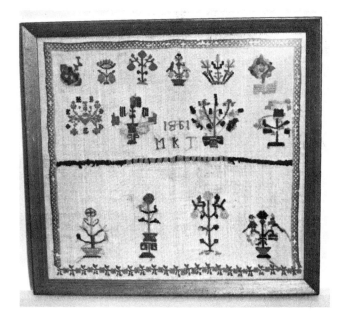

NEEDLEWORK: A very charming example of Civil War period needlework. It was done in South Carolina and very probably by a young (and patriotic!) lady. The colors are still fairly bright. **Dimensions:** 19¾ inches long and 18⅛ inches wide. **Markings:** 1861
M.K.T.

124 NEW HAMPSHIRE DRUM

NEW HAMPSHIRE DRUM: This is a non-regulation drum used by a member of the 12th New Hampshire Infantry band. **Dimensions:** 14 inches tall and 24½ inches in diameter. **Markings:** Painted on the side of the drum is a shield and 12 N.H. Inf.

NEW YORK SOLDIER'S BLANKET: Made of **very** coarse light brown material, much resembling the material used in a horse blanket! This blanket is 6 feet 9 inches long and 6 feet wide. The letters **U.S.** in the center of the blanket are 5½ inches tall and 4¼ inches wide. Carried during the war by THEODORE J. SOUTHWORTH, Co. "A" 184th New York Infantry.

NOSEBAG

NOSEBAG: These were extensively used in both armies since it was definitely a "horse war". The specimen shown here is of white canvas with a leather bottom; and is 13½ inches tall. Equipped with a black leather strap.

Markings: on bottom — MANUFACTURED
                                              BY
                                              J. E. CONDICT
                                              57 WHITE ST.
                                              NEW YORK

NUTCRACKER: Used obviously only in rear echelon establishments and on the home front. Made of cast iron, with a length at the base of 8½ inches. **Markings:**
BATTLE OF CHATTANOOGA
         1863
[TOM RYAN; Nashville, Tennessee]

OFFICER'S HOUSEWIFE

OFFICER'S HOUSEWIFE: Most of the "housewives" of the Civil War era were made for the enlisted man. Here is definitely a deluxe specimen which was of much better material and contents than the ones made by mothers, sisters or sweethearts. This specimen is leather covered, 3¼ inches tall, 3 inches wide and 1¾ inches deep. It is very finely made! There is a mirror in the cover and it contains scissors, a thimble, tweezers, a nail file, a small glass vial, a metal toothpick, and a holder for pen points. Truly a classy outfit! **No markings.**

OIL CAN: Made of heavy tin with handle. It is 4¾ inches tall, 3¼ inches wide and 1¾ inches deep. The pouring spout screws into the can and the spout itself has a screw on top secured by a chain. No markings.

PADLOCKS: Every lock shown here was used in the Civil War. Several specimens are stamped **U.S.** to show government issue if not manufacture. The locks were used primarily for protecting magazine storage areas, buildings, paymaster's safes and satchels privately owned. All the measurements are at the longest and widest points.

Top Row — Left to Right:
1) 4¾ by 3¼ (steel). **Markings:** VR CROWN   COLUMBIA, S.C.
           A. THOMPSON   [ARSENAL]

2) 4¼ by 3 (steel). **Markings:** U.S.
           ST. LOUIS, MO.

3) 3½ by 2 1/3 (steel). **Markings:** V.[?3W CO.]
    Spotsylvania

4) 3¼ by 2½ (steel). **Markings:** THOMPSON & CO.
    Fredericksburg   NEWARK

Second Row:
1) 3¼ by 2½ (steel). **Markings:** W. W. & CO
    Fort Morgan, Ala.

2) 3½ by 2½ (steel). **Markings:** D. M. & CO
    Fort Morgan

3) 3½ by 2⅝ (steel). **Markings:** PATENT V.R. CROWN
    Fort Morgan

4) 3½ by 2½ (steel).
    Chancellorsville

Third Row:
1) 4 by 2⅝ (brass)
    Libby Prison — Luray, Virginia Museum

2) 3¼ by 2⅜ (brass)
    Washington Naval Yard, 1861-1865

3) 2⅛ by 1⅜ (brass). **Markings:** RITCHIE & SON
    Maj. S. K. Williams   NEWAR, N.J.
    Ohio Cav

4) 1⅝ by 1¼ (steel)
    Champion's Hill

Bottom Row:
      1⅛ by ¾ of an inch (brass). No markings.
      Maj. S. K. Williams
      Ohio Cav

PAINTING: Samuel Bell Palmer on March 1, 1862, joined "Mabry Artillery" of Tennessee. Was captured and sent to Federal prison camp at Camp Douglas, Illinois. While there, a Federal officer, Major Samuel K. Williams, Jr. befriended Palmer and provided him with materials to paint. This painting is one of the results — it was painted in the prison camp and presented to Major Williams who also provided Palmer with tobacco and "other luxuries". The two men remained friends after the war.

Major Williams had been in service since 1861. In late 1864 he was ordered to Camp Douglas. Discharged September 9, 1865.

PALL BEARER'S BADGE: Black silk 10 inches long including gold tassels. Worn at services for Lincoln's funeral escort in Columbus, Ohio, 1865. Markings: PALL BEARER.

Funeral Usher's Ribbon: White silk 35½ inches long including gold tassels. Has a gold star 6 inches from bottom of silk material. Worn by Captain Watson C. Squire, 7th Independent Co., Ohio Sharpshooters, and one of "Sherman's Escort". Possibly worn at Lincoln's funeral ceremonies in Ohio, 1865.

PAPER HOLDER

PAPER HOLDER: Made of thin brass, 1½ inches in diameter and ⅝ of an inch deep. Marked with a eagle and **PAPER FASTENERS.** What the fasteners themselves looked like is not known since the container was empty when acquired.

Also shown here is a shield-decorated clip board type of paper fastener for use in unit headquarters. This item was used to hold the various orders and circulars emanating from higher headquarters. The clip is 4 inches tall and 2½ inches wide at the widest point. It is decorated with an eagle, stars, shield, and **E. PLURIBUS UNUM** on a scroll. The material is of thin brass, with a spring separating the front and back sections.

PARAPET BAYONET(?)

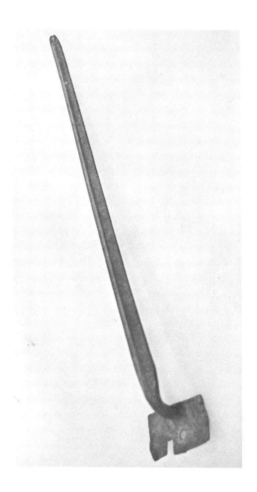

PARAPET BAYONET(?): A bayonet item of some sort — possibly for attachment to a log parapet. The bayonet proper is identical to the regulation triangular bayonet for the M. 1861 Springfield rifle musket except that the blade is only 15¼ inches long. Instead of the normal attachment section (i.e. the sleeve that slips over the barrel with a locking ring) the bayonet flares out to a flat section with a hole (possibly for a nail or screw) and an open slot. This flange section is 2½ inches by 1¾ inches in size. The item is very obviously original and made as one piece. No markings. From the battlefield of Fisher's Hill, Virginia.

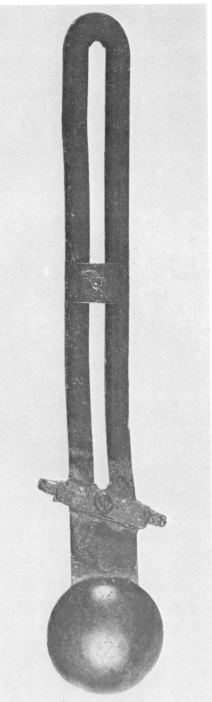

PENDULUM HAUSSE: Found on a battlefield — these items are rare and doubly rare when found where a battle took place. The artillery implements are rare anyway — but battlefield recovered items are extremely scarce! The artillery crews were very careful about their gun instruments! [TOM S. DICKEY; Atlanta, Georgia]

PERCUSSION CAP ARMLET

PERCUSSION CAP ARMLET: This is a most unique item. The leather base is 6¾ by 3¼ inches and is curved to fit the arm. Percussion caps are arranged in 5 rows with each row holding about 10 caps. This armlet was captured at Fort Donelson, Tennessee by Lieutenant H. L. BRICKETT of the 25th Indiana Infantry. The lieutenant was killed a few months later at Shiloh, April 6, 1862. [T. SHERMAN HARDING, II; Orlando, Florida]

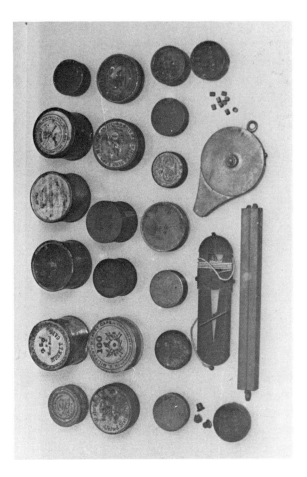

PERCUSSION CAPS AND LOADERS: Shown here are containers of both musket and pistol percussion caps. Note also the two types of percussion cap loaders and the infantry "STADIA", a device for measuring range. The long brass capper came from the Charlestown Navy Yard.

PEWTER CARTRIDGE BOX LINER: The Confederacy accomplished miracles in supplying its troops with the sinews of war. Here is a good example. This is a pewter cartridge box liner for holding cartridges. It is 5½ by 3½ inches and came from the battlefield of the Wilderness.

PICTURES: "A picture is worth a thousand words." This is most certainly true for our understanding of the Civil War. Through the **very** generous cooperation of RONN PALM of Monroeville, Pennsylvania, we are showing some unusually interesting pictures of Civil War soldiers. These pictures speak for themselves! [RONN PALM; Monroeville, Pennsylvania]

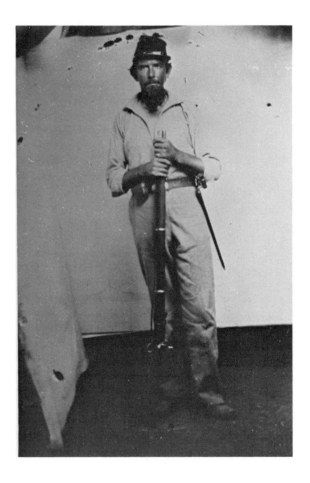

PILLS: Concerned mothers urged their soldier sons to take pills with them to the war. Only in this way could they have protection against "swamp fever" and malaria. Shown here are two examples of the many antidotes prescribed by the soldier's relatives.

Pill Box by Herrick's Sugar Coated Pills. "Price 25 Cts." Thin wooden box is 2 inches long.

Pill Box by Sawyer's "Cholic Pills". Cost 25 cents. Box is 2⅛ inches long. Some pills are still inside!

PINFIRE AMMUNITION: Foreign pinfire revolvers were used quite extensively in the Civil War as attested to by the pinfire ammunition recovered from battlefields and camp sites. Here are two boxes of original ammunition. Both boxes are of cardboard, 4½ inches long, 1½ inches wide, and 1⅜ inches high.

The box on the left holds 25 cartridges, caliber 12 mm, packed in sawdust. The box is marked: FABRIQUE
          DE BALLES ET CARTOUCHES
                              LEFAUCHEUX
          DE 12 MILLEMETRES

The box on the right also contains 25 cartridges. It is marked:

          CARTOUCHES
          12 MILLEMETRES
HOULLIER — BLANCHARD
ARQUEBUSIER BREVETE
          PARIS
A LONGUE PORTEE

PORTHOLE (C.S.N.)

PORTHOLE (C.S.N.): Rarest of the rare! A C.S. porthole recovered from a salvage dump in England. Made of very thick glass with brass rim and fixtures. **Dimensions:** A diameter of 19½ inches overall with the glass diameter of 13½ inches. **Markings:** C.S.S. COTTON.

POSTER: In the days before radio and television and when even newspapers were rare in some rural areas, the poster was used extensively to disseminate news. At times, these posters departed from their usual norm of "straight reporting" and were couched in humorous lines. Here is such a poster — announcing a Fourth of July program in Connecticut. It was written before the North was aware of the long, costly war ahead of it. **Dimensions:** 23⅞ inches tall and 8½ inches wide. Only about 2 weeks after this celebration, 3 Connecticut regiments fought at First Bull Run. Many of the men came from Meriden, Connecticut — locale of the July 4th celebration.

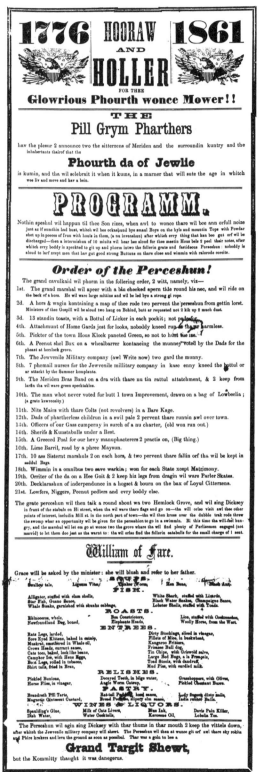

POWDER CANS: Although most ammunition in the Civil War was "fixed", i.e. already prepared for use in weapons by both sides, some powder was used — either from large containers like metal or wood barrels, or from smaller cans as shown here. In fact, a surprisingly large number of cans like these have been recovered from battlefield and camp sites.

The large can is 4½ inches tall, 4½ inches wide, and 2 inches deep. it is of tin, painted black. The paper label says: -CKY RIFLE GUNPOWDER
                      HAZARD POWDER CO.

The small can is of japanned tin, 3⅛ inches tall, 2¾ inches wide, and 1⅛ inches deep. There are no markings on the metal of the can, but the old paper label **says:** MADE "FOR SMALL PISTOLS".

PROJECTILES: This is definitely one of the very best collections of Civil War projectiles in existence. Not only are the main types here but many rare types as well. Only an extremely dedicated and knowledgeable expert could have assembled so fine a collection as this. It is truly fantastic! [TOM S. DICKEY; Atlanta, Georgia]

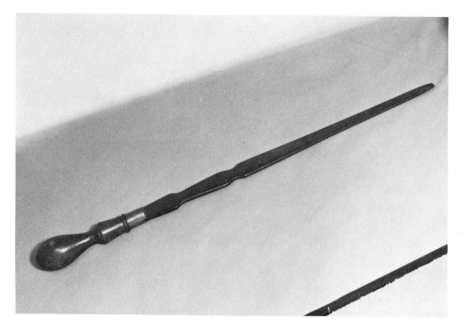

RAILROAD ITEMS: One of the baffling mysteries of Civil War collecting is whatever happened to all the railroad items used. We know that railroads were very extensively used by both sides. Yet railroad items which definitely were used **during the war** are rare indeed. Shown here are some examples:

Screwdriver (Railroad): Steel screwdriver with wooden handle. Overall length is 24½ inches; the blade is 18 inches long. Used during the Gettysburg campaign on the Western Maryland Railroad by locomotive engineer John Nelson Hymiller. (See data on this railroad in author's *Herman Haupt: Lincoln's Railroad Man.*) **No markings.**

Oil Can (Railroad): For steam locomotive. Made of brass with an overall length of 23 inches. The spout is 17 inches long; diameter of the can is 4 inches. **No markings.**

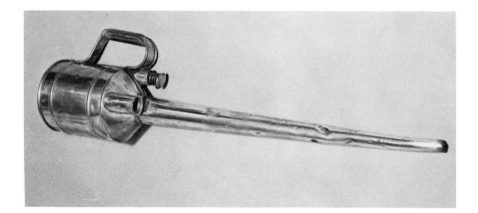

Rail: Section of iron "strap rail" from a C.S. camp at Nickerjack Cove (north of Chattanooga). This rail is 2½ inches wide with 14 inches between holes where the rail was fastened to the "stringers".

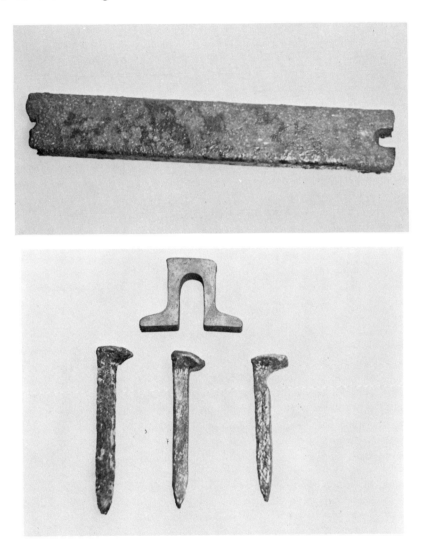

Miscellaneous Railroad Items: Three spikes: Left to Right: The longest is 6 inches in length and was found in a fort on the **Orange and Alexandria Railroad** (Virginia). The second longest is 5½ inches in length and came off the sunken Federal ship CAIRO. The shortest is 5⅛ inches long. Note the wear under the head of this spike — the wear being made by the flange of the rail. From the **Memphis and Charleston Railroad** at LaGrange, Tennessee. With this spike was found a U.S. eagle "I" button.

Also shown is a cross-section of a rail from Ezra Church, Georgia. This section is 2¾ inches tall and 3⅞ inches wide at the bottom.

RAINCOAT

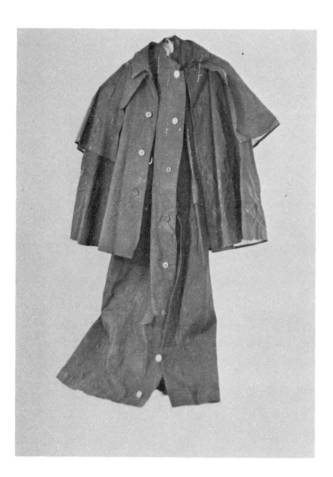

RAINCOAT: An interesting raincoat because it differs markedly from the more common rubber coat. This raincoat is light blue in color and made of a water-proofed canvas material. The cape is detachable. Worn early in the war by Lyman Stowe of the 2nd Michigan Infantry.

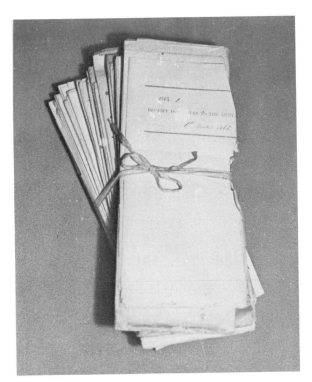

RED TAPE: The term "red tape" has a definite — and really negative — connotation in American military parlance. There was a great deal of red tape in our Civil War — literally! Shown here is a photograph of documents enclosed by a cloth strip which is definitely **RED**. These documents are all dated in 1863 and have not been untied since that time. They came from the field desk of Colonel J. B. McCown of the 63rd Illinois Infantry and were issued during the Vicksburg campaign.

RELIGIOUS MEDAL: Thin medal — "Immaculate Heart of Mary" found in Sherman's lines, siege of Savannah. Only 1 inch long and ¾ of an inch wide. Is decorated with religious symbols of the Roman Catholic Faith.

REVOLVER: Here is one of those "unique" weapons imported from Europe in the early months of the war. It is a caliber .44 LaFaucheux revolver with a folding bayonet 4¾ inches long. This weapon is 6-shots and 12 inches in length. The lettering on top of the barrel is illegible. The weapon came from Nashville, Tennessee.

RIFLES AND MUSKETS: Various long arms are constantly turning up that are of interest to the Civil War student and collector. Shown here are four:

Ohio Rifle Musket: Heavy octagonal barrel, with brass bands. Caliber .58. Length overall is 43½ inches with a 28 inch barrel. Has a cheekpiece. Equipped with a sword bayonet 28 inches long with a 23½ inch blade. The black leather scabbard is stamped: OHIO. **Markings:** On the top of barrel — SEDERL; on lock plate — (1)861.

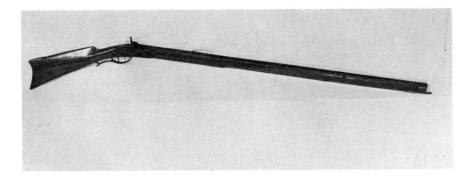

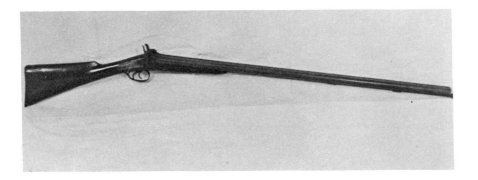

Hunting Rifle: Used by a C.S. volunteer in 1861. Length 58 inches with a 41 inch barrel. Heavy octagonal barrel with brass furniture throughout. Caliber — about .36. Wood ramrod. **Markings:** On lock plate — A. W. SPIES. Spies made rifles in New York during the period 1820-1851.

Shotgun: Used by a South Carolina cavalryman, it is 52½ inches long; each barrel is 36½ inches long. 12-gauge. Steel ramrod. **Markings:** J. MANTON. Joseph Manton of London made this shotgun about 1850.

C.S. MUSKETOON

C.S. Musketoon: This weapon is very probably C.S. made but complete identification has not yet been made. It is 39 inches long with a 24-inch barrel. There is a stud for a sword bayonet. Brass furniture. The weapon is of the Enfield type but is caliber .58. **Markings:** (On lockplate) A E
1864

The lettering is crude.

SABER BOX: Very similar to the musket box as described on page 116 in this volume. Made of plain pine, 4 feet 5½ inches long; 19½ inches wide, and 14¼ inches deep (including the cover). **Markings:**

30
CAVALRY SABRES
HEAVY AM.
SMALL GRIP — FLAT BACK
AMES   1st CLASS
AGH

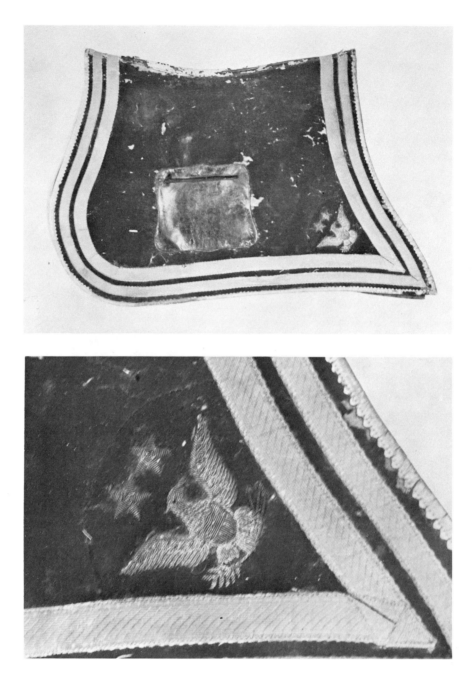

SADDLE CLOTH: Worn under the saddle by officers, generally of field grade or higher. Very finely made — very expensive — and today, very rare! This particular saddle cloth was for a major general as can be seen by the two stars. Made of blue woolen cloth and trimmed with gold-colored bands. It is leather-reinforced with slots for the stirrups straps. Length — 3 feet at longest point; width 21½ inches on each side.

SASH: Officer's red silk sash, about 9 feet long, and 3⅝ inches wide at the middle and tapering to the tassels. Beautifully stitched on this sash (probably by wife or sweetheart!) is: CAPT. C. C. SHULTAS
                CO. H 22d REG.
                C.V.

The 22nd Connecticut Infantry was a nine-month's unit.

SECRETARY

SECRETARY: A fine homemade, crocheted pocket secretary. It is 8 inches long when closed; open it is 8 by 8 inches. White on the outside and bright red on the inside. Was carried in the war by Captain A. H. ALEXANDER, Co. "A" 103rd Pennsylvania Infantry. [ARTHUR LEE BREWER, JR.; Durham, North Carolina]

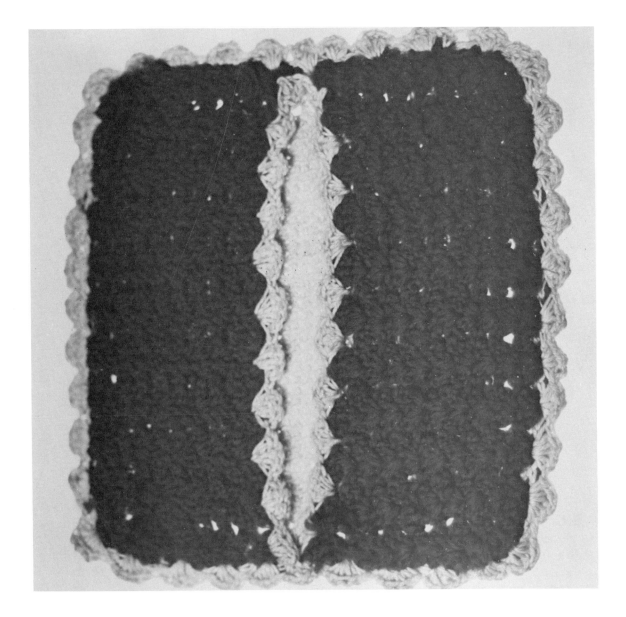

SHARPSHOOTER'S GLASSES: Glasses made especially for a sharpshooter. Note the circular clear lens on the right glass. The glasses themselves have dark glass except for the lighter circular lens which is barely perceptible in the photograph. Frames are of brass and are adjustable. These glasses only saw limited use in the field but apparently were used some. [BILL HOWARD; Delmar, New York]

SHAWL: This luxury certainly was not used at the front very long! It is a 10 by 5 foot shawl made of beautifully pure wool. There is a fringe on both ends. Used in the war by First Lieutenant WILLIAM S. AMES of the 38th U.S. Colored Troops. **No markings.**

SHELTER HALF: Although shelter tents were used by the thousands during the war, this specimen is one of the few authenticated examples known to exist today.

Dimensions: 64 inches by 64 inches. All four corners are reinforced with 4 inches by 5 inches pieces of canvas. There is a total of 31 button holes. This specimen is made of canvas. Used by NATHAN RUSSELL, Co. "F" 38th Massachusetts Infantry.

Markings: In an oval shield —   JOSEPH LEE
64 & 66
Lispenard &
62 Walker Sts.
New York

[From the collection of WILLIAM C. McKENNA, Westmont, N.J. Photographs by STEVEN MILLER, Audobon, N.J.]

SHOT LADLE

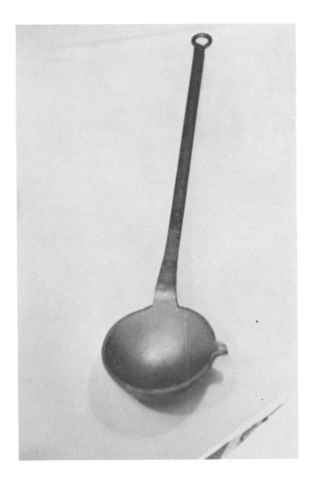

SHOT LADLE: Iron shot ladle weighing about 5 pounds with an overall length of 31 inches. The bowl is 6⅞ inches in diameter and 3 inches deep. **No markings.**

Also shown is a shot-making outfit — probably Confederate. This came from Lancaster, South Carolina. **No markings.**

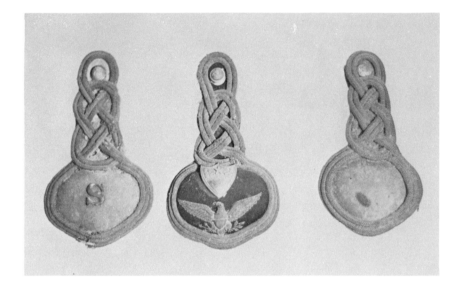

SHOULDER KNOTS: Although this type of shoulder insignia was to become very popular in the post-Civil War era, some officers did wear the shoulder knot during the 1861-1865 period. The three examples shown here were worn during the Civil War.

Left to Right:

Marked **S.** Gray with red and blue cording and a New York State button.

Colonel's shoulder knot with a silver shield decorated with stars. The cloth is dark blue with gray cording, and a U.S. staff officer's button. **Markings:** HARTLEY & GRAHAM
    NEW YORK

Red shoulder knot with green cording. The button has a harp motif. Worn by an Irish regiment — the 69th New York Infantry.

SOUVENIRS:

Wooden Plaque: Plaque made from a hardtack box on which is fastened some battlefield bullets and other relics from the 1864 siege of Petersburg. The long piece of wood at the top is marked: PIECE OF CHEVEAUX DE FRISE
FROM REBEL FORT "MAHONE"
CALLED BY THE SOLDIERS
FORT DAMNATION!

The round piece of wood is marked: SABOT
3-INCH CANISTER
FROM REBEL FORT MAHONE
PROBABLY FIRED _____

The piece of wood at bottom of the plaque is marked:

PIECE OF "BOMB PROOF"
FROM FORT SEDGWICK,
CALLED BY THE SOLDIERS
FORT HELL!

Brick: Complete brick 8½ by 4 by 1¾ inches. Marked: CANNON DESIGN
and MALVERN HILL
JULY 1st 1862

Small piece of brick: taken from the Dunkard Church at Antietam. **Dimensions:** 1 inch square and 3¾ inches long.

Piece of wood from the Andersonville Prison stockade. Dimensions: 1 inch square and 2⅝ inches long. A label on the wood reads: SOLD BY A MEMBER OF
THE GAR WHO GOT IT
WHILE ASST. ADJ. GEN. OF
THE DEPT. OF GEORGIA.
36th ANNUAL ENCAMPMENT GAR

BULLETS IN MEDICINE BOTTLE

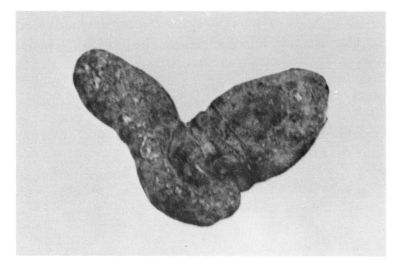

Bullets in Medicine Bottle: This bottle contains 2 bullets taken from a wounded soldier. He was PETER S. CHASE, Co. "I", 2nd Vermont Infantry. CHASE was wounded twice — at Fredericksburg (Dec. 13, 1862) and at the Wilderness (May 5, 1864). The two bullets were taken from his leg after Fredericksburg. The label on top of the bottle gives the information cited above. The medicine bottle is 3 inches tall and 1¾ inches in diameter. Chase died September 16, 1927.

Extracted Bullet: Bullet extracted from leg of a Federal soldier by Assistant Surgeon ROBERT W. ELMER, 23rd New Jersey Infantry. The soldier's name and battle are not recorded. The bullet fragment has a nail in it (probably used to put up on display); the bullet itself is caliber .44.

Bullets That Met in Mid-air: ARTHUR LEE BREWER, JR. of Durham, North Carolina contributes this photo of two bullets which met in mid-air at Gettysburg.

SPIGOTS: Pewter spigots from barrels used in the field. The top spigot came from an Alabama camp at Dumfries, Virginia. **Markings:** NEW YORK
NO. 3

The bottom spigot top came from a campsite at Eastport, Mississippi. **No markings.**

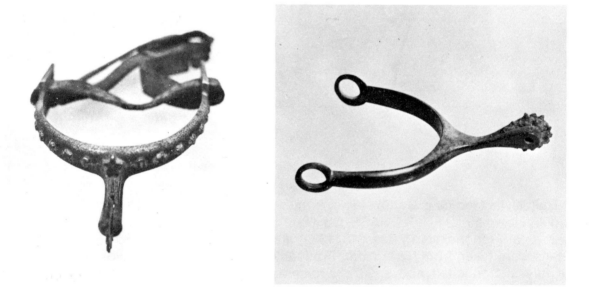

SPURS: Shown here are contrasting types of spurs. The Federal spur (with the spur strap) is of ornately decorated brass. It is of regulation size and shape. There are 6 stars on each side of the spur with **U.S.** in block letters separated by a large star just over the rowel projection. [RONN PALM; Monroeville, Pennsylvania]

The C.S. spur is made of brass. Its total length is 5¼ inches and came from the 1861 battle at Dranesville, Virginia.

STATE DOCUMENTS: The collecting of Civil War documents is, of course, a field in itself. The three shown here are self-explanatory. These colorful items were highly prized and were hung with pride in the family livingroom. [TOM MacDONALD; Eustis, Maine]

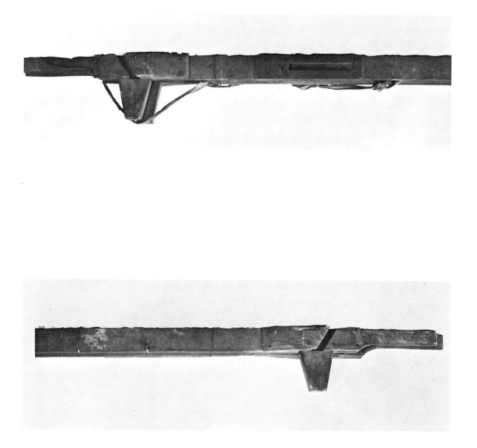

STRETCHER: A heavy stretcher used in the field. It is 8 feet 2 inches long, about 2¾ feet wide, equipped with a thin canvas material of which only fragments remain. This stretcher was used at the battle of ANTIETAM, September 17, 1862.

SUSPENDERS: Civil War soldiers used suspenders, **not** belts to hold up their trousers. Many did not even wear suspenders; they merely buttoned their trousers tight enough to keep the trousers up around their waists. I have never even seen a pair of Civil War suspenders; they are rare! But here are photographs of a pair worn by GEORGE W. BARNES, Co. "H", 36th Massachusetts Infantry. The cloth of these suspenders is 1⅝ inches wide. The clips are the same type as shown on page 188 of Vol. II of the *Encyclopedia*. [ROBERT CORRETTE; Fitzwilliam, New Hampshire]

TASSEL FOR HOSPITAL PATIENT: A yellow wool tassel worn by patients in U.S. military hospitals. Total length 6¾ inches. The original paper package holding this tassel had the following written in faded ink: WORN BY HOSPITAL PATIENTS ON UNIFORM.

TELEGRAPH KEY: Thin brass, 2⅜ inches long. Found at Civil War site on Polegreen Road, Hanover County, Virginia in 1962. **No markings.**

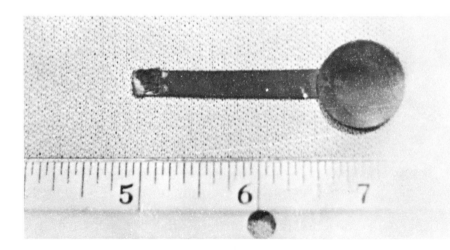

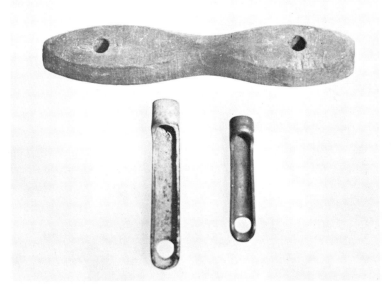

TENT ROPE TIGHTENERS: Apparently there has been little change in the basic types of tent rope tighteners since 1865. The three shown here are from the Civil War. The large wooden specimen is 8 inches long, 1½ inches wide at widest point, and 1 inch thick. It is made of hard pine.

The larger of the metal specimens is of heavy brass, 4 inches long. It came from Cold Harbor. The smaller specimen is also of heavy brass, but is only 3 inches long.

TOILET ARTICLES:
Toilet Kit: Made of heavy black cardboard with a small lock. Kit is 7 inches tall, 5⅝ inches wide, 3½ inches deep. A very elegant outfit. Included in the contents are various

brushes, shaving items, mirror, a pearl handle bottle opener, large needle, pearl handle shears, steel boot hooks, a bottle. **Markings:**   J. B. WILLIAMS CO.

MUG
SHAVING
SOAP

Used during the war by a soldier from Carmel, Maine.

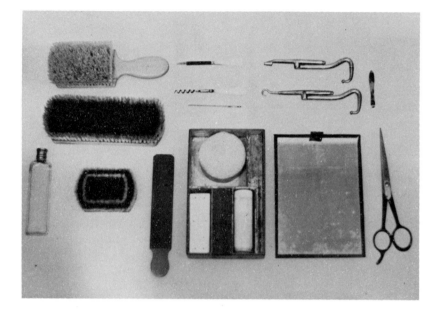

Tooth Brushes:

Top: Bone handle, 6½ inches long. **Markings:** EXTRA FINE PARIS FRANCE. Used by W. L. Ames, 117th New York Infantry.

Bottom: Bone handle, 6½ inches long. **Markings:** STURTEVANT'S SPECIAL NO. 45, FRANCE. Used by Surgeon ENOCH PEARCE, 61st Ohio Infantry.

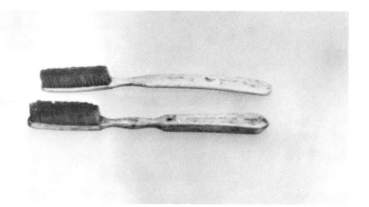

Toiletry Bottles: Left to Right

1) Clear glass, 6⅛ inches tall. **Markings:**
    TRICOPHEROUS
    FOR THE SKIN AND HAIR
    NEW YORK
    BARRY'S

2) Clear glass, 5⅞ inches tall. **Markings:**
    LYON'S
    NEW YORK
    KATHAIRON
    FOR THE HAIR

3) Brown glass, 4⅞ inches tall. **Markings:** BUCKINGHAM
    WHISKER DYE

TOMPION STAR: Made of medium heavy brass. Greatest width — 6¼ inches. From the tompion of a large naval cannon.

TOMPIONS

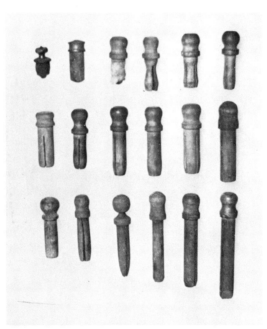

TOMPIONS: The tompion was a wooden or cork plug inserted into the muzzle of a gun to keep out water, dirt, etc. Shown here are 18 different types and calibers. All were used during the war.

TOOTH EXTRACTOR: Crude iron extractor found in the CHINN HOUSE on the battlefield of FIRST BULL RUN (FIRST MANASSAS). This extractor was found in the rafters of the CHINN HOUSE which served as a hospital. Total length 6¼ inches. **No markings.**

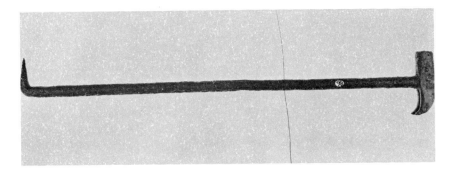

TOW HOOK: This is an artillery implement used for unpacking ammunition chests. The one shown here is 14⅞ inches long. Length of the hammer head is 2 inches. From the battlefield of SHILOH. [TOM DICKEY; Atlanta, Georgia]

VETERAN RESERVE CORPS BELT: Beautiful buff leather belt for noncomis-sioned officers of the Veteran Reserve Corps. The belt is 36¾ inches long, 1¾ inches wide, excluding the buckle. **Markings:** (on inside of the belt) HERMAN OTTO
Co. H 17 r
2nd V.R.C.

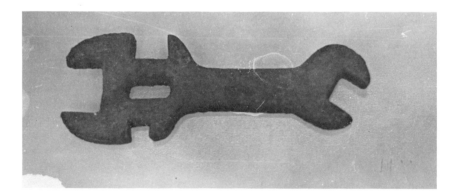

WAGON WRENCH: Very unusual iron wrench for use by army teamsters on their wagons. Overall length 7¾ inches. Width at widest place is 2¾ inches. This wrench is ⅝ of an inch thick! No markings. From Falmouth, Virginia camp of the Army of the Potomac.

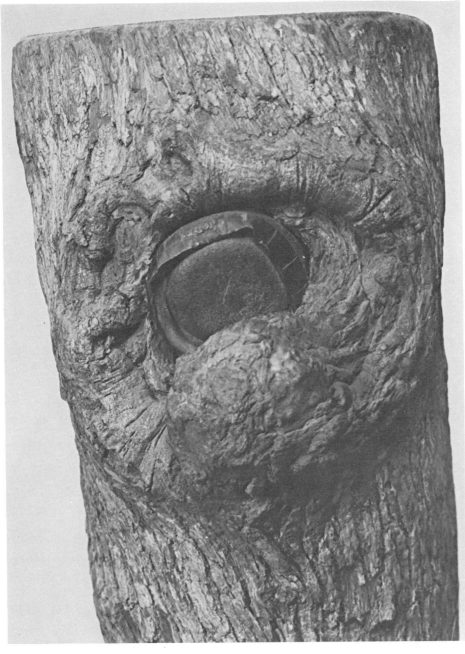

WAR LOG: Shown here are three "war logs" from Western Theater battlefields. As can be seen from the photographs, the term "war log" applies to a section of a tree which has a projectile in it. For many years after the war the "war log" was a prized souvenir. But all too often the wood rotted away and eventually only the projectile was left. However, here are three excellent "souvenirs".

No. 1: Oak log with the base end showing of a C.S. 3.8-inch Reed shell. Probably from CHICKAMAUGA.

No. 2: Pine log with a C.S. 3-inch Archer projectile imbedded in it. From CHICKAMAUGA.

No. 3: This log has a 10-pounder Parrott shell and 2 bullets plus an iron canister shot imbedded in it. (For the bullets and iron canister shot — look to the left of the picture.) From KENNESAW MOUNTAIN, Georgia. [TOM DICKEY; Atlanta, Georgia]

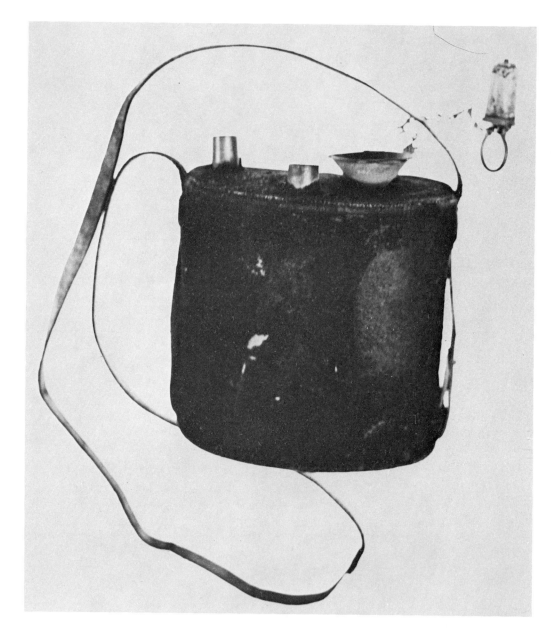

WATER FILTER CANTEENS: Since most roads of the 1861-1865 period were unpaved, mud and dust were often very much in evidence for soldiers as they moved around camp or on the march. Because of the mud and dust the soldiers had difficulty in finding clear drinking water. Accordingly, especially in 1861, some soldiers carried the "water filter" canteen. Shown here are two types.

3-spout: Has a blue wool cover. This canteen is 6¼ inches tall and 6¼ inches wide. **No markings.** [ARTHUR LEE BREWER, JR.; Durham, North Carolina]

2-spout: This specimen is very probably Confederate. It is 6¼ inches tall and 6¾ inches wide. **No markings.** [ARTHUR LEE BREWER, JR.; Durham, North Carolina]

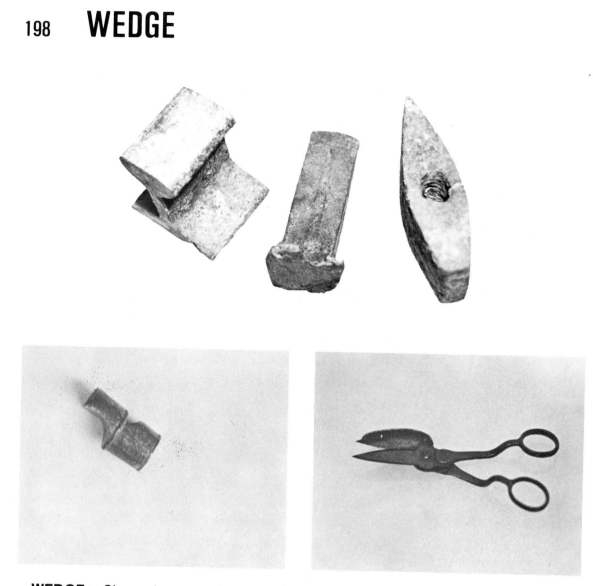

WEDGE: Shown here are three excavated items from the site of the Federal FORT MACGILVRAY at PETERSBURG. Of especial interest is the splitting wedge shown in the center of the picture. This type of wedge was used in splitting logs for construction of huts or for use on the fortifications.

WHISTLE: Whistles and any reference to their use during the Civil War are very rare. This pewter whistle dug up at Port Hudson was probably used by an officer. Length 1¼ inches, with a diameter of ¾ of an inch. **No markings.**

WICK CUTTER: Used with candles. This specimen is made of good steel, 5¾ inches long. **Markings:** W. B. BARNARD
PATD.
DEC 27th 1864

WOODEN BOOT JACK: Front and rear views of a wooden boot jack used by a Federal soldier. (The wooden canteen is used as a prop only for photographing purposes.) **Markings:** (on reverse side of boot jack) U.S.A.
W W

These letters are crudely carved in the wood. [KEN MATTERN; Wayne, Pennsylvania]

WRITING KIT

WRITING KIT: Very attractive writing kit; 1 foot long with a diameter of 1⅝ inches. The cylinder is made of hard wood protected by a water-proofed cover. One end of the cylinder unscrews; this end contains a glass inkwell as shown in the photograph. A pen is included in the kit. **Markings:** (on the cover) PATENT APPLIED FOR.

Also stencilled on the inside of the cover is: LIEUT. A. W. CLOUGH
                                            Co. H. 13th ME REGT

The 13th Maine Infantry served in the 19th Army Corps and lost a total of 195 during battle, disease, in prison, etc.

BIBLIOGRAPHY

In addition to the bibliographies found in Volumes I and II, the following specialized studies are recommended to the reader and collector.

ALBERT, ALPHAEUS H.
Buttons of the Confederacy. Hightstown, N.J. 1963.

Record of American Uniform and Historical Buttons, 1775-1968. Bayertown, Penn. 1969.

[ANONYMOUS]
Civil War Maps in the National Archives. Washington, D.C. 1964.

CAMPBELL, J. DUNCAN AND EDGAR M. HOWELL
American Military Insignia 1800-1851. Washington, D.C. 1963.

COGGINS, JACK
Arms and Equipment of the Civil War. New York, N.Y. 1962.

COLE, M. H.
A Collection of U.S. Military Knives, 1861-1968. Birmingham, Alabama 1968.

CORBITT, D. L. AND ELIZABETH W. WILBORN
Civil War Pictures. Raleigh, North Carolina 1964.

DAVIS, ROLLIN V., JR.
U.S. Sword Bayonets 1847-1865. n.p. 1962.

DONNELLY, RALPH W.
The History of the Confederate States Marine Corps. New Bern, North Carolina 1976.

EDWARDS, WILLIAM B.
Civil War Guns. Harrisburg, Pennsylvania 1962.

GAVIN, WILLIAM G.
Accoutrement Plates North and South 1861-1865. 2nd Edition. York, Pennsylvania 1975.

HARDEN, ALBERT N., JR.
The American Bayonet. Philadelphia, Pennsylvania 1964.

[HARWELL, RICHARD]
Uniform and Dress of the Army and Navy of the Confederate States of America. Philadelphia, Pennsylvania 1960.

HOWELL, EDGAR M. AND DONALD E. KLOSTER
United States Army Headgear to 1854. Washington, D.C. 1969.

HOWELL, EDGAR M.
United States Army Headgear 1855-1902. Washington, D.C. 1975.

KEENER, WILLIAM G.
Bowie Knives. n.p. 1962.

202 BIBLIOGRAPHY

KERKSIS, SYDNEY C. AND THOMAS S. DICKEY
Field Artillery Projectiles of the Civil War 1861-1865. Atlanta, Georgia 1968.

Heavy Artillery Projectiles of the Civil War 1861-1865. Kennesaw, Georgia 1972.

KERKSIS, SYDNEY C.
Plates and Buckles of the American Military 1795-1874. Kennesaw, Georgia 1974.

LEWIS, WAVERLY P.
U.S. Military Headgear 1770-1880. n.p. 1960.

LORD, FRANCIS A.
Civil War Collector's Encyclopedia. Vol. I Harrisburg, Pennsylvania 1963; Vol. II West Columbia, South Carolina, 1975.

Civil War Sutlers and Their Wares. New York, N.Y. 1969.

Uniforms of the Civil War. New York, N.Y. 1970.

McKEE, W. REID AND M. E. MASON, JR.
Civil War Projectiles. n.p. 1966.

MILHOLLEN, HIRST D. AND DONALD H. MUGRIDGE
Civil War Photographs 1861-1865. Washington, D.C. 1961.

PHILLIPS, STANLEY S.
Bullets Used in the Civil War 1861-1865. Laurel, Maryland 1971.

Excavated Artifacts from Battlefields and Campsites of the Civil War 1861-1865. Ann Arbor, Michigan 1974.

REILLY, ROBERT M.
United States Military Small Arms 1816-1865. Baton Rouge, La. 1970.

RIPLEY, WARREN
Artillery and Ammunition of the Civil War. New York, N.Y. 1970.

STEPHENSON, RICHARD W.
Civil War Maps. Washington, D.C. 1961.

TODD, FREDERICK P.
American Military Equipage 1851-1872 (Vol. 1). Providence, R.I. 1974.

WEBSTER, DONALD B., JR.
American Socket Bayonets 1717-1873. Ottawa, Ontario 1964.

CIVIL WAR COLLECTOR'S ENCYCLOPEDIA

Volume IV

TO

My Wife Marjorie

Whose support and expert assistance
have been a continuing inspiration
in my writing and our lives.

VOLUME IV

ADDITIONS AND CORRECTIONS TO VOLUME IV CIVIL WAR COLLECTOR'S ENCYCLOPEDIA

According to Roger S. Durham, Curator of Fort Bliss Museum, Texas, the following notes are added:

Page 2: C.M.A. cartridge box. Probably is post Civil War.

In a recent letter Robin Reynolds of Bloomington, Ill. informs me that the G.M.A. should read C.M.A. and stood for Culver Military Academy, an Indiana institution, and the cartridge box dates from the 1890s.

Page 27. Mr. Durham identifies these blanket roll buckles as hardware from horse harness. He is very probably correct.

Page 83. The grenade fin identification was merely an educated guess. Mr. Durham, while admitting he does not know what it is, believes it is not a grenade fin. He dug one out of a colonial town site in Georgia which would place it back in Revolutionary War times.

Page 86. Probably the decorations in heel plates are just that — decorations, and not intended to be corps insignia of any sort.

Page 111. Not an oil can, but the handle off an old safety razor.

Page 175. Sword sling is most likely post Civil War.

My sincere appreciation of these comments submitted by Mr. Durham.

In another recent letter Lieutenant Commander John Stott of Virginia Beach, Va. very kindly sent some corrections and pertinent photographs explaining the corrections. He shows, as did Durham, that the "oil can" on p. 111 is indeed the handle of a safety razor. LCdr Stott also clarifies another point which has been debated for many years. On page 86 is depicted a "star" style heel plate. Stott sent the author a photograph of such a heel plate (not complete, but enough of the heel plate for correct identification) and this one was found at Lee's Mill, Virginia at a site occupied by Union forces only early in the war, 1862. Thus this heel plate predates issuance of corps badges by at least a year. Moreover, it was found far from any railroad and in the Eastern theater of war (the Army Corps which had as its badge the star — the 20th Army Corps — served in the Western theater). Therefore, it is reasonable to assume that the emblem on the heel plate was only decorative.

FOREWORD

As new material has come in, the author has found it necessary to incorporate this material in permanent written form. Although excellent basic works on the various phases of Civil War collecting are now available, such diverse but virtually unknowns as the OVI buckle and "Comrades of the Battlefield" are still surfacing. The author is **greatly** indebted to the loyal assistance of many individuals interested in perpetuating the history of the Civil War. [See the list of contributors!] Their contributions are noted in the captions. If not otherwise noted, items described are from the author's collection. When any markings are present on an item, those markings are given exactly as they appear on that item. Otherwise, no comment is made on markings.

LIST OF CONTRIBUTORS

WILLIAM S. ARIAIL, Little River, S. C.
BOBBY ARMSTRONG and MARY LOU BERBERICH, Montclair, New Jersey
ED AND MARGIE BEARSS, Arlington, Va.
ROBERT BORRELL, SR., Clinton, Maryland
FREDERICK W. CHESSON, Waterbury, Conn.
WILLIAM COLEMAN, Canoga Park, California
DAVID CORCILIUS, Phelps, N. Y.
ROBERT S. CORRETTE, Fitzwilliam, N. H.
ROGER DAVIS, Keokuk, Iowa
W. E. ERQUITT, Atlanta, Ga.
MARTIN J. FOWLER, Medford Lakes, N. J.
WILLIAM D. GORGES, Westboro, Massachusetts
ROD GRAGG, Surfside Beach, S. C.
MICHAEL HAMMERSON, London, England
D. C. HANNAH, Rexburg, Idaho
CHARLES S. HARRIS, Ooltewah, Tennessee
GLEN HAYES, Pleasantville, N. Y.
DAVID HOLDER, West Sussex, England
JOHN HUGHES, Battle Creek, Michigan
G. B. HUNT, Reno, Nevada
FRANK A. HUNTSMAN, Hutchinson, Kansas
MICHAEL JOHNSON, Charleston, S. C.
JESSE LIVINGSTON, Troy, Tennessee
DR. JOHN L. MARGREITER, Chesterfield, Missouri
JOHN A. MARKS, Memphis, Tennessee
WILLIAM MOORE, Baton Rouge, La.
SAM PADGETT, West Columbia, S. C.
JOHN F. POWELL, University City, Missouri
LEO REDMOND, Cayce, S. C.
IRWIN RIDER, Erie, Pa.
LEE SANZO, Winchester, Indiana
THEODORE L. SCHOFIELD, Watertown, N. Y.
VINCE SPITALE
CLYDE HODO STRICKLAND, Tuscaloosa, Alabama
HOWARD B. TOWER, JR., Jacksonville, Florida
KEN WELLER, Fithian, Illinois
GARY WOLFER, Allentown, Pa.

ABOUT THE AUTHOR

Since his retirement as Professor Emeritus in History from the University of South Carolina, the author has concentrated his research on Civil War artifacts. This fourth volume in the series is the result of his continuing effort to utilize his extensive knowledge of Civil War memorabilia with the enthusiastic support of qualified experts, both here and abroad.

As governor of the Company of Military Historians and Associate Curator of Military History, South Carolina Museum Commission, he maintains close contact with other Civil War experts and museums. This contact is constantly expanding by his frequent appearances as guest speaker to Civil War Round Tables and similar historically oriented groups interested in the 1861-1865 struggle. By means of an extensive correspondence with collectors all over the world as well as his specialized displays of Civil War items at gun shows, Dr. Lord keeps on top of new discoveries in the field of Civil War collecting.

For over thirty years the author has contributed specialized studies on the Civil War to American and foreign journals. In addition, he has written the following:

> *They Fought for the Union* (1960)
>
> *Civil War Collector's Encyclopedia,* Volume I (1963)
>
> *Bands and Drummer Boys of the Civil War* (1966)
>
> *Civil War Sutlers and Their Wares* (1969)
>
> *Lincoln's Railroad Man: Herman Haupt (1969)*
>
> *Uniforms of the Civil War* (1970)
>
> *Civil War Collector's Encyclopedia,* Volume II (1975)
>
> *Civil War Collector's Encyclopedia,* Volume III (1979)

SPECIAL ACKNOWLEDGEMENTS

In addition to the contributors duly noted, I want to thank: Gordon Brown, photographer, and Roland Mann of Mann Photographers, whose professional abilities have done so much to enhance the quality of this book's visual presentations.

I am also sincerely appreciative to *North-South Trader* for permission to include my own articles on "Veterans' Reunion" and "Hooker's Personal Corps Badge."

U. S. CARTRIDGE BOX: This oddity shows that even with inspectors scrutinizing the quality of workmanship, mistakes in manufacturing were sometimes missed. In this instance the cartridge pouch has the U.S. stamped upside down, but has still been passed by the inspector. (T. J. Sheppard)

David Holder

C. S. CARTRIDGE BOX: There is considerable speculation about this cartridge box. It is of tarred leather, 6½ inches by 4¾ inches. Contains a plain tin liner with no divisions. The shoulder strap is heavy cotton webbing — 50 inches long — and attached to the box by brass studs at the base on the box and a leather retaining strap at the top. The brass box plate is marked GMA possibly for Georgia Military Academy.

David Holder

U. S. AND MISCELLANEOUS: Unusual breast plate with only two brass hooks.

Lee Sanzo

Extremely rare OVI belt buckle — the only one the author has ever seen. It is 3¼ inches long and 2⅛ inches wide at its widest point. On the lead-filled back of the buckle are "arrow head" hooks. Until I saw this buckle I thought Ohio units used only the "U.S." or OVM buckles and plate.

National Guard cartridge box letters. Made of thin brass, 1¾ inches wide and 1½ inches tall. The designation "National Guard" is as we know, of general use, much later than the Civil War. However, New York State had "National Guard" units which guarded the "home front" while volunteer and militia units were confronting the enemy in the Civil War.

All items shown here were dug in the Western theater of operations.

Top Row (Left to Right):

C.S.A. rectangular brass. Found at Oxford, Mississippi.

C.S. oval brass with rope inner border. Found at La Grange, Tennessee.

C.S.A. rectangular pewter. Found at La Grange, Tennessee.

Second Row (Left to Right):

U.S. oval brass, 2.13 inches by 3/36 inches. Found at La Grange, Tennessee.

U.S. rectangular, two-piece sword belt plate. Cast brass. Applied German wreaths. 2.14 by 3.20 inches. Found at Germantown, Tennessee.

U.S. oval, model 1839, small size. Stamped brass. 1.63 × 2.80 inches. Found at La Grange, Tennessee.

Third Row:

U.S. oval, showing rear of buckle with original leather fragment still adhering to the hooks. 2.30 × 3.48 inches. Found at La Grange, Tennessee.

U.S. rectangular, two-piece sword belt plate (showing rear of buckle) 2.03 × 3.38 inches. Found at Germantown, Tennessee.

U.S. oval, model 1839, small size. 1.63 × 2.80 inches. Found at Germantown, Tennessee.

Fourth Row:

C.S. sword belt plate, cast brass. Found at Lumpkins Mill, Mississippi.

C.S. sword belt plate, wreath only, cast brass. Found at Eastport, Tennessee.

C.S. belt plate, cast brass. No designation. Found at La Grange, Tennessee.

Fifth Row:

U.S. improvised belt buckle. Heavy brass plate with rounded corners. Three iron wire hooks soldered on back. Rectangular, size 1.78 × 2.72 inches. Scratched on face of buckle: JAMES HASTIE
                 15TH ILL. REGT.
Found at La Grange, Tennessee. (NOTE: Hastie was a 21 year-old, redhead, First sergeant of Company E. His hometown was Apple River, Illinois. The 15th Illinois was in Veach's Brigade of General Stephen A. Hurlburt's Fourth Division in the Battle of Shiloh. Hastie was killed the first day, April 6, 1862, and is buried in Grave No. 1742 in the National Cemetery at Shiloh. Hurlburt's Division camped at La Grange, Tennessee in the Summer of 1862.)

English "snake" buckle. Cast brass snake, heavy brass (0.165 inches diameter) loops and rings fabricated by brazing. 2.80 × 3.50 inches. Found at La Grange, Tennessee.

8

Curious adaptation of a C. S. buckle for U. S. use.

Lee Sanzo

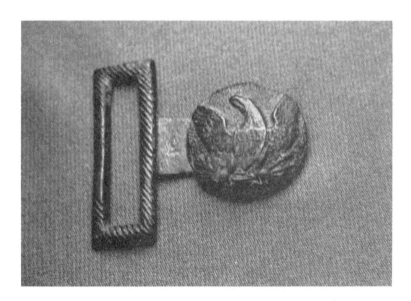

Military buckle as used by U. S. officer in the early months of the Civil War.

Lee Sanzo

Militia plate used by the C.S. Found at Fort Fisher, North Carolina. There is a nail hole at each corner, and a small one in the center, but no traces of any hooks or wires.

Michael Hammerson

C.S. Texas rectangular buckle. Found at New Bern, North Carolina.

William D. Gorges

CITADEL BREAST PLATE: This plate has never appeared so far as I know. It is made of heavy brass, 2½ inches in diameter. Found at Tullifinny Creek, S. C. where a battalion of Citadel and Arsenal cadets (forming a battalion of "State Cadets") was stationed in December, 1864, to guard the Tullifinny trestle of the Charleston and Savannah Railroad. These cadets fought Sherman's men December 7-11, 1864, and then went into C.S. defense on James Island, S. C.

Leo Redmond

L.S.I. CROSSBELT PLATE: Made of heavy brass, with silver block letters. The buckle is 3¼ inches long and 2¼ inches wide. Each letter is ¾ inches tall. This buckle was acquired in Louisiana and possibly was worn by a Louisiana militia unit.

12

C.S. SHAKO MILITIA PLATE: Brass with silver letter "W" on a black center. The plate is 2¾ inches in diameter, with a motif of a cannon and spear (or flag staff) heads. The unit "W" is unidentified.

Unidentified (C.S.?) militia crossbelt plate. This dug plate is 2⅝ inches tall and 1⅞ inches wide at the widest point.

William S. Ariail

C.S. BREAST PLATE: Made of heavy brass, 2⅜ inches in diameter. There are no signs of the original fastenings for a crossbelt plate, but rather has three small holes in the outside rim. Unidentified unit. From C. S. trenches, siege of Savannah, Georgia.

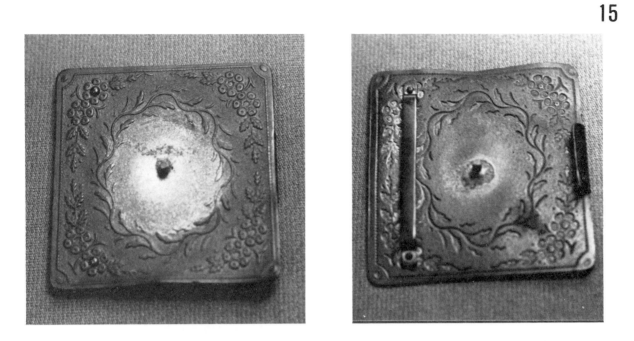

SASH BUCKLES: These fancy but impractical buckles, made of very thin brass, were used with a cloth belt and worn over the officer's sash. They were for dress only and not strong enough to support revolver or sword. Many different variations were sold by dealers in military supplies and by the ubiquitous (and money-grabbing!) sutlers. Two variations are shown here, courtesy of Lee Sanzo.

Front and back of a sash buckle found at La Grange, Tennessee.

Small C.S. sash buckle dug in a camp of Miles Legion at Port Hudson, Louisiana.

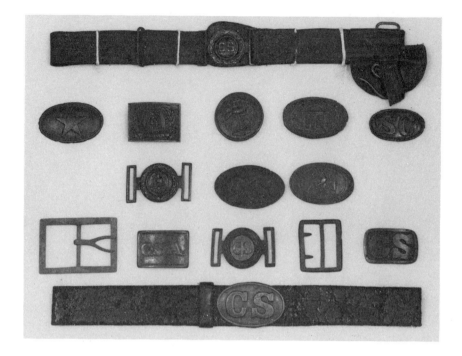

C. S. BUCKLE DISPLAY: (Sam Padgett Collection)

Top Row: (Left to Right)
C. S. belt and buckle. The buckle has the distinctive lettering, suggesting it was manufactured by Haiman of Columbus, Georgia.

Second Row:
Texas oval box plate.

Virginia.

South Carolina breast plate. Worn by a soldier from Lancaster, S. C.

Georgia oval buckle dug near Fredericksburg, Virginia.

South Carolina oval belt buckle.

Third Row:
Two-piece officer's buckle from Louisiana.

C. S. oval box plate from Port Hudson, Louisiana.

Mississippi oval box plate, converted to use as a belt buckle.

Fourth Row:
C. S. "forked tongue" buckle.

C.S.A. buckle

Two-piece buckle found at Cold Harbor, Virginia.

C.S. frame buckle.

C.S. buckle dug at Kenesaw Mountain, Georgia.

Fifth Row:
C.S. oval buckle on its original belt.

The cow bells found on Civil War campsites and picket posts were not necessarily there because some bovine "accidentally" strayed into military custody. It is now clear that these civilian cow bells were attached to rope lines at picket posts to serve as a warning if the enemy approached. For example, a small iron cow bell (2½ inches tall) with an iron clapper, which was one of a series of such bells, were all found in a straight line — regularly spaced out — in front of a C.S. trench position at Port Hudson, Louisiana.

Not shown here is a large C.S. cow bell, 6¾ inches tall, with an iron clapper. Found in Confederate lines at Grand Gulf, Mississippi. (NOTE: This bell is very similar in appearance to the bell shown above except it is much larger.)

AMMUNITION BOX OPENER

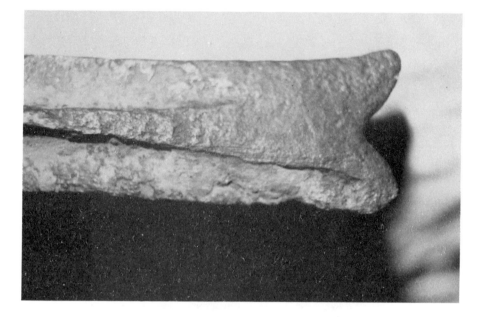

The box openers issued with ammunition boxes were easily lost. Hence, it was necessary to improvise. Shown here is a bayonet, cleverly adapted, to use as a box opener. The blade portion of the bayonet is 10 inches long, and is four-sided. The tip has been flattened and spread to form a "Y".

John Hughes

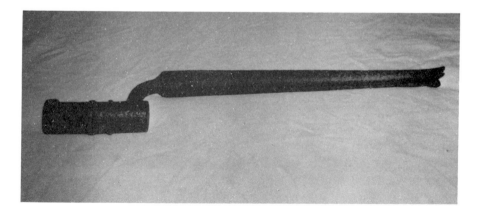

(A) U.S.

U.S. Axe. Unusually large, this specimen came from Headquarters of the 17th Army Corps, seven miles south of Savannah, Georgia. It is 9¼ inches long and 4¼ inches at the widest part of the blade.

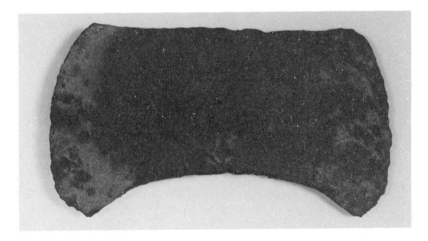

TWO-BLADED AXE HEAD. Dug out of a sandy soil artillery bunker at Battery Halleck on the causeway approaching Big Tybee Island, (today known as Savannah Beach), Georgia. Eleven batteries were set up under General Quincy A. Gillmore to bombard C.S. Fort Pulaski into submission. After a two-day bombardment (April 10 & 11, 1862) the Fort surrendered. **Dimensions of Axe Head:** Length — 9 inches; greatest width of each blade is 5 inches. (NOTE: Excavated two bladed axe heads of the Civil War era are comparatively rare.)

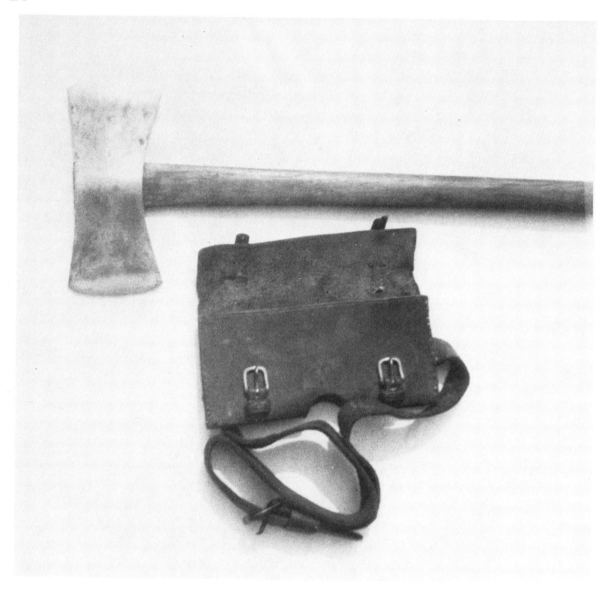

TWO-BLADED HATCHET AND HOLDER. The hatchet is 17 inches long overall, while the hatchet head itself is 6½ inches long and 3 inches wide. The head is marked "Colclessor, R. and E.L." The rest of the marks are obliterated. "R. Cook" is crudely carved on the handle. The leather scabbard is 7 1/3 inches long and 3¾ inches wide. There are no markings on the scabbard.

David Corcilius

(B) C.S.

A fireman's axe found in a C.S. trench at Port Hudson, Louisiana. This axe is 11¾ inches long and 4½ inches wide at the widest part of the blade. The use of such fire fighting equipment as axes in the field shows the desperate straits of the Confederacy by 1863.

AXE HEAD: Dug from inside the confines of Confederate Spanish Fort. This Fort and also Fort Blakely connected with Mobile by means of a causeway over the bay and the Blakely River. The battle of Spanish Fort took place March 27 to April 8, 1865. **Dimensions:** Length — 6¾ inches; width of blade at widest part — 4¼ inches.

HATCHET: Dug up many years ago at Confederate Fort Blakely, Alabama. At this fort was fought the last major infantry land battle of the Civil War (April 1-9, 1865). Fort Blakely (and Spanish Fort) had to be subdued before General E.R.S. Canby's forces could cross the bay and establish themselves in Mobile on April 12th. **Dimensions:** 4¾ inches long and 2½ inches at the widest part of the blade.

BALDRICK

[No picture shown] This decorative item of military dress was a wide sash commonly worn by drum majors or band majors. Occasionally, it was worn by aides-de-camp. After 1865 the baldrick was in common use by musicians in both military and civilian bands.

The monotony of camp life was often broken by soldiers voting for their choice of officers and political figures up to and including the President himself. Also, members of some secret orders had their elections. Therefore, there has survived a variety of ballot boxes. The one shown here is a regimental ballot box, wooden with black and white glass marbles. It is stenciled '1 ME CAV' (1st Maine Calvary).

Michael Hammerson

Of equal interest, certainly, is one used by Company A, 12th Massachusetts Infantry. This ballot box (illustration not shown) is of one-eighth inch walnut and is 13 inches long. Inside are eight wooden balls, ⅝ inch in diameter, and ten wooden balls, one-half inch in diameter. There are also five black squares, three-eighths inch square. The cover is fastened with a pair of small brass hinges. Width of the box is 5⅜ inches. The German silver plaque which is fastened with two brass nails is engraved.

Co. A
12
Ms. Inf.
(Company A 12th Massachusetts Infantry).

David Corcilius

U. S. BANK NOTE: St. Albans Raid, October 19, 1864

The Confederates were a daring bunch. Among their most audacious projects was a raid on a St. Albans, Vermont bank on October 19, 1864. The leader of this raid was a young Confederate lieutenant, Bennett H. Young (21 years old.) His plan was to terrorize New England and get some much needed money from U. S. sources! The raiding party — 22 in number — were successful in getting money — about $200,000. in gold, securities, and currency and, forced to retreat, went back into Canada, their original base of operations. The leader, Young, lived until 1919, and was commander of the United Confederate Veterans. Although the town of St. Albans invited him to return for a visit after the war, he declined, for reasons of prudence!

The bill shown here came from money seized by Young's raiders in the raid. It was given to W. O. Shewmaker of Kentucky in 1892 or 1893 by a Confederate veteran, Ben B. Bigstaff. When Young appeared in Jackson, Kentucky in a lecture tour, Shewmaker showed him the bill and Young was "curious to know where I had got it."

John A. Marks

Because of many requests received from collectors as to the basic type of binoculars actually used in the Civil War, there is shown here the "normal" type used. It is of unquestionable authenticity and is inscribed:

Captain William Badger
4th N. H. V. Sept. 20, 1861

It is also marked "Superior Glasses".

Roger Davis

26 BLANKET

Dimensions are 62 inches long and 54 inches wide. Carried by Augustus Call, 1st Michigan Sharpshooters. The blanket is of light brown color, with red and blue stripes.

Roger Davis

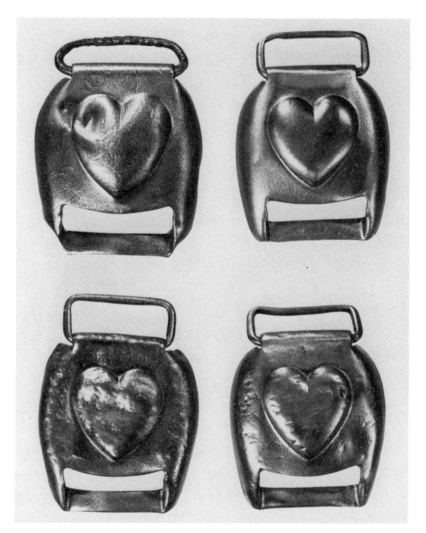

These Confederate blanket roll buckles are made of brass and are in two sizes. The larger size is 2 inches long and 1⅞ inches wide. The smaller type is 1⅞ inches long and 1½ inches wide. In the group photograph of these buckles, they came from the following areas:

Top Row: (Left to Right) Virginia; New Hope Church, Georgia.

Bottom Row: (Left to Right) Port Hudson, Louisiana; New Hope Church, Georgia.

28 BOTTLE LABEL

Label from a champagne bottle made in New Orleans and found in C. S. lines at Big Black River battlefield in Mississippi. The green glass label is 1¾ inches in diameter and stamped in the glass is an eagle and "F. Seignovret & C. New Orleans".

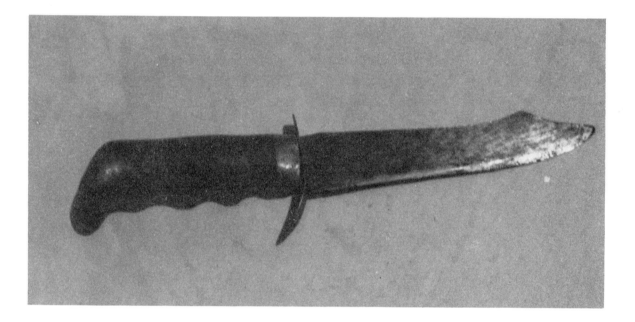

This crude C. S. Bowie knife is 12⅝ inches long. The blade is 1½ inches wide at the hilt. The guard appears to be either brass or copper. The ferrule is pewter. Inlaid in the butt of the grip is a crude 4-pointed star also of pewter. Otherwise, there are no marks on the knife.

David Corcilius

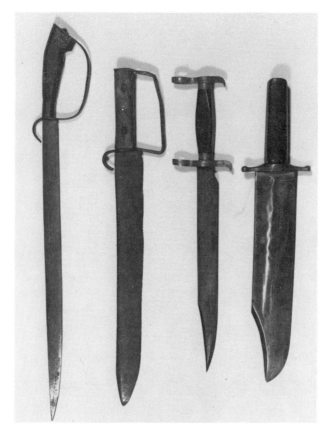

BOWIE KNIFE COLLECTION: Sam Padgett

Grouped in this illustration are four types of C.S. edged weapons, including two Bowie knives and a Bowie knife-bayonet. (The knife-bayonet is also shown here in a photograph by itself.)

Left to Right:

Knife found in a cave near Decatur, Alabama, along with several other items. Overall it is 24½ inches long and has an 18½ inch sword type blade with a carved wooden grip.

A blacksmith made "D-Guard" Bowie knife. Very crudely made. This knife has a 15½ inch blade and was carried by a Texan named ? Miller.

Potts Bowie — bayonet with a 12¼ inch blade. This knife came from Kentucky and is a very handsome piece.

Handsome and large Bowie knife from Texas. The blade is 12½ inches long and 2½ inches wide. It has a wooden handle. Inlaid in the handle was a silver star which was removed by the descendants of the original owner.

This 4-band brandy barrel came from France originally and was used by Company "C" 9th New York Infantry. This unit, famous in the war as "Hawkins Zouaves" was raised in May 1861 for two years' service. During the war it lost 71 killed and 25 by disease. At Antietam (September 17, 1862) it lost 45 killed, 174 wounded and 14 missing and a total of 233 in one battle! The barrel was carried by a 'Vivandiere' — a female who served the regiment, usually as a nurse. The barrel was used to carry brandy to the wounded. Only a very few Vivandieres served in the Civil War, usually with regiments composed of men of French extraction. This wooden barrel is 9¼ inches long with brass suspension loops and stopper. It is painted brown and blue. The brass letters identify the barrel. As can be seen from the illustration, it has a script NG on one end (National Guard), and 9, C, and Z.D.A. on the other (Company "C" 9th [Zouaves D'Afrique].

Martin J. Fowler

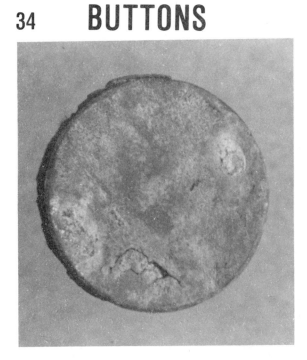

Despite several excellent books on military buttons, occasionally unusual types appear which should be described to the Civil War collector. Two such buttons are shown here.

A 1st Connecticut Heavy Artillery button is shown here. It was found at Bermuda Hundred, Virginia in September 1981. The button is made in a two-piece construction and appears to have been hollow. The 1st Connecticut Heavy Artillery served at Bermuda Hundred, Virginia from May 1864 to April 1865.

Robert Borrell, Sr.

The Chaplain's button shown here is 1 3/16 inches in diameter and made of hard black rubber. The front is plain but the back of the button is marked:

NOVELTY RUBBER CO.
GOODYEAR
PATENT
1851

This button came with a letter of recommendation from Rev. Albert Case for appointment as Chaplain in the 42nd Massachusetts Infantry. Thus far, I have found no indication that Reverend Case served in the 42nd or any other regiment. But the button may well have come with his chaplain's uniform — purchased with the belief he would serve, but not receiving his commission.

CANDLESTICKS

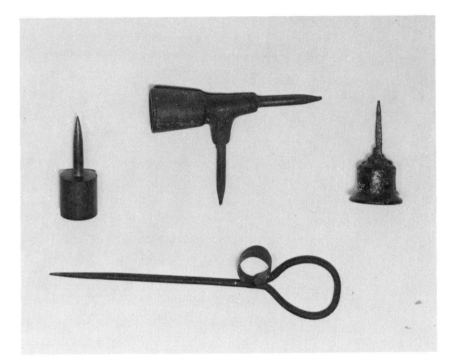

These four Confederate candlesticks were all designed for service in the field. All are of iron with sharp points for sticking into a tree or board. The one on the left is 2⅝ inches tall and 1½ inches in diameter. It was found in General Stephen A. Hurlburt's division at La Grange, Tennessee. The one at the top of the photograph is 8 inches long with ⅞ inch aperture, while the one on the right is 2¾ inches tall and a 1 inch diameter. The bottom candlestick is 4½ inches tall with a 1⅛ inch diameter. Note that this specimen can be stuck in either an upright or horizontal tree or board. I have never seen another specimen like this one.

The Confederate candlestick shown here is 2 inches tall, 1¼ inches in diameter, and was found on the site of a Confederate picket post at United States ford at the crossing of the Rappahannock River, west of Fredericksburg, Virginia.

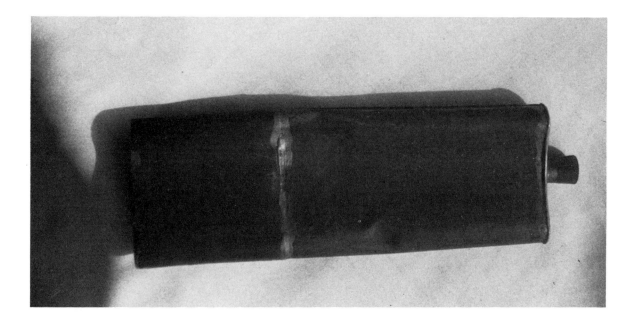

Shown here is a very rare "boot canteen" probably Confederate. It is 11½ inches tall, 3¼ inches wide and has no markings.

David Corcilius

Not shown but of historic interest is a U.S. canteen still filled with sorghum or molasses, although in a crystalized state. It was captured by a Confederate soldier and hidden in a barn in Ashland, Virginia. This U.S. canteen was most assuredly captured or picked up by a Confederate soldier at some Richmond, Fredericksburg, or Petersburg battle. Sorghum, or molasses was very popular with soldiers of both sides. Many of the Shenandoah Valley farmers in August 1864 had finished their sorghum-molasses prior to the arrival of Federal troops under Sheridan. Men of the 14th New Hampshire Infantry came in possession of a barrel of sorghum. "Canteens and cups were filled; men ate until nauseated; in their greed the stickly treacle dripped everywhere, smearing clothing from head to foot, gluing beards and dust in remarkable compounds, slopping, spilling, running: sorghum left its imprint on thousands of highly flavored and thoroughly sweetened defenders of the Union." F. H. Buffum, *History of the 14th N.H. Inf.,* 1882.

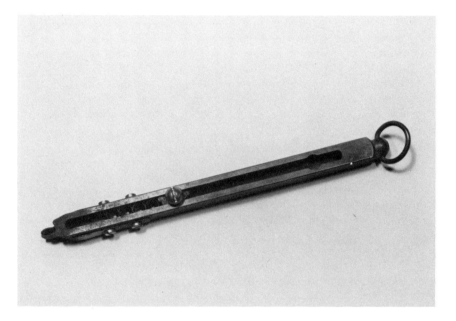

This unique capper is of heavy brass, 5⅜ inches long including carrying ring, and 5/16 inches square. There are no markings. This capper can hold about 15 percussion caps for the revolver. Compare this capper with the two shown on page 118 of Vol. 1 of the *Encyclopedia*.

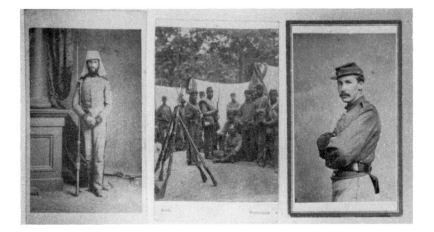

These "cartes de visite" of New York militiamen date from the early months of the war. They show men in the very early days and weeks of the North's preparation for the first battle.

Left to Right:
Charles During, 8th New York State Militia. June 1861.
Brady photo of camp scene of the 8th New York State Militia.
Unidentified member of the 37th New York Infantry.

Left to Right:
    Unidentified — in ink — "Departure from New York April 23, 1861."
    Charles During, 8th New York Militia.
    Unidentified — in pencil — "Washington 9 June 1861".

The 8th New York State Militia was organized in April 1861 to serve three months. Known as the "Washington Grays" the regiment left for Washington April 20, 1861. It served in the Capital city until July and then participated in the Battle of Bull Run, July 21, 1861. It was attached to Porter's First Brigade, Hunter's Second Division, McDowell's Army of Northeast Virginia. The regiment was mustered out at New York, August 2, 1861. The 37th New York Infantry was organized in June 1861 to serve two years. It lost 74 killed and 38 dead by disease.

42 CARTRIDGE HOLDER

This all metal cartridge holder is 3½ inches tall, 4½ inches wide, and 1½ inches deep. It has a hinged top which is marked:

B. KITTEREDGE & CO. CIN. O.
PATENTED JAN. 27, 1863
REISSUED APL. 14, 63.

There are loops in back for carrying in the belt. This cartridge holder had several caliber .36 pistol balls in it when it was found in an attic.

As students of the Civil War are well aware, soldiers on both sides helped pass the long monotonous hours in camp by carving just about everything imaginable. As examples, we show both lead and wood carvings. The bar of lead shown here stands 1¾ inches tall and was carved into the form of a Minie bullet. It was dug in the camp of the 39th Mississippi Infantry at Port Hudson, Louisiana.

Exceptionally well done is this carved "B" — a Company letter, probably of an Iowa regiment since it was found near some Iowa items. It measures ¾ inch by ½ inch.

Lee Sanzo

44 CATHOLIC PRAYER BOOK

This is a truly beautiful prayer book for Catholic use. It was printed before the war (New York, 1856) and has 256 pages of prayer text plus a "Catalogue of Catholic Bibles" as an appendix. It is 3¾ inches tall and 2½ inches wide. Written in ink on the inside cover are the words:

JAMES DOUGHERTY
Co. "G" 72 P.V.
Philadelphia Fire Zouaves
Colonel Baxter
Commanding

The 72nd Pennsylvania Infantry, known as "Baxter's (Philadelphia) Fire Zouaves" was organized in August 1861. It served in Hancock's 2nd Army Corps and was one of the 300 "Fighting Regiments" of the Federal Army, losing 736 killed and wounded, and 165 captured and missing. At Savage Station, Virginia (June 29, 1862) it lost 14 killed, 85 wounded, and 20 missing. Shortly afterwards, at Antietam (September 17, 1862) the 72nd lost 38 killed, 163 wounded, 36 missing. And at Gettysburg (July 1-3, 1863) this regiment lost 44 killed, 145 wounded, and 2 missing.

When collectors and museum archivists come across newly-acquired Civil War items — especially those of a non-military nature — they are often uncertain as to the material used in making the item. This is especially true of items the material of which resembles modern plastics. It is well known that bone, ivory, rubber, and gutta — percha were used. But what is not so generally known is that celluloid appeared in the middle of the war (1863). It was discovered by John Wesley Hyatt in response to a $10,000. prize offered for the discovery of a substitute for ivory. Celluloid, a very useful substance, is composed essentially of camphor and celluloid nitrate.

CHAIN BRIDGE BOLT

One of the landmarks of war-time Washington, D.C. was "Chain Bridge" which crossed the Potomac River about three miles from Georgetown. The reservoir which supplied most of Washington and Georgetown was also about the same distance from the bridge. To protect the bridge and reservoir a block house was constructed at the approach to the bridge. In addition, the approach from the Maryland side of the Potomac River was guarded by **Batteries** "Vermont", "Kemble" and "Martin Scott". The more vulnerable approach from Virginia was guarded by **Forts** "Ethan Allen" and "Marcy". A relic of Chain Bridge is shown in the accompanying photograph. This massive bolt weighs over 3 pounds, is 6¾ inches long, 1 inch in diameter. A large nut, 1¾ inches square and 1¼ inches thick turns freely on the threads. This bolt came from the Virginia end of the bridge.

This campaign chest was used by Almond B. Wells who enlisted as a First Lieutenant in Co. "A" 1st Battalion, Nevada Territory Cavalry on May 1, 1863. He was promoted Captain of Company "D", April 9, 1864. Wells remained in the U. S. Army, retiring August 16, 1903, with the rank of Brigadier General.

The chest is 40 inches long, 18¾ inches high, and 19½ inches wide. It still has the original paint (red) and the name is stenciled in large black letters.

David Corcilius

Civil War soldiers spent an inordinately large percentage of their time in the service polishing and cleaning their weapons, accouterments, and uniforms. This was certainly more true for the Federals than for the Confederates, and, within the Federal Army, more time in the Eastern than in the Western theaters of operations. The Army of the Potomac and the garrison troops in the East were truly "spit and polish" outfits. Accordingly, cleaning supplies (usually sold by the sutlers) were in great demand. However, surprisingly little is known about these necessities. Most of them were used up during the course of the war, and few collectors have made any serious attempt to collect these unspectacular but essential items. In previous volumes of the *Encyclopedia* I have shown some of these cleaning materials. Here are some more.

Shown here are two blacking containers and a can of polish.

Left to right:

Can of blacking found at La Grange, Tennessee. This can is 2¾ inches in diameter with no discernible markings.

A can of William R. Warner's "Union Oil Polish" 3½ inches in diameter. Dated 1861 the can is also marked:

47 & 48 Market St. Boston
"Apply it thin and polish at once."

The third can was found at Falmouth, Virginia (where the Army of the Potomac spent the winter of 1862-1863). This can is 2⅝ inches in diameter and is marked:

Army & Navy
Made By
B. F. Brown & Co.
Boston
Blacking

Brushes were used to polish the metal or black the leather equipment. Shown here are three brush handles recovered from Civil War sites. Two of the handles are 5½ inches long each, and the longest is 6 inches long. The latter has "T.A." carved on the back of the handle. Material is hard, wood-like substance. (The bristles disappeared in the soil before these handles were found.)

Here, as with so many of the categories covered in this volume of the *Encyclopedia*, we are merely adding newly-discovered items; there is no attempt to be definitive in an overall coverage.

Two views are given here of one-half of a **Pewter** quarter. Dug on the site of Big Black River, Mississippi.

Lee Sanzo

Both sides of a sutler's token are shown here. Dug at Port Hudson, Louisiana in the position held by the 1st Arkansas Infantry. It reads on both sides:

Post Exchange
5¢
1st Ark. Inf.

Lee Sanzo

52 CONFEDERATE BALLOON FRAGMENT

Contained within the frame is a small fragment of a Confederate gas balloon as similarly used by Federal balloonists until 1863. The fragment is made from silk — now discolored with age — and is 2¾ inches by 3 inches in size.

The balloon was manufactured by gathering all the silk dresses in the Confederacy and sewing them together. However Confederate dreams of a balloon corps were shortlived. According to General James Longstreet (*Battles & Leaders* Vol. 2 pages 512-513): "It was done and soon we had a great patchwork shop of many hues which was ready for use in the seven days campaign. We had no gas except in Richmond, and it was the custom to inflate the balloon there, tie it securely to an engine, and run it down the York River Railroad to the point at which we desired to send it up. One day it was on a steamer down the James when the tide went out and left the vessel and balloon high and dry on a bar. The Federals gathered it in, and with it the last silk dress in the Confederacy. This capture was the meanest trick of the war and one I have never forgiven."

David Holder

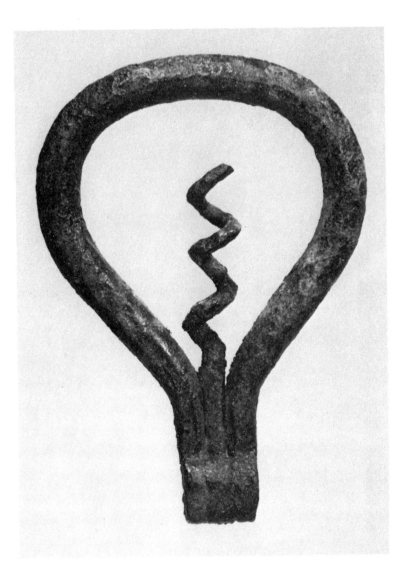

The great profusion of wine and liquor bottles at Civil War campsites is conclusive evidence that officers and men of both armies drank something besides water. Of course the percentage of those who indulged and the amount consumed varied greatly with units and individuals. However, the sutlers did a thriving business in dispensing

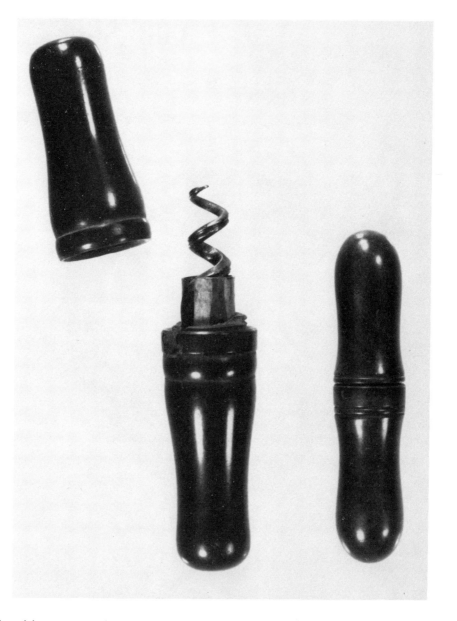

liquor and sold many corkscrews to go along with the bottles. Two different types of these corkscrews are pictured here.

The iron corkscrew was found in the Federal camp at Falmouth, Virginia. When closed it is 2¾ inches long and when open it is 4 inches long. There is no doubt that this corkscrew saw much use during the Army's stay in Falmouth during the long and discouraging winter of 1862-1863!

Much fancier than the "rough and ready" iron corkscrews are these specimens with their elegant wooden containers. The two are similar in design, differing only in size. The smaller is 2⅛ inches long; the larger is 3⅛ inches long. Both were designed to be carried in the pocket safely, since the wooden top screwed tightly on the bottom section.

Corps badges intrigue us all and collecting them is a delight because of their great variations in design and materials. Much research has been done on them; some excellent books and articles have appeared in print in recent years. But new types are constantly turning up!

Badges of the 2nd Army Corps and its veteran association are shown here. These badges belonged to Private Lucius Matlock Mason, Battery "B", 1st Rhode Island Light Artillery. Mason enlisted August 13, 1861, and was mustered out August 12, 1864. He was taken prisoner near Warrenton, Virginia on November 23, 1862, and was held prisoner for about eleven months until he escaped.

Robert Borrell, Sr.

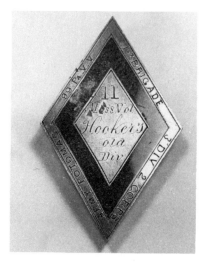

HOOKER'S PERSONAL CORPS BADGE:

The badge shown here is of special historic interest. It was the personal property of Major General Joseph Hooker and was sold along with his sword at a recent auction. On March 21, 1863, "Fighting Joe" Hooker as commander of the Army of the Potomac, issued a circular concerning the adoption of corps badges 'for the purpose of ready recognition of corps and divisions of this army, and to prevent injustice by reports of straggling and misconduct through mistake as to their organizations.' A corps was normally divided into three divisions and the color of the badge was determined by the number of the division — 1st Division, red; 2nd, white; and 3rd, blue. When more than three divisions, green was used for 4th, and orange for the 5th.

Equipped with its own special leather case, this beautiful badge is as follows:

Description

Made of sterling silver — diamond-shaped, with each side of the diamond 1 5/16 inches long. Total length from top tip to bottom tip is 2 3/16 inches. The dark portion of the badge is a glass-like material — red in color. No maker's name on the badge. A silver pin on the back was used as a fastener.

Inscription

On the "center diamond" is inscribed:

> 11
> Mass Vol
> Hooker's
> old
> Div.

On the outer edge of the badge is inscribed:

> 99 Pa. V.V.
> 1st Brigade
> 3 Div 2 Corps
> Army Potomac

As can be seen from the photograph, the center diamond is inscribed with the

legend: **11 Mas Vol** and **Hooker's old Div.** This refers to the 11th Massachusetts Infantry which served in 1862 in Hooker's Division of the 3rd Army Corps. (It will be noted that the badge is that of the 3rd Army Corps.) The 11th Massachusetts was transferred to the 2nd Army Corps in March, 1864. Like the 11th Massachusetts, the 99th Pennsylvania Veteran Volunteers originally served in the 3rd Army Corps, but was transferred late in the war to the 2nd Army Corps.

"Fighting Joe" led his division from Yorktown until just before Antietam, when he was given command of an Army Corps. As commander of the Army of the Potomac he was soundly defeated by Lee at Chancellorsville May 1-3, 1863.

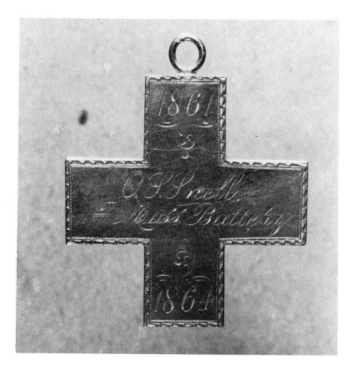

The attractive corps badge shown here is typical of the fine quality of many badges which were sold by dealers. This silver badge is of the 6th Army Corps and belonged to Oliver S. Snell, 1st Massachusetts Light Artillery. Snell enlisted April 20, 1861 in Cook's Battery of the regiment for three months' service. He was mustered out August 3, 1861. Three days later (August 6, 1861) he enlisted again — this time as a sergeant — in the same regiment. But he was reduced in rank to a private on September 1, 1862 (I wonder why!) and was mustered out as a private October 19, 1864. He died August 5, 1912.

Robert Borrell, Sr.

COUNTERSIGN SIGNALS (Illustration Not Shown)

The "countersign", according to Civil War definition was "a particular word given out by the highest in command, intrusted to those employed on duty in camp and garrison, and exchanged between guards and sentinels." So by definition, a set of "countersign signals" given out by General Henry M. Naglee on November 26, 1862, is mis-named. But for a student of Civil War signal intelligence, the order is of interest. The order was issued by General Naglee for — as he termed them — "countersign signals" between Yorktown and Gloucester Point, Virginia. These signals consisted of rockets and lights. Among the signals were:

"The Enemy Approaches"
"The Enemy have attacked Picket"
"The Enemy retreated", etc.

The original document is 12½ inches by 16 inches in size and is entitled "Special Orders No. 90."

Catholic soldiers of both armies wore the crucifix, i.e. the symbol depicting Christ on the cross. Shown here is a brass crucifix, 1⅝ inches long. Only the cross is left; the crucified figure of Christ has broken off. Found in a U.S. camp at Bardstown, Kentucky.

The cruciform is also a religious symbol but is only the cross without Christ on it. This cruciform was found at Chancellorsville in the immediate vicinity of where Stonewall Jackson was shot. It is brass, 1 inch long and ¾ inches wide. It is decorated with a cross, heart, and the words "Kingdom Come".

William Coleman

Many examples of cutlery of the Civil War era are being dug up or located in Grandma's attic, and there is much confusion about the types used. Although previous volumes of the *Encyclopedia* show some of the types, the following collections will increase our knowledge of them.

Mess Knives and Forks

Variations of the products of Lamson & Goodnow Manufacturing Company are shown here.

Top Knife and Fork

Naval mess knife with anchor motif. Ornate handles — ivory grips with pewter blade and tines.

Middle Knife and Fork

Bone grips — crude. Marked as being made in the "S. Falls Works".

Bottom — Knife

Plain ivory handle also made in the "S. Falls Works".

Martin J. Fowler

The knives in this collection are made by the Meriden Cutlery Company and vary in length from 9⅜ inches to 9¾ inches.

W. E. Erquitt

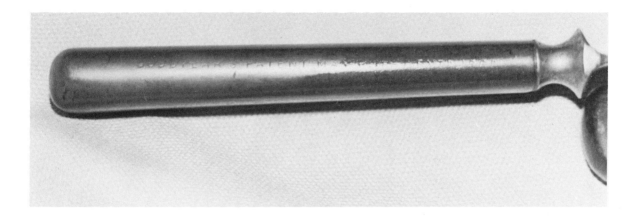

Handle of a Civil War knife which is of unusual interest. It is of hard rubber and is marked:

Meriden Cutlery Company
Goodyear's Patent May 6, 1851.

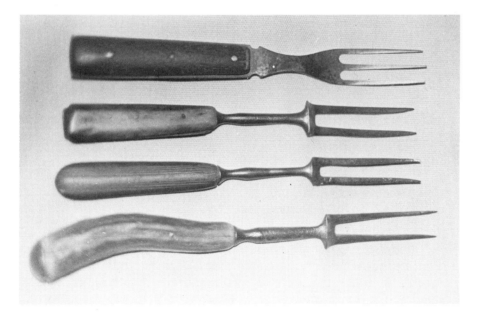

Collection of four early Civil War forks.

64   DICE

Because of the many games involving dice which were popular with both sides during the war, dice like the bone one shown here, are being found on camp sites quite frequently. As with the specimen shown, these dice are often crude in appearance; in fact, this specimen is homemade. Found near the Pentagon Barracks at Baton Rouge, Louisiana.

Lee Sanzo

DOCUMENTS

The collecting of military documents is a whole field in itself and Civil War military and allied documents have been generally neglected by all but a few zealous students of the war period. Perhaps the very vastness of the varied accumulations of 1861-1865, especially the routine military ones, has discouraged most collectors. Accordingly, there are shown here a few types of documents to pique the reader's curiosity and interest.

EIGHTH REGIMENT, THIRD BRIGADE AND FIRST DIVISION

NEW-YORK STATE MILITIA.

TO ALL TO WHOM THESE PRESENTS SHALL COME OR MAY CONCERN:

KNOW YE, That *Charles A. During* is a Private in the Company under my Command, designated as " " Company, in the EIGHTH REGIMENT OF NEW-YORK STATE MILITIA, and as such is entitled to all the privileges and advantages appertaining thereto.

IN WITNESS WHEREOF, I have hereunto set my hand, the *Twenty second* day of *November* in the year of our Lord one thousand eight hundred and *Fifty four*.

Countersigned.

Geo Lyons
Colonel of said Regiment.

Samuel H. Ley Captain of said Company.

(A) **U.S.**

Militia Enlistment Certificate, showing that Private Charles A. During was a member of the 8th New York State Militia. The certificate states Private During was a member, dated November 22, 1854, and signed by Colonel George Lyons. The back side of this certificate, shows that on November 22, 1861 Private During was "fully uniformed, armed and equipped." This certificate is 13 × 7⅞ inches.

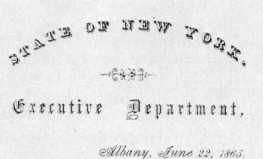

STATE OF NEW YORK.

Executive Department,

Albany, June 22, 1865.

To all whom it may Concern:

The bearer of this note is a meritorious soldier by the name of **Alfred A. Stratton.** He lost both arms in the battle at Fort Steadman, Petersburgh, 8th June, 1864, in the celebrated charge by our brave boys on the Fort. His life was for a long time apparently suspended in the balance, but finally under skillful medical treatment and kind attention he recovered, and to-day stands before our loyal people the noble exponent of the courage, devotion and patriotism of the American Soldier.

I knew him when he was not armless. A poor, honest orphan boy, residing in Chautauque County, this State.

He went into the service upon small pay and with large patiot= ism. His situation appeals to the liberality of a grateful and generous people.

Very truly, yours,

R. E. FENTON.

Wound certificate, stating that Alfred A. Stratton, lost both arms in the Battle of Fort Steadman (Petersburg, Virginia), June 18, 1864. The certificate is dated June 22, 1865, and is 11 × 8½ inches in size.

David Corcilius

HEADQUARTERS UNITED STATES FORCES,

Marion, Ala., June 12, 1865.

The bearer hereof, K. L. Griffin, Priv't Co. F & Ala. Cav., Confederate States Army, of the Army of _____ Tenn _____ now a prisoner of war, has this day given his parole of honor not to take up arms against the United States of America, nor give aid or comfort to their enemies until properly exchanged. He is therefore permitted to return to his home in Perry Co. Ala., and there remain unmolested so long as he observes and abides by the conditions of his parole, and the laws in force where he resides.

J. H. Marsh,
Colonel 9th Minnesota Volunteers.

Colmdg at Marion
Ala

(B) **C.S.**

Certainly one of the most historically interesting documents is the one issued the Confederate soldier. The text is self-explanatory and needs no elaboration. The size is 8 × 5¼ inches.

C.S. Naval Broadsides

(All of these rare broadsides are largely self-explanatory.)

The LAUREL served mainly to take the men, cargo, and weapons out to sea for their transfer to the SHENANDOAH. The U. S. Consul in Liverpool was very suspicious of the loading of the LAUREL and consequently sent his superiors a warning of her probable use by the Confederacy. However he was too late and the LAUREL did get the crew and equipment out to the SHENANDOAH on the High Seas. Size of these broadsides — 10 × 8 inches.

"LAUREL,"

Iron built Screw Steamer, Fore and Aft Schooner, of Glasgow, 296 tons register, Captain J. F. Ramsey, for Nassau and Matamoros, H. Lafone consignee.

Length 207 feet, breadth of beam 27 feet, marked draught of water 10 feet, fore and aft; Hull black, plain stern, round stern with mouldings, name and port in yellow letters on same, 8 deadlights in port and starboard sides aft, and 7 each side forward (Boats in iron swing davits on each quarter, and one each side in her waist.)

Poop, wheel, binnacle, square box athartships, skylight, capstan, companion, iron railed and netted, a wooden rail fore part of same, main hatch, patent winch, mainmast; house over main deck, iron railed and netted round, a house built over the works of the engine, with ventilator each side, funnel, steam pipe, fore part ventilator each side, wheel and binnacle, galley and rooms underneath; middle hatch, patent winch, foremast, fore hatch, companion, ventilator, companion; rooms each side against the rails, windlass; topgallant forecastle; Bell, engraved thereon "Laurel," 1863; Works of patent windlass, capstan, iron swing davit on port side for fish tackle two iron stocks and anchors.

Masts and booms bright; mastheads and gaffs black; companions, skylight, houses, boats and bulwarks cream colour; funnel red, white, and black.

Built for a passenger boat to sail between Liverpool and Sligo.

UNITED STATES CONSULATE,

LIVERPOOL, 11TH OCTOBER, 1864.

SIR,

The Screw Steamer " LAUREL" of about 300 tons burthen, sailed from Liverpool on Sunday the 9th inst., with Captain Semmes, eight other Confederate Officers, and about one hundred men.   She has six 68-pounder Guns, in cases in her hold, with Gun Carriages ready for mounting.

There is no doubt but this expedition has been fitted out for a Piratical Cruise against the United States, either in this or some other vessel.   It is quite probable that there is some other vessel to which the Men and Guns are to be transferred.

The " LAUREL" cleared for Matamoras, via Havana and Nassau, but this does not indicate her destination.

Inform any United States Naval Officer who may be within your reach.

I annex a description of the " LAUREL".

I am SIR,

Very respectfully,

Your obedient Servant,

THOMAS H. DUDLEY,

Consul.

The ship CHAMELEON, the subject of the second broadside described here, had a checkered career. She was originally called the ATLANTA, a blockade runner, and made two trips from Wilmington, North Carolina to Bermuda in 1864. She was commissioned a Confederate cruiser (commerce destroyer) and re-named the TALLAHASSEE, under command of John Taylor Wood. She then embarked on a successful three-week cruise extending from Wilmington to Halifax where she destroyed some 30 coast and fishing vessels. In October, 1864, she became the OLUSTEE and took seven more prizes. This ended her career as a cruiser. She then was pressed into service as a blockade runner, was re-named CHAMELEON and was sent to Bermuda with a cargo of cotton and brought back much needed medical supplies for Lee's army. In 1865 she was unable to enter either Wilmington or Charleston, the only ports still in the hands of the Confederacy. So her captain was forced to take her to Liverpool where she was seized by U.S. authorities. This broadside was the "Order-for-Sale" for this ship. Size of broadside — 9¼ × 5¾ inches.

The dominoes of this delightful set are incredibly small. Each domino piece is only ½ inch long and ¼ inch wide! The mahogany box has a sliding cover and is 2⅛ inches long and ¾ inch wide. This is truly an amazing set. The domino pieces are made of ivory.

DONALDSON ITEMS

Occasionally a collector acquires several items all used by the same soldier. Such was the case with the effects of Thomas B. Donaldson. For purposes of simplicity and over-all interest, these items are all shown together in this section of the *Encyclopedia*. The warrant, picture, and medal belonged to Donaldson who was "Wagon Master" of the 19th Ohio Infantry.

The daguerreotype shows Donaldson at enlistment at age fifteen.

This unusual warrant is of heavy parchment, 14⅝ inches long and 9½ inches wide. It states that Donaldson was appointed "Wagon Master" August 10, 1861. It is dated November 15, 1861 and was signed in Louisville, Kentucky by the regimental commander Samuel Beatty who went on later to become one of the outstanding generals in the West.

The silver medal is especially unique. It very probably is "one of a kind". The silver clasp is marked:

THOMAS DONALDSON

The medal proper is 1½ inches in diameter and suspended from the clasp by blue silk.

The front of the medal shows the head of a Roman centurion in bas-relief.

The back is beautifully engraved as follows:

THOMAS DONALDSON
CLERK OF ADJ. GEN. OF OHIO
MARCH 15 to APRIL 15
1861
FIRST PERSON EMPLOYED
IN ORGANIZING SOLDIERS
FROM
GEN'L. H. B. CARRINGTON
ADJ. GEN'L. OF OHIO

EAR TRUMPET

This unusual item is not included in the *Encyclopedia* for comic relief; it actually was used by soldiers suffering from noise damage. This particular ear trumpet is one of the smallest issued. It is a brass, cylindrical horn, 3 inches across the top tapering to 1 inch at the bottom. It has a 3½ inch curved ear tube.

William Coleman

As shown by the photograph, this copy of *General Regulations for the Military Forces of . . . New York* (1858) was the personal property of Elmer Elsworth. The book was presented to Ellsworth during the spectacular tour of his famous Zouaves in 1860. Much was made in the North by the young Ellsworth's death — "the first to fall". He was killed by the proprietor of the "Marshall House Tavern", Alexandria, Virginia, May 22, 1861, when Ellsworth was removing a Confederate flag from the roof of the tavern. Lincoln was among the mourners at the somber funeral ceremony which received extensive newspaper coverage in the Northern press.

ENFIELD CARTRIDGE BOXES

Much uncertainty still exists among many Civil War collectors about Enfield musket accouterments. This is due, in large part, to the almost complete lack of basic documentation on the subject. Moreover, actual war-time photographs of soldiers wearing the Enfield accouterments are surprisingly few and far between. Accordingly, the photograph here of two Enfield cartridge boxes should be helpful. Both are of thick black leather with buff leather closing tabs. The box on the left is 8¼ inches long, 3¼ inches wide and 4 inches tall. It has a tin liner, divided into 2 sections for cartridges, and a small section with its own cover for percussion caps. This box is marked:

21   6   42   1855

The box on the right is about the same size but its tin liner is divided into 5 equal sections and has no markings at all.

Shown here is an unusual epaulette box because it has a patent date and also has 3 tin boxes which fit inside the epaulette box and were used to hold extra buttons and other miscellaneous items. The box itself is made of heavy tin, painted black, with a brass plate on the front with the lettering:

PATENTED JANY. 28, 1862

Dimensions of the box are: 12⅝ inches long, 5 inches wide, and 6½ inches high. This epaulette box came out of an antique shop several years ago and the owner thought it was a fish bait box!

David Corcilius

FILE

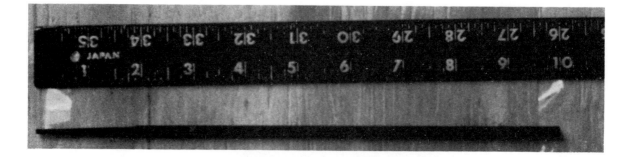

Gradually we are learning more about the tools used by both sides during the war. Shown here is a rat tail file about 10 inches long.

Glen Hayes

FRUIT CAN

There is much research left to do in the field of food containers of the Civil War period. Previous volumes of the *Encyclopedia* have contained several items in this category. To assist the interested collector we are showing the largest container of its type the author has ever seen. This fruit can is 8½ inches tall and 6 inches in diameter. It was found on the site of the Battle of Pleasant Hill, Louisiana. (The battle took place on April 9, 1864.)

Soldiers of both sides played games when in winter quarters and during lulls in active operations. Illustrating this is the collection of game items shown here. The ivory dice and the star design button were found together in a C.S. artillery position at Bermuda Hundred, Virginia. The dice are 5/16 inch square! The playing cards are marked as being patented April 5, 1864. These cards were exported from England (made by **Goodall**). There are 52 cards. Suits are not numbered but, for example, the card deuce of spades is shown only by two spades with no numbers at all on the card. This deck of cards advertises the Corticelli spools of thread.

82 GOFF ITEMS

As with the "Donaldson Items" (see above), it was decided to include items under one heading.

The inscription on the inside cover of the dictionary reads:

> This dictionary was on my Father's person — David Goff — when he was shot in the battle of Gettysburg, July 2, 1863.
> Mrs. W. F. Humphrey

David H. Goff enlisted July 28, 1862, to serve three years. He was mustered in as a corporal in Company "A" 126th New York Infantry. He surrendered with his regiment at Harpers Ferry on September 15, 1862, and was paroled the next day. Promoted sergeant and later first sergeant. Wounded in action in Gettysburg July 2, 1863, and died of his wounds July 4, 1863.

David Corcilius

Recently a varied assortment of grapeshot was found in a Confederate battery near Georgetown, South Carolina. These grapeshot vary in diameter from 1¼ to 2¼ inches. In February 1865 the Federals captured the battery.

Rod Gragg

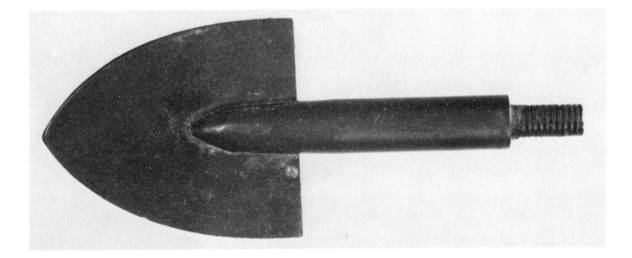

GRENADE FIN (?)

As yet this item has not been definitely identified but it may be a grenade fin. The "spade" is 1⅜ inches wide at its widest part — made of good steel and is threaded to screw into some item — possibly a hand grenade or "booby trap". The item is 3½ inches long and is from Pocataligo, South Carolina, where a battle took place on October 22, 1862.

84 GRENADE LAUNCHER (?)

As with the preceding item (e.g. "Grenade Fin"), identifying this item as a grenade launcher is only an educated guess. But obviously it is something! It is made of steel and is 6¼ inches long and 2 inches in diameter. From Harpers Ferry.

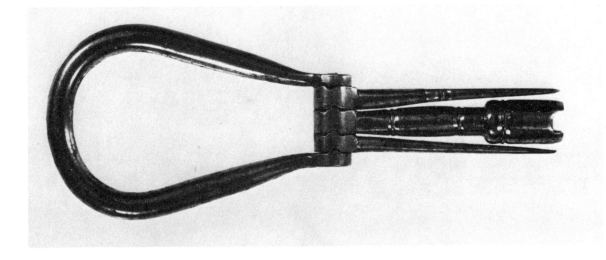

A handsome, well-made useful combination gun tool of bright steel. The length is 5 inches when open and 3 inches when closed. It has a screwdriver, cone pick, and nipple wrench. Rare!

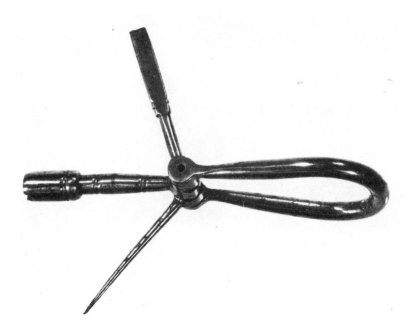

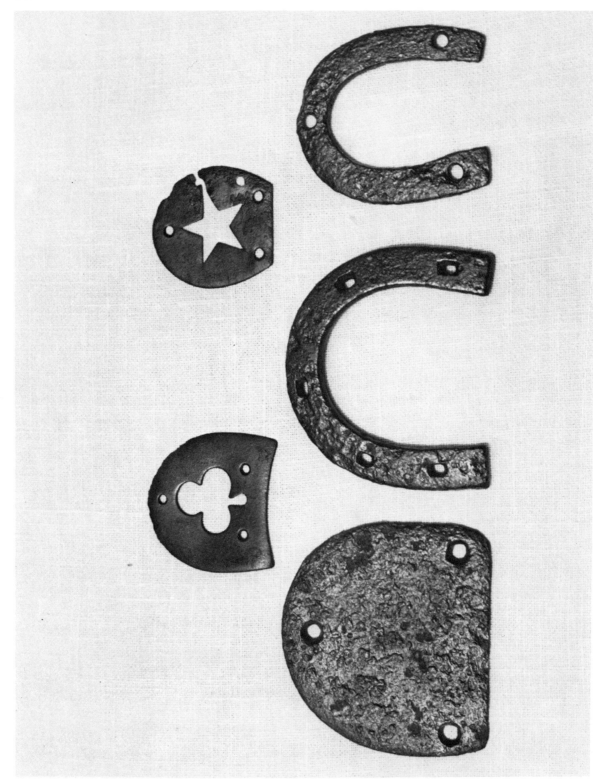

Shown here are five heel plates that were used on the heels of the boots or shoes of Civil War soldiers. These plates are typical of a number that have been found in the camps located in North Mississippi and West Tennessee.

Description: The three plates in the lower row are made of either wrought iron or steel, and were in the range of ⅛ to 3/16 inch in thickness. All have punched holes for the securing nails. Measuring from front to back and side to side, the plates are from left to right: 2 9/16 by 2 11/16; 2½ by 2¾; and 2⅜ by 2 1/16 inches. The holes in the full plate are countersunk to allow nail heads to be flush.

The two plates in the upper row were made of thin brass, probably 1/32 inch thick, and each has holes for securing nails. The plate on the left has a considerable amount of bright plating remaining on its inner surface. Measuring in the same manner as indicated above, the plates are 1¾ by 1⅝ and 1⅝ by 1½ inches. These two plates have openings in the shape of the Union 2nd Corps and the Union 12th and 20th Corps badges. These two plates were apparently from quite fancy shoes or boots that may have been worn by officers. Their reason for being in the Western theater of the war is uncertain. However, it is interesting to know that these two plates were found in camps located within one quarter of a mile of two different railroads.

All of the plates have been used as indicated by the uneven wear from side to side. One side of each of the two brass plates is worn to a knife edge. The two additional holes in the plate with the star were clearly caused by raised nail heads being beneath the plate.

John A. Marks

All students of the Civil War readily appreciate the role of horses in military operations. And many photographs have survived showing care of horses including traveling blacksmiths with their forges in the field. It is obvious that care of their horses was a continuing concern for all commanders on active operations. But on several occasions the cavalry of the Army of the Potomac was largely immobilized because their horses were not shod. The Federal general Pleasanton's chief excuse for his failure to catch Stuart after the Chambersburg raid of October 1862 was that he had only 800 shod horses out of 4500. Also, during the Gettysburg campaign apparently the Confederate general Jenkins had to stop from time to time to have civilians along the way shoe his horses. Apparently there was no great problem of supply of horseshoes. As early as 1835, Henry Burden had patented a "horseshoe machine" and this machine had received later patents up to 1862. So effective was the machine that it was the type used for making horseshoes for Federal armies in all the war theaters.

Shown here is a very unusual horseshoe which is as odd as another strange specimen on page 88 of Volume III of the *Encyclopedia*. The horseshoe here may well have been for correcting some injury to the horse's hoof. It was found at Spotsylvania and is 6½ inches long, and 4 inches wide at the widest part. The projection on top of the shoe (the 'cleat') is 2 inches long.

Because of their inherent value, and their strong aesthetic and historic appeal, Civil War identification discs and pins continue to be much desired by experts and beginner collectors alike. And new variations are constantly coming up. Since most of them are of metal a surprisingly large number in a good state of preservation have been recovered from battlefield and camp sites.

(A) **U. S.**

Silver 5th Corps badge ¾ inches tall and ¾ inches wide. "J.L." in stippled letters in center. Worn by John Lanigan, Co. A 9th Massachusetts Infantry. At age 26, Lanigan, a bootmaker from Boston, enlisted on February 10, 1862. He was captured at Fredericksburg, December 13, 1862. He re-enlisted on February 16, 1864, was wounded at Wilderness, May 5, 1864 and killed a week later at Spotsylvania (May 12, 1864). The 9th Massachusetts Infantry lost 160 killed, or 15.3 percent of its original enrollment.

Identification pin, probably 22nd Army Corps, marked "L.G." in script letters. Well-made. The diameter is 1½ inches.

Identification disc made from a large penny. Worn by Charles Gleice, bugler of Company B, 1st New York Artillery. After his service with this artillery regiment, Gleice joined Company L, 8th New York Cavalry. He deserted from this regiment October 25, 1862 and on July 6, 1863, he enlisted in Battery "B" 1st Maryland Light Artillery after changing his name to Charles Clay. On February 16, 1864 he joined Battery "A" Junior Artillery Maryland Volunteers. Four days later he was transferred to Battery "D" 1st Maryland Light Artillery and served with this battery to the end of the war. He died at the age of 46 in Baltimore, Maryland on August 1, 1883. [Shown here also is a tin-type of Gleice].

Robert Borrell, Sr.

U. S. CHRISTIAN COMMISSION

over

Address my ....

....

....

....

☞ Suspend from the neck by a cord, and wear
over the shirt--in battle, under.

See

IDENTIFIER.

over

I am...

Co....................*Reg't*...

............*Brig.*...........*Div.*..............*Corps.*

"God so loved the world, that he gave his only begotten Son,
that whosoever believeth in him should not perish,
but have everlasting life."

See

Identification tab issued by the U. S. Christian Commission. This unique tab is of strong paper and is reminiscent of hastily written pieces of paper pinned by the Federal soldiers on their backs before the insane attack of Cold Harbor. This tab, of course, was made expressly for the purpose of identifying the soldier on the battlefield or in the hospital. It is 2¾ inches long and 1¾ inches wide. The lettering is self explanatory. (For a brief discussion of the U. S. Christian Commission see Author's *They Fought For The Union,* page 132.)

David C. Hannah

94

Iowa lead piece. Use is unknown. The piece is marked:

H 11 IOWA

It is 2½ inches long and 1½ inches wide and was found at Shiloh.

Lee Sanzo

B. **C. S.**

This identification pin was dug up in Mississippi. It is made of silver and has "2" and "Independence" on the front. On the back is engraved.

J. Froment
Joined Co. Sept. 12, 1864
Exempted June 10, 1872

J. Froment was a private in the 5th Co. 4th Regiment, French Brigade, Louisiana Militia. His name appeared on the rolls — not dated — and his unit was ordered into service of the State of Louisiana.

Another Louisiana identification is the one shown here. It is of silver, 1¼ inches in diameter. This pin is marked:

"J. Post"

The owner was Private John Post, Co. "D" 7th Louisiana Infantry. He enlisted June 7, 1861 at Camp Moore, Louisiana. Post was present on all rolls up to October 1861. But he was later drummed out of the service. He was born in Ireland. At his enlistment he lived in New Orleans. By occupation he was a laborer, aged 25, and single.

C. **Miscellaneous discs and pins**

(The following items are not military, but are of definite Civil War interest.)

The slave identification tag shown here is of copper, 1 13/16 inches in diameter. On the front is the following:

Charleston
No. 191
Servant
1801

On the back of this disc is a hallmark and C. Prince.

"Peace Democrats" Identification Disc

This U. S. copper cent was worn by a member of the "Peace Democrats" or "Copperheads". Some members wore the head of Liberty cut out from the coin itself. Some historians believe the epithet "Copperhead" was used by loyal Northerners against anti-Administration individuals who attacked treacherously as the dreaded copperhead snake. The coin is the regular copper cent of the period (1847) —about one inch in diameter and perforated with a small hole of the use of a carrying string. Presumably, it was worn around the neck. This coin was found at McClellan's base at White House — Peninsular Campaign.

This Masonic saddle shield was dug in the camp occupied by Sherman's troops near Shiloh, May 13, 1862.

Lee Sanzo

Shown here are both sides of a Civil War lady's reversible pin. One side holds a tintype of an artilleryman while the other side has a shield motif. The "T" bar is missing.

Robert Borrell, Sr.

The small patriotic pin shown here was dug in the Shiloh area.

Lee Sanzo

100 INSIGNIA

Due to uncertainty among some collectors as to what constitutes "insignia" the following discussion should be of some assistance.

Definition: (from the Latin) means a distinguishing mark or badge —

Singular — Insigne
Plural — Insignia

But now — **Insignia** — is used generally both in the singular and plural.

TYPES OF INSIGNIA

Rank — officers and men

Length of Service — only enlisted men (Dates from the Revolution. One stripe for a specific number of years. (Usually 3 or 4.)

Unit Designation — Armies to Companies

Special Awards — Bravery, Competence in Weapons, etc. or Campaign Participation (usually medals)

Because of some confusion as to the term "insignia", it should be pointed out that "insignia" includes badges, distinguishing marks of rank, and membership in units.

A "decoration" is conferred on an individual for an act of gallantry or for meritorious services, while a "medal" is issued to an individual for his participation in a designated war, campaign, or expedition. Much confusion exists because of the fact that some decorations have the word "medal" in their title. A "badge" is awarded an individual for proficiency in a specific field, such as rifle marksmanship.

Collecting Insignia: Family Reasons
Inexpensive
Colorful
Historically Interesting
Small — Light in weight
Endless Variety!

Rank Designation

Before the Revolution the Colonial troops naturally followed the example of the British forces. There were some notable (and sensible!) exceptions. For example: Roger's Rangers.

During the Revolution the uniform of the Continental Army was similar to that of the French Army — but State militia units wore their own. As a matter of fact, for the most part, it was an army without uniforms. There was no apparent distinction between officers and men. It was not possible to supply uniforms in 1775 but it was possible to distinguish the different grades. Accordingly, in a general order, Washington ordered the following insignia to be worn:

Commander-in-Chief:	Light blue ribbon across the breast between the coat and waistcoat.
Major General:	Purple ribbon
Brigadier General:	Pink ribbon
Aide-de-Camp:	Green ribbon
Field Officers:	Red on pink cockades in their hats
Captain:	Yellow or buff
Subaltern:	Green
Sergeant:	Shoulder knot of red cloth on the right shoulder
Corporal:	A green knot

In 1780 it was ordered that rank be indicated in shoulder epaulettes. Major Generals wore two epaulettes with two stars on each; Brigadier Generals — one star on each.

In 1832 the spread eagle for Colonels was prescribed.

In 1833 the first uniform for enlisted ranks — corporal and sergeant were established; in 1847 it was set as two stripes for a corporal and three stripes for a sergeant.

These and later additions of various grades of sergeants were used by both Federal and Confederate forces from 1861-1865. All chevrons during this period were worn with the point down.

About 1840 it was decided to distinguish the branches of service by a distinctive color for the trimmings and facings on the uniforms; blue for infantry; yellow for cavalry; red for artillery; etc. This custom prevails to the present day.

In 1872 epaulettes were abolished in favor of shoulder knots. But shoulder boards came back and have been worn on dress uniforms right up to today. For active field service the shoulder loop has been in use since the Spanish American War. Rank designation has remained the same for about 150 years. The one exception outside more stars for higher generals was the addition of the gold bar for second lieutenants in 1917.

C. S. Insignia

When war broke out in April 1861, the Confederate War Department faced an influx of volunteers in uniforms of various hues and designs. Standardization was only a hope — since Southerners despised regimentation and many units refused to part with their special uniforms. Therefore, regulations set forth by Secretary of War Leroy Walker in August, 1861 were only a "style".

Colors — the same as U. S. except medical was black, and staff and engineers were buff.

Enlisted men wore chevrons like the U. S.

Officers' rank was designated by braid on the sleeves and insignia on the collars.

Color Insignia

2nd Lt.	1 bar
1st Lt.	2 bars
Captain	3 bars

Major	1 star
Lt. Col.	2 stars
Colonel	3 stars
General Officer	Stars in a wreath

Unit Designations

Army Corps — U. S. 1863-1865

U. S. Navy

Insignia is unique! (Army and Marine Corps use only one system of designation rank.)

But the Navy and Coast Guard are different.

In the Revolution the U. S. Navy **generally** followed the French Navy. By 1812 a regulation uniform had been prescribed for officers but the seamen wore what they wished. However, bell-bottomed trousers, which could be rolled up easily when washing the deck became standard. We tended to copy the British after 1783. The black kerchief was adopted after the Battle of Trafalgar, as an emblem of mourning for Lord Nelson (October 21, 1805). And the three white stripes worn around the edge of the collar were to commemorate Nelson's three great Naval victories: COPENHAGEN, THE NILE, AND TRAFALGAR.

In 1835 the first "rating badge" was authorized. These badges indicate a sailor's rating of job speciality aboard ship.

U. S. Marine Corps

Rank designations for both officers and men follow closely those of the U. S. Army. These designations go way back and were well set down in the 1859 Marine Corps regulations. The emblem of the Corps is a globe of the Western Hemisphere. Above this is an American eagle, wings spread and facing left. Behind the globe is a naval anchor fouled with rope.

Awards

Oldest — Purple Heart. Originally issued during the Revolution as a "Badge for Military Merit". Not reactivated for over 100 years. In 1931 General Douglas MacArthur had the medal classified and appropriate ribbon added. These were the Silver Star, Distinguished Flying Cross, and the Purple Heart.

Early in the Civil War medals were awarded to the commands which had defended Forts Sumter and Pickens. Generals like Quincy A. Gilmore and Benjamin F. Butler issued special medals to their men. But there was no medal for bravery for general issued by the U. S. Medals were objected to on the grounds that wearing of decorations was "contrary to the spirit of American institutions". But, finally "Medals of Honor" were authorized by Congress. About 1,000 Medals of Honor were added for Civil War service as compared with 95 for World War I and about 300 to all branches of the Armed Forces in World War II and 131 in the Korean War.

Throughout the last century, the U. S. practically avoided giving awards. The fact can plainly be seen in a photograph of the U. S. Army's ranking general (1883-1888) Phillip H. Sheridan. The picture shows him wearing seven medals — but **all** are veteran society medals. As late as 1888, the professional head of the Army had to make do with Society medals!

Shown here is a carte de visite of a young artilleryman wearing a 4-button sack coat and on his cap is an odd-shaped crossed cannon of brass with a silver letter "A" above them.

Robert Borrell, Sr.

INTRENCHING TOOLS

As with several other types of Civil War items, intrenching tools are being dug up in large numbers and in wide variety of types.

A. **U. S.**

Hoe found at site of Sherman's headquarters in LaGrange, Tennessee. It is 5 inches in length from the edge of the blade to the outer edge of the handle socket. The blade itself is 6 inches wide at its widest part.

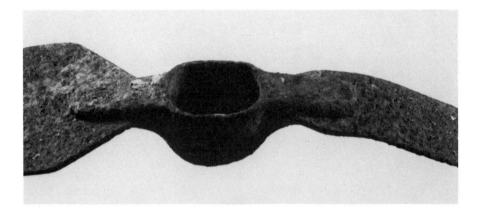

This adze was found at Cold Harbor. Its over-all length is 10½ inches. The large blade is 2¾ inches wide and the small blade is 1¼ inches in width.

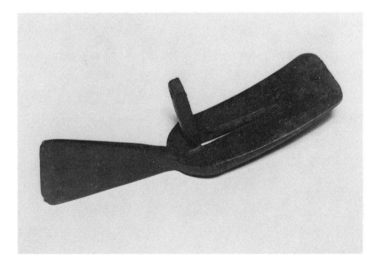

A non-dug adze, of heavy iron, stamped "U.S." It is 11¾ inches long. The large blade is 3⅜ inches wide at its widest part, while the small blade is 2¾ inches wide at its widest part.

106

B. **C. S.**

This large and heavy hoe was found in a Confederate camp in C.S. trenches six miles south of Savannah, Georgia. This hoe is 8¾ inches long, including the hole for the handle. The width of the blade at its widest point is 5⅝ inches.

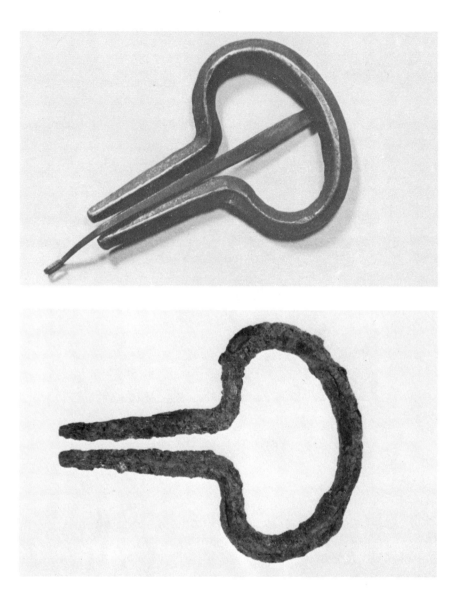

Because they are small and inexpensive, the Jew's harp was a favorite with many soldiers to pass away the time in camp. Shown here are examples from both armies. The unusually large iron Jew's harp was carried by a soldier from Massachusetts. It is 4½ inches long and 3⅜ inches wide at the widest part. This Jew's harp is rather crudely made and has a steel spring.

The Confederate Jew's harp — unlike the one described above — was dug. It is 3½ inches long and 2¾ inches wide at its widest part. This is of iron and was dug up in Confederate Fort Fisher on the Cape Fear peninsula, North Carolina. A land-sea battle was fought here January 6-15, 1865.

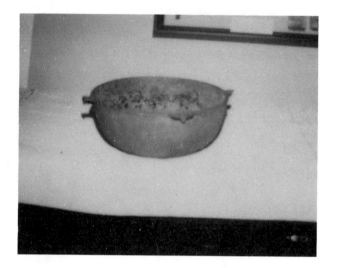

All Confederate items are of interest to the collector, and mess and camp equipment is no exception. Most of the C.S. camp equipment encountered by the Author is unmarked. But occasionally a collector comes up with a marked specimen. For example, there recently was located in Corinth, Mississippi an iron kettle marked on the bottom:

Confederate States
1863
of America

The dimensions of this **very** rare kettle are:

    Diameter at top — 9 9/16 inches
    Diameter at bottom — 5 1/16 inches
    Depth — 4 inches

  The lid and handle are missing.

Roger Davis

The kettle (with the handle) is a splendid iron specimen, recovered from inside the C.S. works at Port Hudson, Louisiana. Made of heavy iron, 9 inches in diameter, and 7½ inches deep, it has three small legs at the bottom. The handle is of very heavy wire.

Found in the same spot as the above is this heavy iron kettle, 10½ inches in diameter and 8 inches deep. The handle was made of baling wire. When excavated, this kettle was about full of human bones — mainly hands and fingers. The kettle was recovered from the site of a Confederate hospital.

110 LAMP FIXTURE

Wick guide from a Barracks Oil Lamp. The wick extended up through the two parallel slots. When the shaft was rotated the wick could be adjusted either up or down.

Michael Johnson

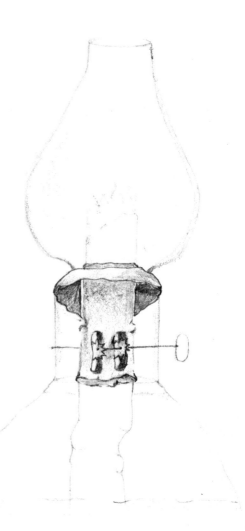

This C. S. lead ingot was recently discovered in Pocataligo, South Carolina. Several of these were discovered in the same cache. Each plate is 7¼ inches in diameter and ½ inch thick. Especially interesting is the way the Confederates marked these lead ingots — they pressed a rectangular C.S.A. buckle into the lead while it was still soft.

Leo Redmond

112 LEG IRONS

Enforcement of discipline was a continuing problem in both Federal and Confederate armies. And, of course, this enforcement involved punishment and restraint of culprits. Accordingly, hand irons and leg irons were in fairly general use. Examples are shown on page 53 of Volume I, *Civil War Collector's Encyclopedia.* But another type of leg iron is shown here.

William Coleman

As with so many non-military essentials described in the various volumes of the *Encyclopedia*, the category of lighting equipment is replete with fascinating variety! Certainly worthy of being so considered is this match and candle holder. It is of tin, painted green.

3⅞ inches long and 2⅞ inches wide; it is 1⅞ inches long and 2⅞ inches wide when closed. This holder came from the estate of Captain E. S. Skilton, Co. "A" 57th Ohio Infantry.

David Corcilius

114

Various types of match boxes are shown in the accompanying photograph. From Left to Right in the semi-circle at the top:

(1) Front side is marked with "Memorial" and "Gen. John A. Logan" and the General's picture. Back side has a figure of a soldier and the words: "The Volunteer" and "40 Rounds". This box is of heavy tin, 2½ inches tall and 1¼ inches wide.

(2) Thin tin, 2¾ inches long, 1¼ inches wide. Original matches. Carried by Surgeon Enoch Pearse of the 61st Ohio Infantry.

(3) Heavy tin, 3 inches long and 1⅛ inches wide. Carried by G. D. Smith of Wayne, Maine.

(4) Iron box — 2⅜ inches long and ⅞ inches wide. This came from North Carolina.

(5) Iron — oval shaped. Decorated with a lyre and cross. It is 2⅛ inches tall. From General Sedgwick's regimental camp sites across the road from Berkeley Plantation of Harrison's Landing of 1862.

(6) Oval box made of hard rubber. This box is 2⅞ inches long and 1 inch wide.

The bottom box is of heavy tin, 2½ inches long and 1½ inches wide. It is marked:

> G. W. Gail & Ax
> Tobacco Works
> Baltimore, Maryland

    This second group of match boxes shows a similarity in size and shape. All six boxes are of painted tin, shaped like the Civil War knapsacks, with hinged covers. All are 1¾ inches long, 1¼ inches wide and ¼ inch deep. Some of the boxes are marked:

> Knapsack Matches
> Licensed

and manufacturer's names. Included in the manufacturers are:

> The United Machine & Supply Co. N. Y.
> The Diamond Match Co.
> Bryant & May Limited

and others.

116 LINCOLN CAMPAIGN RIBBON

A very rare item of Lincoln's 1860 Presidential campaign. Made of woven silk.
Lee Sanzo

This trunk lock is very probably military-oriented, since it has an eagle motif on the front over the key hole. The lock is made of brass, 1⅝ inches tall and 2½ inches wide. It is marked with the eagle and:

— AC — Lock Co.

The lock came from the site of the 92nd New York Infantry's position on the skirmish line outside Fort Anderson, North Carolina on March 14, 1863.

The combination lock is heavy brass, 1⅜ inches tall and 1⅛ inches wide. There are five rotating discs, each marked with letters of the alphabet.

Extremely rare and interesting U. S. Mint loyalty oath. Made of bronze 1⅛ inches in diameter. This is a truly beautiful medal! On the front is the head of Washington and the words:

"The Constitution is
Sacredly Obligatory
On All."

On the back of the medal are wreaths and the words:

U. S. Mint
Oath of Allegiance
Taken By The
Officers and Workmen
Sept. 9, 1861
Jas. Pollock, Dir

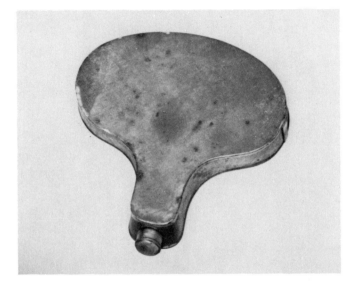

The subject of medical canteens was discussed in the first volume of the *Encyclopedia.* Since publication of that volume, however, I have found the two shown here. They are included here because they are different from the types already discussed.

122

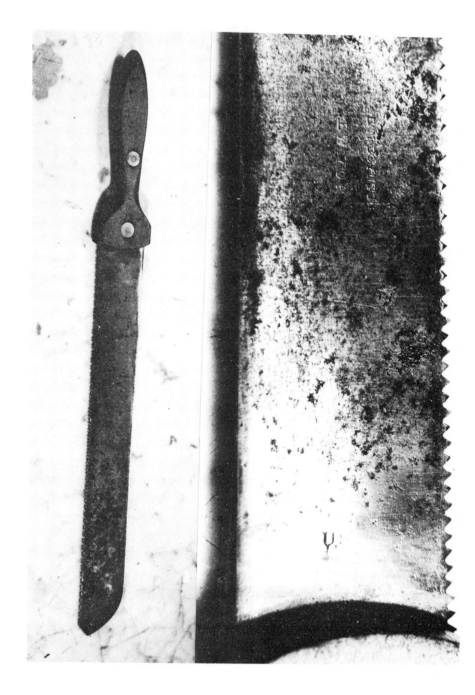

U. S. Medical Department bone saw. Both sides of the blade are stamped "U.S." and the blade is also marked:

E. M. Boynton

I. W. York

The saw has a 12½ inch blade, wood handle, and brass fittings.

Martin J. Fowler

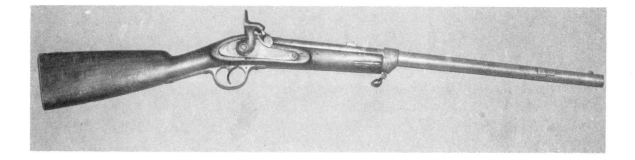

This C. S. musketoon is another specimen of the type described as probably Confederate on page 166 of Volume III of the *Encyclopedia*. The specimen shown here was purchased in North Carolina. It has the AE markings on the screw heads, the nipple vent, and the brass nose cap. It also has:

ALA 1864

crudely stamped on the lock plate. As can be seen by the photographs, this musketoon (or carbine) shows use by the 1st South Carolina Cavalry.

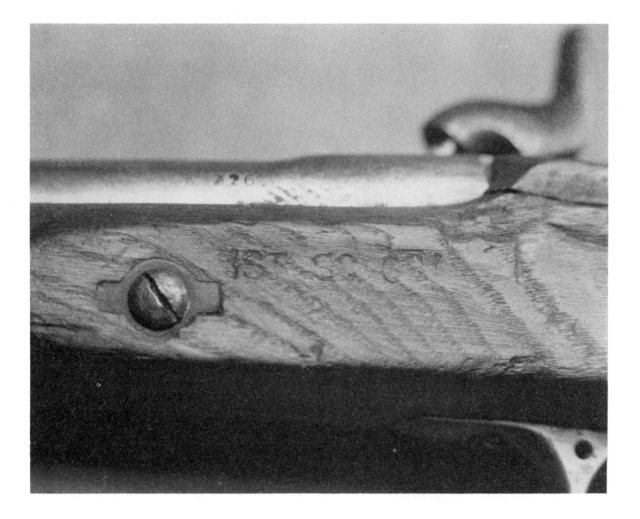

Another interesting Confederate weapon is the carbine shown here. It was used by a cavalryman from York, South Carolina. It is 33½ inches long with an 18¼ inch barrel. This carbine has a single barrel band. Caliber .52.

Sam Padgett

This is a very attractive bit of carving. It is a neckerchief holder carved of bone by a New York Artilleryman. Completely done by hand, this holder is decorated with a shield, crossed cannons, numbers, and letters — all painted red in much the same way the scrimshaw was made.

Robert Borrell, Sr.

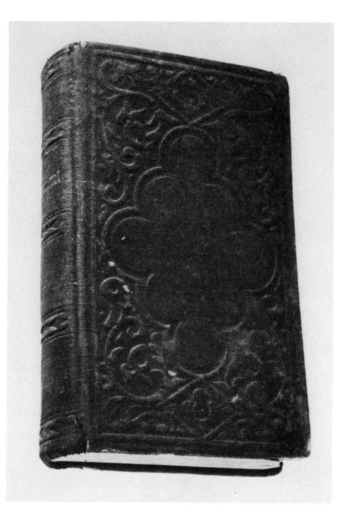

A first glance at the New Testament shown here would make most readers wonder why it is included in this volume of the *Encyclopedia*. In outer appearance the New Testament here does not differ from thousands of others of the Civil War period. In fact, I believe this particular binding is the most common of all Civil War pocket Bibles and New Testaments. But this particular specimen is shown because it is in German and was used by one of the many thousands of soldiers of German extraction who served during the War. Like most pocket New Testaments it is 4¾ inches by 3 inches — the "normal" size. It contains 453 pages, completely in German and is entitled *Das Neue Testament* (The New Testament) and was published by the American Bible Society in New York, 1863

130 OIL CANS

The metal parts of weapons needed oiling from time to time in the field. This was especially true for the gun locks of pistols, revolvers, and long arms. Shown here are two oil containers. Both are from the Fredericksburg, Virginia battle area. The container with the screw top is of steel, 2⅝ inches long and ⅜ inch in diameter. The screw top has a cone pick attached (used to clean out the nipple of the musket).

This container is of corrugated iron but with the screw top missing. It is 3 inches long and 7/16 inch in diameter.

132   OPENER

Here is another unsolved mystery, but very probably the item shown here is an opener. My educated guess is that it was used as a nail puller, perhaps for tops of hardtack boxes or the wooden ammunition boxes. It is metal (probably iron), 3 inches long and 1¼ inches wide at its widest part. From a Federal camp at La Grange, Tennessee. (Late information indicates this could be a button board.)

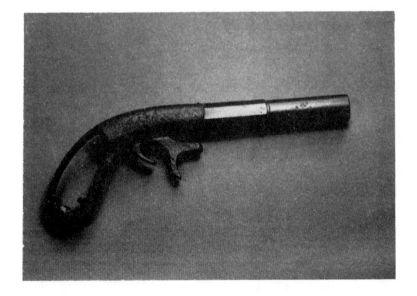

This "boot pistol" was recovered at the site of the great cavalry battle at Brandy Station, Virginia (June 9, 1863). This is a underhammer pistol. Its barrel is marked on top:

BACON & CO. NORWICH, CONN.

and underneath the barrel are the words:

CAST STEEL

Lee Sanzo

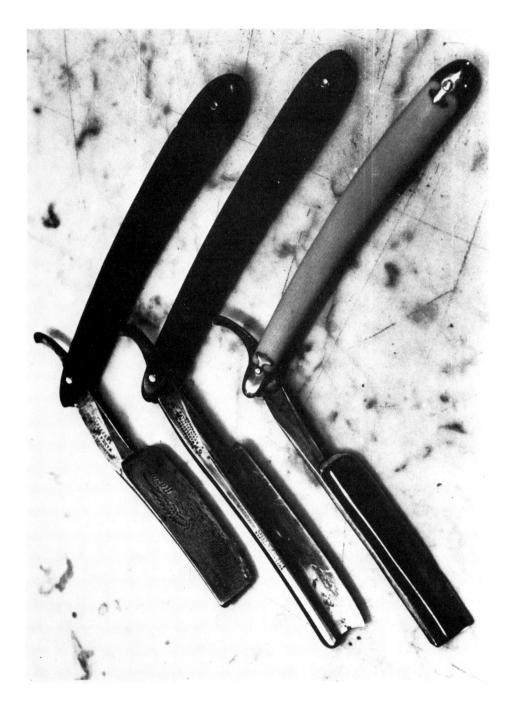

Razors have been discussed in other volumes of the *Encyclopedia* but these specimens are shown here because they give a fairly good representation of the various types in general use during the War. Note the eagle motif on the top specimen of the group of three.

Martin J. Fowler

Included in this category of **Relics** are varied items of Civil War interest, all of which have been recovered from the land or sea.

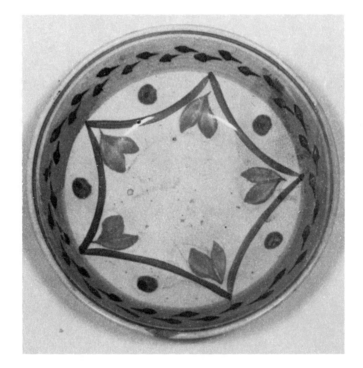

C. S. Dish

This dish is one of a large assortment of dishes recovered from the sunken blockade runner *Georgiana,* lost off Charleston in 1863. The photograph does not do justice to the bright colors (red, green, black) which are still so bright that the dish truly looks as though it was made only yesterday. The dish is 5½ inches in diameter and 1 inch deep.

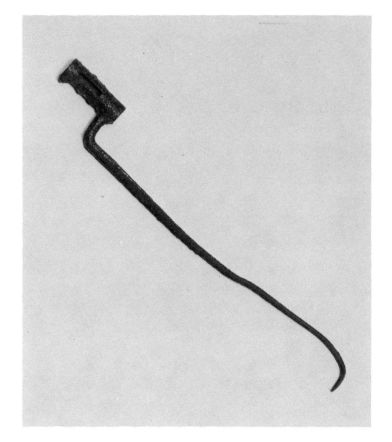

Clothing Hook

This is the regulation U.S. caliber .58 musket bayonet which was adapted as a hook for dragging the bodies of dead soldiers to the burial site. It came from the Antietam (or Sharpsburg) battlefield of September 17, 1862. Members of burying parties used these bayonets (presumably still attached to their muskets) in order to stay as far as possible from the decaying corpses which emitted extremely foul odors — both from internal gas as well as the inevitable stench of human excrement released from the body at death.

Insignia and Accouterment Plates

All items shown here were recovered from sites in the Western theatre of operations.

(1) **Shoulder scales.** Both shoulder scales shown are from the camp of the 2nd Iowa Cavalry at La Grange, Tennessee. The one on the left is 3 5/16 inches and 2 3/16 inches wide and 6⅜ inches long. The one on the right is 4 7/16 inches and 2 3/16 inches wide and 6⅞ inches long. Both are of brass with steel reinforcement.

(2) **Pompom Eagle, Model 1851.** Later this plate became known as the Jefferson Davis Hat Plate. Pressed brass, 1⅞ inches wide, 2½ inches tall. Two brass wire fasteners soldered on back. Found at La Grange, Tennessee.

(3) **Crossed sabers.** Pressed brass, 3⅜ inches wide, 1¾ inches tall. Four brass wire fasteners soldered on back. Found in the 2nd Iowa Cavalry camp at La Grange, Tennessee.

(4) **Company letter.** Letter **K**. Cast brass, 1 1/16 inches wide and 3/16 inch tall. Two spikes on back for securing. Found at La Grange, Tennessee.

(5) **Infantry insignia.** This infantry "bugle" is of pressed brass. 3 9/16 inches wide and 1⅝ inches tall. Two wire fasteners soldered on back. Found at La Grange, Tennessee.

(6) **Regimental number.** Number **4**, pressed brass, 11/16 inch wide and 11/16 inch tall. Wire fasteners soldered to back. Found at La Grange, Tennessee.

(7) **U. S. Cartridge Box Plates.** Upper specimen is 2 1/5 inches by 3 2/5 inches. Lower specimen is 2.19 inches by 3.44 inches. It is marked **HUNTER**. Both plates were found in the 2nd Iowa Cavalry camp at La Grange, Tennessee.

(8) **U. S. Shoulder Belt Plates.** Both of these "Eagle" plates are 2.55 inches in diameter and marked:

W. H. Smith
Brooklyn

They have a stamped brass face with two wire loops imbedded in solder filled back. Both were found at La Grange, Tennessee.

(9) **Buttons.**

(Left row — top to bottom)
Confederate Army officers coat button. Brass, two-piece, gold wash. (See Albert, CS26B) Found at La Grange, Tennessee.

Confederate infantryman's coat button. Two-piece, brass face, ferrous back. (See Albert, CS182A). Found at La Grange, Tennessee.

Mississippi militia coat button. Brass, two-piece. Plain star with **Mississippi** encircling on a lined field with border. Marked:
C. Bellenot
N. O.
(Albert, MPI). Found at La Grange, Tennessee.

140

Mississippi cuff button. Brass, two-piece, gold wash. The letter "I" in a star with **Mississippi** encircling. Marked:

       Hyde & Goodrich
        N. O.

(Albert, MP4AV). Found at La Grange, Tennessee.

Louisiana coat button. Brass, two-piece, with border. The pelican's head is to the right on a plain field. (Albert, LA9A). Found at La Grange, Tennessee.

(Right row — top to bottom)

Missouri staff officer's coat button. Brass, three-piece, gold wash. Missouri state seal on a lined field. (Albert MO2A). Marked:

       Scovill Mfg. Co.
       Waterbury

Found at La Grange, Tennessee.

Union infantry officer's coat button. Two-piece, brass, gold wash. Spread eagle with letter "I" on a recessed shield. Marked:

       Extra Quality

Found at La Grange, Tennessee.

Union cavalry officer's coat button. Two-piece, brass, gold wash. Spread eagle with letter "C" on a recessed shield.

Found at Germantown, Tennessee

Union rifleman officer's coat button. Two-piece, brass, gold wash. Spread eagle with the letter "R" on a recessed shield. Found at La Grange, Tennessee.

Union artillery officer's cuff button. Two-piece, brass, gold wash. Spread eagle with the letter "A" on a recessed shield. Found at Jacinto, Mississippi.

Union staff officer's cuff button. Three-piece, brass, with heavy gilt. Spread eagle with shield on a lined field with 19 stars encircling. Found at Oxford, Mississippi.

John A. Marks

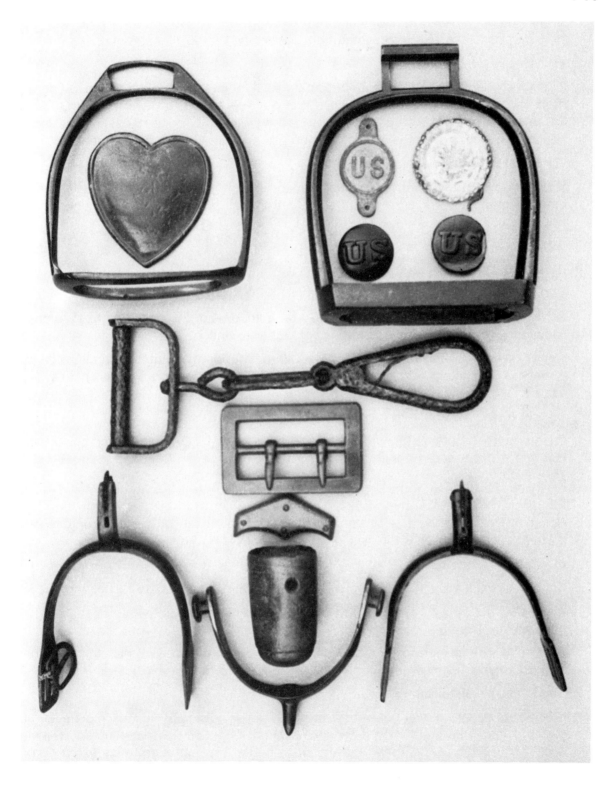

Shown here is a nicely representative collection of accouterments associated with the mounted service. All were recovered from sites in the Western theatre of operations.

(1) Stirrups

The left stirrup is a cavalry stirrup of cast brass. It is the lightweight pattern, 5⅛ inches high and 4⅝ inches wide. Found in the camp of the 2nd Iowa Cavalry at La Grange, Tennessee. The right stirrup is one used by the artillery. It, too, is of cast brass. Heavy pattern, 5⅞ inches high and 5⅛ inches wide. Found at La Grange, Tennessee.

(2) Cavalry martingale

Heart-shaped of stamped brass. Face has a raised border. Three pronged fasteners embedded in solder filled back. It is 2 15/16 inches high and 2 13/16 inches wide. Found in camp of the 2nd Iowa Cavalry at La Grange, Tennessee.

(3) Cavalry rosettes

(Within the stirrup — Left to right)

Top Row

Federal cavalry rosette, cast brass, "U.S." on a lined field. 2⅛ inches high, 1¼ inches wide, 5/32 inches thick. Found on the approaches to Shiloh.

Cavalry pewter rosette with a silvered face. Wire loop for attaching to strap is soldered to back. 1¾ inches in diameter and ¼ inch thick. Found in a North Mississippi cavalry camp.

Bottom Row

Cavalry bridle rosettes, stamped brass faces with raised "U.S." Solder-filled backs with wire loops imbedded. 1¼ inch in diameter and 3/16 inch thick. Found in La Grange, Tennessee.

(4) Carbine sling swivel

Roller, swivel, link and snap for a cavalry carbine sling. All pieces made of iron or steel. 2⅞ inches wide at roller, 8½ inches long. Found at Pulaski, Tennessee.

(5) Carbine sling buckle

Cast brass with wrought brass prongs. 1 15/16 inches wide, 3 3/16 inches high, 5/32 inch thick. Found at Germantown, Tennessee.

(6) Carbine sling tip

Cast brass with four brass rivets. 2¼ inches long, 1 inch wide, and ⅛ inch thick. Found at Germantown, Tennessee.

(7) Saddle pistol holster tip

Heavy cast brass with two holes for riveting to leather holster. 1½ inches in diameter at the open end; 1¼ inches in diameter at closed end. It is 2 9/16 inches long and ⅜ inch thick in the bottom. Apparently these tips are made heavy enough to contain a pistol bullet in case of accidental discharge. Found at Germantown, Tennessee.

(8) **Spurs**

(Left to right)

Confederate cavalry spur. Cast brass frame with steel rowel. Brass strap buckle attached. Frame is 3⅛ inches wide and 3⅜ inches deep. Rowel prong ⅜ by ⅜ inches square, projecting 1⅜ inches. Found on Shiloh battlefield just south of the Park.

Cavalry spur of cast brass with a "jabbing" prong instead of a rowel. Has two applied studs for attaching straps. Some nickel plate remains. 3 9/16 inches wide at open end and 4¼ inches wide overall. The arch is 2⅜ inches deep. 3⅜ inches long over the prong. Found at Pulaski, Tennessee.

Federal cavalry spur of a cast brass frame with steel rowel. The frame is 4 inches wide, 2⅞ inches deep. Rowel prong is ⅜ inch in diameter, projecting 1¼ inches. Found in camp of the 2nd Iowa Cavalry at La Grange, Tennessee.

John A. Marks

MESS GEAR

The mess shown here was all recovered from sites in the Western theatre of operations. (Read left to right)

Top Row

(1) Pewter teaspoon, 4⅞ inches long, marked:
    C. Parker & Co.
Found at La Grange, Tennessee.

(2) Wrought steel tablespoon, 7⅝ inches long. Found at La Grange, Tennessee.

(3) Pressed steel tablespoon — two-piece with applied handle. 7¼ inches long. Found at La Grange, Tennessee.

(4) Steel for sharpening knives, 9 inches long and 9/16 inches in diameter. Wooden handle is missing. Found at La Grange, Tennessee.

(5) Pressed steel tablespoon — two-piece with applied handle. 7¾ inches long. Found at La Grange, Tennessee.

(6) Wrought steel teaspoon — one-piece, 5¼ inches long. Found at Lumpkins Mill, Mississippi.

(7) Brass tablespoon — one-piece, 7 inches long. Marked BNF. Found at Lumpkins Mill, Mississippi.

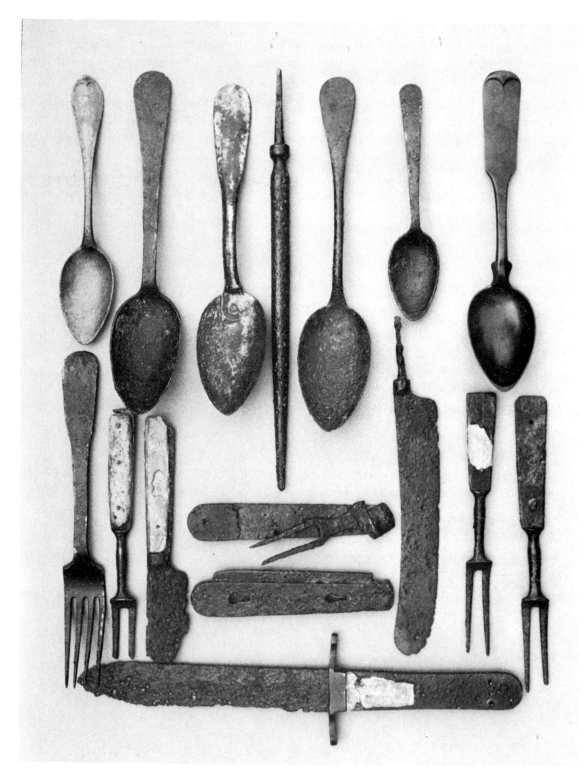

(1)   Steel mess fork — one-piece, four-tine, 7¼ inches long. Found at La Grange, Tennessee.

(2)   Steel mess fork, two-tine, with front and back bone handle attached with brass pins. Originally about 6¼ inches long. Found at La Grange, Tennessee.

(3)   Steel mess knife with two bone handle pieces attached with two brass pins. Found at Pulaski, Tennessee.

(4)   Steel knife and fork combination, with one folding blade and one folding two-tine fork. Two brass rivets on the fork fit into two slotted holes in the knife. Each section originally had an applied handle (probably wood) on one side. Length is 4⅝ inches closed. Found at La Grange, Tennessee.

(5)   Steel mess knife, 7⅜ inches long. Originally this knife had an applied handle of wood or bone. Found at La Grange, Tennessee.

(6)   Steel mess fork, two-tine. Front and back bone handle pieces are attached with two brass pins. Length of fork is 5¾ inches long. Found at La Grange, Tennessee.

(7)   Steel mess fork, two-tine, with front and back wood handle pieces attached with two brass pins. Length of fork is 6⅜ inches. Found at La Grange, Tennessee.

Bottom of Picture

Steel side knife with a brass guard. The two bone handle pieces are attached with four brass pins. Knife is 10⅛ inches long. Found at Eastport, Mississippi.

John A. Marks

Musket Barrels

Shown here are two musket barrels recovered from battlefields. The top specimen is an 1862 Springfield musket barrel, dug at Cold Harbor, Virginia. It came from a grave that was uncovered recently. The bottom barrel is from an Enfield musket and was dug at Petersburg, Virginia. The rear sight is still able to be adjusted!

Ken Weller

A Confederate-marked Le Fauchaux revolver. This revolver was found in the razing of an old house in Lexington, South Carolina. It is a six-shot weapon, 6¾ inches long. Marked:

1862
C.S.

Used the pin fire cartridge.

Leo Redmond

A collection of eight cavalry rosettes — all from the Western theatre of operations.

(Read left to right)

Top Row

Atlanta — Vicksburg — Tennessee — Dalton

Bottom Row

Port Hudson — Atlanta — Kenesaw Mountain — Atlanta

These are made of heavy brass or pewter. The largest is the one from Dalton, Georgia (2⅜ inches in diameter); the smallest is the one from Vicksburg (1⅝ inches in diameter).

150

(A) **U. S.**

This copper rosette is 2 inches in diameter. It has a U. S. shield and 13 stars with stripes running up and down. Very rare rosette! Found at Kenesaw Mountain battlefield.

(B) **C. S.**

Heavy brass, 2⅜ inches tall and 1¼ inches wide. This is a very unique Confederate rosette; evidently it was originally a civilian item adapted to military use. This rosette came from Joe Wheeler's cavalry camp at Lovejoy, Georgia, which was over-run by Kilpatrick at the start of the "March to the Sea".

SARDINE CAN

These sardine cans have been found in substantial numbers on many camp sites. The specimen shown here was selected for inclusion in this book because of its fine state of preservation. It is shown here through the courtesy of VINCE SPITALE who is its owner and who supplied the photographs shown here. The sardine can is marked:

> DUBOIS ALLAIN
> SARDINES A L'HUILE
> PORT-LOUIS PRES LORIENT
> DUMONTI (MORBIHAN) A PARIS

Ed & Margie Bearss

(A) **U. S.**

Officers folding scissors (Originally invented in England in 1801 and called "pocket scissors"). These scissors fold compactly into a small size, for travel as well as for safety. Only 2 inches long when folded, the 3-inch blades nestle inside the handles to insure safety in carrying.

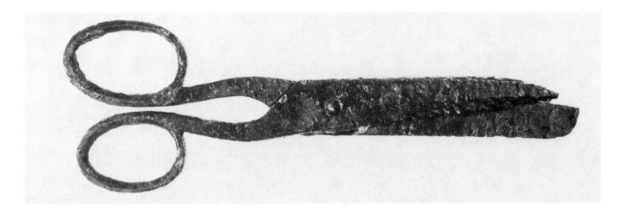

(B) **C. S.**

Confederate scissors of unusually large size (8 inches long). Were dropped in the "open" position. These scissors were dug out of Spanish Fort, Alabama several years ago.

Truly a unique item! This "dispatch case" was carried by couriers in Mosby's famous 43rd Virginia "Partisan Ranger Battalion." It is of heavy brass, 5⅞ inches long, and 1 5/16 inches in diameter. Both ends are removable. As can be seen by the photograph the case is marked:

43rd Virginia
Partisan Ranger Battalion
Not to be opened by any soldier
with less than field or staff
commission on penalty of death.

Irwin Rider

(A) **U. S.**

Solid copper spike from the hull timbers of the Civil War ship New Hampshire. The spike is stamped "U.S." and was made by the firm of the famous Paul Revere silver-and-coppersmith. The spike weighs 11 ounces, is 9¼ inches long with a thick flat head ⅞ inch square. The **New Hampshire** served with the Gulf Blockading Squadron, mainly as a supply ship. The ship is shown here in a modern photograph. The **New Hampshire** sank off Massachusetts shortly after World War I when she was en route to Nova Scotia where she was to serve as a coaling ship.

(B) **C.S.**

Spike from the Confederate ship, originally called the **Nashville**. About the middle of the War, she was refitted and named the **Rattlesnake** and served as a blockade runner. On February 27, 1863, she was sunk in the Ogeechee River by the U. S. monitor **Montauk** and the U. S. S. **Wissachickon** off Fort McAllister.

SHOULDER SCALES

Because of considerable confusion about what type of shoulder scale was worn by the various enlisted ranks, these photographs are included here in this volume. Shoulder scales were worn by enlisted men in the different branches of service; they varied only to show differences in rank and **not** to designate any particular branch of service. The three basic army types are shown here. The smallest of the three was worn by privates while the similar but larger one was worn by non-commissioned officers.

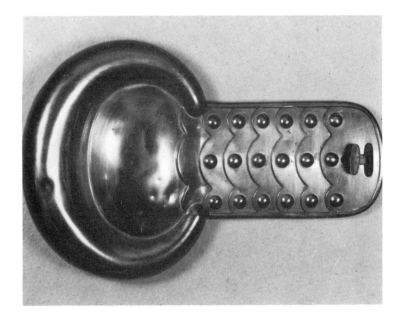

The NCO staff wore the same size scales as the NCO's but with three rows of imitation rivets. All three types are of brass.

Robert Borrell, Sr.

Much research remains to be done by future students of the 1861-1865 period with respect to the entire field of military outfitters. Shown here are two sets of shoulder straps; each set was supplied by a different dealer. The shoulder straps of an artillery lieutenant colonel are the type advertised in the 1864 illustrated catalogue of Schuyler, Hartley, and Graham.

Shown here also is a beautiful pair of an artillery captain's shoulder straps. These have stamped imitation embroidery borders and captain's bars. On the reverse of each shoulder strap is a maker's label marked:

Very few Civil War shoulder straps have any markings to indicate patent date or marker.

Robert Borrell, Sr.

162   SIGNAL FLARE CARTRIDGE CASE

The item shown here is an enigma. My educated guess is that it is the expended case of a signal flare cartridge. Up to now I have not seen a similar item nor a drawing or photograph of anything resembling it. This "case" is of heavy copper, 3⅝ inches long and 1¼ inches in diameter. It was dug on the battlefield of Bentonville, North Carolina (March 19, 1865).

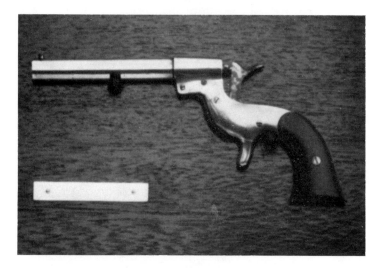

The owner of this rare type of U. S. Army signal pistol is a British collector. Let him tell us of his find in his own words:

"The present owner of this signal pistol was asked by a friend in midsummer of 1979 to look at the contents of an old Victorian seaman's chest which had been found in the loft of a cottage he had just inherited.

The chest was found to contain every conceivable type of weapon from almost

every country. It was assumed the original owner had accumulated these during his seafaring days.

Tucked away in the bottom of the trunk was the pistol shown here. One can only speculate as to how it came to be where it was — what a tale that would be!

As can be seen, the pistol is in excellent condition — a crisp action and clear markings with very little pitting considering its 120 year rest in a damp loft."

David Holder

Pipes

Two clay pipes from the siege of Savannah. The larger pipe (on the left) is decorated with soldiers holding flags. The smaller pipe (on the right) has a castle motif **very** similar to the engineers insignia of the U. S. Army — and it also has some indecipherable lettering. By way of contrast there is a plain clay pipe shown here as an example of the clay pipe in very common use by soldiers of both sides.

W. E. Erquitt

Pipe Tamper

This brass pipe tamper, about 2 inches tall is one of the unique Civil War finds resulting from underwater search. It was recovered from the U. S. Army transport **Boston** which was sunk by the Confederates at Chapman's Ford, South Carolina on May 26, 1864.

Howard B. Tower, Jr.

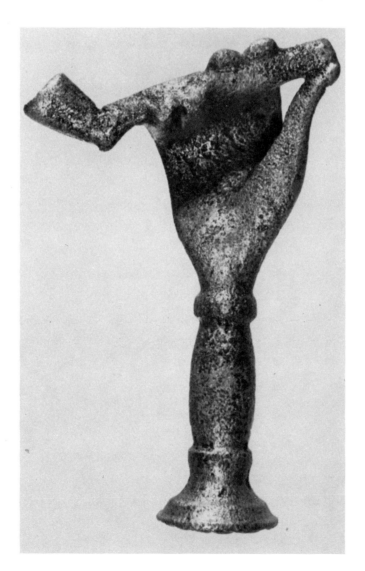

Smoking Kit

This handsome smoking kit is made of japanned tin, 4⅝ inches long, 1¾ inches wide, and 1 inch deep. It has a small inner compartment, possibly for paper. Both ends of the kit fold out; one end has a compartment for matches, the other end apparently held a small pipe (pipe is missing from kit).

David Corcilius

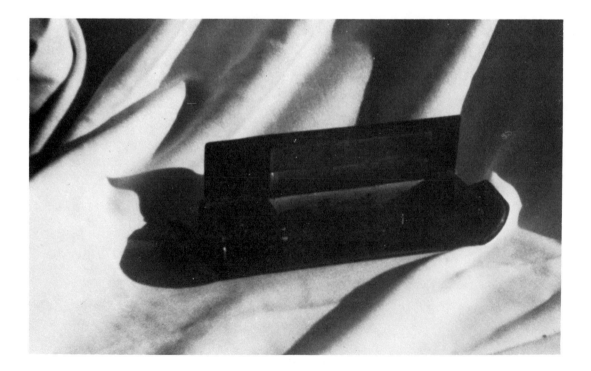

Tobacco Containers

The four tobacco containers shown here are all of heavy tin.

(Left to right)

Rectangular box, 3 inches long, 2¼ inches wide, ⅞ inches deep. From Annapolis, Maryland.

Oval box, 3⅛ inches long and 2⅛ inches wide at widest point. There is a sunburst design on the lid and on the bottom.

Oval box, 3¼ inches long and 2⅛ inches wide at widest point. No design but is marked:

Pat Jan 24 (?) 1860
C. Parker

Rectangular box, 3 inches long and 2 inches wide. Stamped on top:

Tobacco

Snuff was rather extensively "enjoyed" by many soldiers of both sides. Shown here are four snuff containers used during the War.

(Left to right)

Japanned tin oval box, 2½ inches long, 1 9/16 inches wide and 1 inch deep. From Maryland.

Amber snuff bottle 2½ inches tall and 1½ inches wide. From a C. S. trench at Savannah.

Tin snuff container, 2¼ inches tall and 1½ inches in diameter. Top is stamped:

BUTTERCUP SWEET SNUFF

This can came from North Carolina.

Tin snuff container, 2⅜ inches tall and 1¾ inches in diameter. The top is stamped.

GEO. W. HELME
SNUFF
COMPANY

Also of interest are the two snuff bottles shown here. On the left is a thick brown bottle, 2¾ inches tall with a bottom 1⅝ inches by 1½ inches. The bottle on the right is green in color, 3¼ inches tall with a bottom 1¼ inches by 1 inch. There are labels on both sides.

One reads:

Dr. Marshall's
Catarrh
Snuff
186-

On the other side a label reads:

"This snuff is superior
to anything yet
known."

(The label goes on to credit Dr. Marshall's snuff with curing colds, headaches, catarrh, etc.!)

Civil War photographs are replete with camp scenes in which barrels are very frequently in evidence. Many of these barrels, as well as the smaller wooden casks, contained whiskey or even water! Frequently these liquid containers were equipped with spigots. Two are shown here. On the left is a pewter spigot, 5½ inches long and 3 inches tall (to top of handle). It is marked:

NEW YORK
FENNS PATENT
NO. 3

This spigot was found at Dumfries, Virginia. The spigot on the right is of brass, 4½ inches long and 3 inches to top of handle. From Camp Nelson, Kentucky.

Individual and unit ownership of uniforms, military equipment, and personal belongings was as important in the Civil War as it is in modern armies. Because of this fact, the stencil was an important item both for the individual soldier and also for his unit. Basically, a stencil outfit consisted of ink (or other stencilling fluid) and the applicator (usually a brush of some sort). The stencil kit shown here consists of a wood container, 3½ inches tall and 1¾ inches in diameter. The top is removable enabling the user to get at the fluid (contained in a bottle inside the wood container) and, in this kit, two glass syringe applicators which resemble writing pens. The patent date of this stencil kit is November, 1863.

Also shown here is a stencil stamp. It is made of lead and on the stencilling surface are an eagle, floral decorations, and a slot in the middle for insertion of a man's name or a unit designation. Dug up at Port Hudson, Louisiana.

This portable camp stove is 14½ inches tall. It has a copper bottom and is marked:

Manuf'd By Peerless Cooker Co.
Buffalo, N. Y.
Pat'd.
David Corcilius

This Confederate sword is by an unidentified maker. The only marks are a 2 over a 10 on the hilt. It is 41½ inches long overall including the scabbard. The blade is 34 inches long and ⅞ inch wide at the hilt. The scabbard is the so-called wrap-around type with a brazed seam. The two bands for the carrying rings are soldered on with the carrying rings brazed to the bands. The wood grip is probably walnut. It is knurled at the front and back. The single-edged blade appears to be hand made, not rolled.

David Corcilius

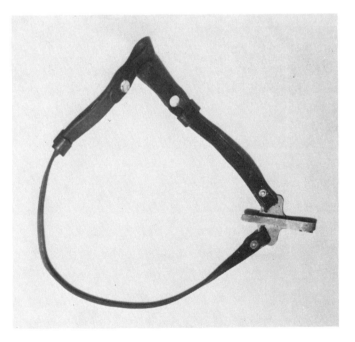

SLING

There is some uncertainty about this item. Some collectors believe it is very possibly post-Civil War. Perhaps its inclusion here will prompt the readers to come up with a definite answer. The brass hanger is stamped:

RIA

which stands for Rock Island Arsenal. This sword sling has two black leather slings — one is 26 inches long and the other is 12 inches long.

176 SYRINGE NOZZLE

Rare example of a Confederate medical item. This porcelain syringe nozzle came from a hospital in Richmond, Virginia. This item is 1 11/16 inches long and is marked:

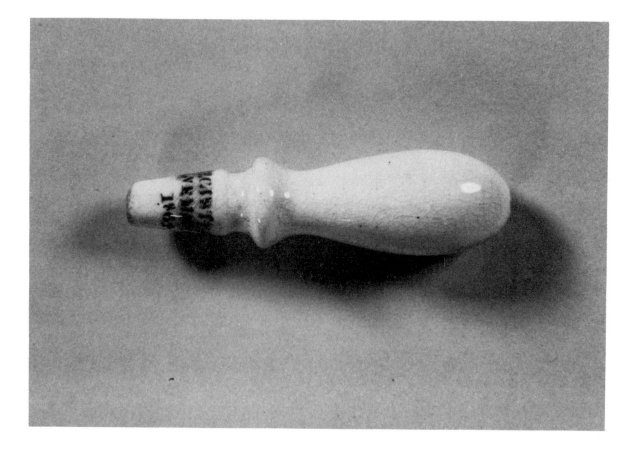

Registered
November 24,
1864

TELEGRAPH BULLETIN!

LATEST NEWS!

Telegraph Office, Concord, 7 o'clock, A. M., June 15, 1861.

J. W. ROBINSON, Publisher. - - PRICE ONE CENT.

Harper's Ferry Evacuated by the Rebels.

Hostile Proceedings of the Missouri Authorities.

NEW YORK, June 14. The *Post's* Washington dispatch says that Gen. Scott has received a dispatch confirming the reported evacuation of Harper's Ferry by the rebels, who have moved on to Leesburg, of which place they are now in possession with several thousand men. Fairfax Court House is also in their possession.

The *Commercial's* Washington dispatch says it is thought that the rebels are at Winchester, whence they will proceed to Strasburg, and thence concentrate at Manassas.

BALTIMORE, June 14. A letter received at the office of the *American* confirms the report of the burning of the bridges at Harper's Ferry. The correspondent says he heard the explosion and went up to see the conflagration. All the troops had gone from the Maryland side, and were hurrying out of Harper's Ferry towards Winchester as fast as possible.

A gentleman at Sharpsburg says, the Virginians had shot at dam No. 5, and that an attack was being made on the warehouse at Mercerville, which people were preparing to resist. The purpose of the rebels is to rob it.

WILLIAMSPORT, Md., June 14. The Shepherdstown bridge was burnt last night by the rebels. The rebel pickets have been withdrawn from all points 20 miles above and 10 below. It is rumored that the enemy are throwing up breastworks at Sheperd Ford, between dam No. 4 and Shepherdstown bridge.

ST. LOUIS, June 14th. The second regiment went out on the Pacific Railroad this afternoon, fully provisioned with camp equipage and munitions of war.

It is conjectured that the 2d regiment will embark on the Louisiana at Herman and follow the expedition under Gen. Lyon.

Under a guarantee of protection from the Federal Government, the Pacific Railroad Company is taking energetic measures to immediately repair the bridges.

ST. ANEERT, Mo., June 14. A special Agent sent down from Jefferson City with the mails, has just returned here. He says the Governor and all the State Officers left there yesterday, and the last of the soldiers this afternoon, taking all the locomotives and cars.

They burnt the bridge at Grey's Crook, three miles west of Jefferson City, and also the one above there.

It is supposed the Governor has ordered his forces to concentrate either at Boonesville or Arrow Rock.

It is thought Gen. Lyon will push on after him, and if he meets with no detention, he will not be over twenty-four hours behind the Governor.

NEW YORK, June 14th. A letter from Bayard Taylor to the *Tribune* says Holland, who was recently bearer of dispatches to the Confederate Government from England, returned there from the City of Baltimore.

He rushed on board a few minutes before the Steamer left New York.— His dispatches were confided to a lady, who concealed them in her dress. He appears to have been greatly frightened.

These one-sheet "flyers" or bulletins were media by which "news flashes" of 1861-1865 were given to an expectant public. These bulletins were posted in public places; they supplied the **only** news where newspapers were absent or only delivered once a week. They fulfilled admirably the need for cryptic reports of news from the war front — whether in New York City, Detroit, or St. Louis. This bulletin was issued by the "Telegraph Office", in Concord [New Hampshire] at 7 A.M., June 15, 1861. Its size is 9¾ inches by 6¼ inches.

178 TENT PEG

    Tent pegs were easily broken or lost in the field and so the men had to improvise. This is an 1842 musket barrel about 18 inches long which was found in a Federal hospital site at Gettysburg. The muzzle has been hammered flat to facilitate the musket barrel being driven into the ground. The breech end of the musket barrel has marks on it, much like a tent peg looks when it has been repeatedly struck with a hammer or blunt side of an axe.

Glen Hayes

While many soldiers who used tobacco preferred smoking the "noxious weed", others liked their chew. This cardboard container was used for both of these examples of Civil War tobacco. On the left is chewing tobacco whose container is 3½ inches by 2 inches. On the front of the package is:

> A. H. Mickle & Sons
> Grape
> Fine Cut Chewing
> Tobacco

On one side is the address:

> No. 110 Water Street, N. Y.

The package on the right is 3½ inches by 2 inches and is marked:

> Mrs. G. B. Miller & Co.
> Fine Cut
> No. 36 Broadway
> New York
> and
> Andrew H. Mickle & Sons
> Successors

(A) **U. S. & C. S.**

This is a finely assorted collection of dug Civil War tools in excellent state of preservation. All are from the Western theatre of operations.

(Read left to right)

Top Row

Hand axe, 4¾ inches long, 2⅝ inches wide, ⅝ inch thick. Marked "U.S." and with inspector's mark "P". Found at Lumpkin's Mill, Mississippi.

Awl, 7¾ inches long with 13/16 inch diameter ring. Found at La Grange, Tennessee.

Wheelwright's chisel, 12 inches long, with ¾ inch wide cutting edge. Found at La Grange, Tennessee.

Wheelwright's rasp, 17 inches long, 1 9/16 inches wide. Flat on one side, and rounded on the other. Found at La Grange, Tennessee.

Wrench. Hand wrought and welded. For one-inch square nut. Handle is pointed at end. 7 inches long. Found at Davis Mill, Mississippi.

Farrier's rasp, 13½ inches long, 1⅜ inches wide, and 5/16 inch thick. Fine on one side and coarse on the other. Found at La Grange, Tennessee.

Blacksmith's pincers, 12¼ inches long, 1 inch wide at jaws. Found at Pulaski, Tennessee.

(Beneath hand axe, left to right)

Mechanic's pincers, 5⅞ inches long, ½ inch wide at jaws. Found at La Grange, Tennessee.

Ordnance or Gunsmith's vise, 5½ inches long, 1¼ inches wide jaws, spike for securing in a stump, block or post. Thumb screw for tightening. Found at Germantown, Tennessee.

Cross-cut saw file, three-cornered, 5⅜ inches long. Found at La Grange, Tennessee.

Bottom Row — (left to right)

Sack needle, used in cavalry camps to sew up sacks of oats or shelled corn. 5¾ inches long, ⅛ inch in diameter. Found in a North Mississippi cavalry camp.

Threading tap for cutting threads in steel parts. For ½ inch diameter threads. 4 inches long. Found at La Grange, Tennessee.

Gunner's gimlet, for clearing the vent (priming hole) in artillery cannon and rifles. Steel stem and cast iron handle. 3⅞ inches long, 2⅛ inches wide. Found at La Grange, Tennessee.

Auger for boring holes in wood. Steel, 7⅞ inches long, for ½ inch diameter hole. Found at La Grange, Tennessee.

Mechanic's dividers, 4½ inches long. Found at La Grange, Tennessee.

Clawhammer. Cast iron, 1⅛ inch diameter face, 4½ inches long. Found at La Grange, Tennessee.

Blacksmith's hardy. Hand forged steel. 1⅞ inches wide cutting edge, 4⅜ inches long. Placed upright in the square hole on back of anvil and used in cutting off ends of heated horseshoes. Found at Eastport, Mississippi.

John A. Marks

(B) **C. S.**

In recent years some interesting Confederate artifacts have been recovered in a river in Columbia, South Carolina. These artifacts were from the arsenal in Columbia and were thrown in the river at the approach of Sherman in 1865. Among the artifacts were the two ordnance tools shown here.

Draw knife, wood handles with a 9-inch cutting blade.

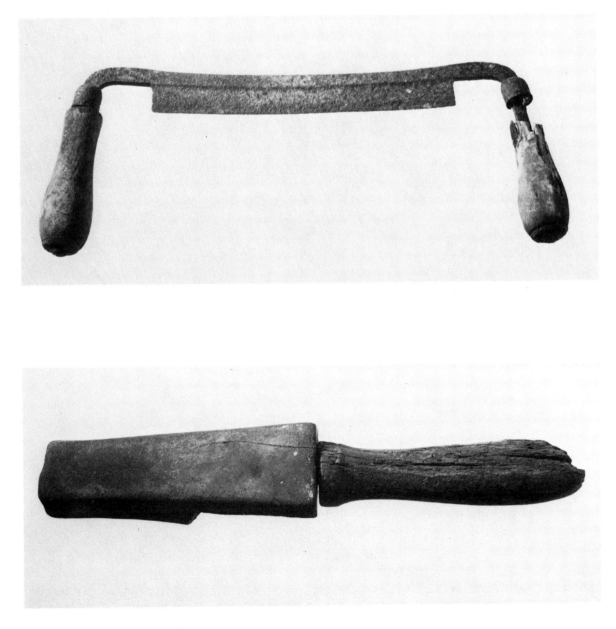

Whetstone, wood handle, 9¾ inches long.

Infantry Band Uniforms

Worn by a member of the band of the 3rd Maine Infantry. Note the stripes on pants and sleeves. The 3rd Maine Infantry was raised in June 1861 and served through the war. It was recruited from Kennebec lumbermen — large, powerful men. It lost 489 killed and wounded. At Gettysburg the regiment went in with 210 officers and men. It lost 18 killed, 59 wounded, and 45 missing or a total of 122 — about 60%.

Robert S. Corrette

Marine Corps Band Uniform Coat

A splendid example of the very rare U. S. Marine Corps band uniform coat. This coat follows the color (red) and all specifications as prescribed by the 1859 Marine Corps regulations.

Bobby Armstrong
& Mary Lou Berberich

Shoes

This is a Confederate shoe, measuring 10 inches in length, heel to toe, and 5½ inches from heel to toe of shoe. It was found in Richmond, Virginia at Dock and 7th Streets on the site of what was once a Confederate warehouse. The warehouse was burned in the evacuation of Richmond April 2, 1865.

William Coleman

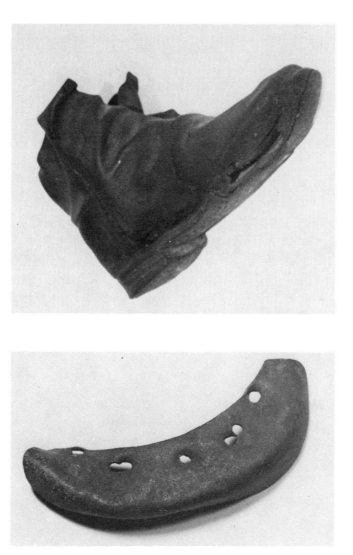

Toe clip for shoes

Thin brass clip for the toe of a soldier's shoe. Worn to prevent wear on the shoe; its counterpart was the heel plate. See page 11 of Volume II of the *Encyclopedia*. This clip is perforated with holes for nailing to the shoe. It is curved, 2 inches long, and came from the site of the 92nd New York Infantry's position in the skirmish of March 14, 1863, outside Fort Anderson, North Carolina.

Militia Hat Box

    Made of heavy tin, 16½ inches tall, with the box 12 × 11 inches at bottom and top. Probably purchased by an officer or soldier from a civilian manufacturer or dealer. This type of hat box was used by militiamen to carry their very elaborate and large-size headgear.

David Corcilius

    A ribbon type veterans' badge belonging to Theophilus Hulett, Co. "D" 5th New York Heavy Artillery. Hulett enlisted as private February 8, 1864 and was discharged July 19, 1865 at Harpers Ferry, West Virginia.

Robert Borrell, Sr.

Another ribbon type badge, belonged to Frank B. Camp, Battery "E" 5th U. S. Light Artillery. He enlisted in Co. "C" 5th New Hampshire Infantry on September 11, 1861. On February 12, 1863 he transferred to Battery "E" 5th U. S. Light Artillery and was discharged from this Battery January 29, 1867. He received a gunshot wound on the scalp at the Battle of Fair Oaks, Virginia on June 1, 1862.

Robert Borrell, Sr.

Collecting veterans' badges has become increasingly popular. This is true because they are comparatively numerous and very attractive. For example here is a beautiful gold badge of the Chicago Mercantile Independent Battery Light Artillery. Around the edge of the badge is listed the battles in which the battery was engaged:

Arkansas Post
Champion Hills
Vicksburg May 22
Siege of Jackson
Port Gibson
Black River Bridge
Siege of Vicksburg
Mansfield

Robert Borrell, Sr.

Two examples of veteran reunion badges are shown here. The one with the larger number of badges is shown here, courtesy of Roger Davis, Keokuk, Iowa. The other is a collection of Confederate veterans' badges. As can also be seen in Davis' collection, these veterans' badges vary greatly in appearance.

Left to Right (bottom picture)

Top Row

Richmond, Virginia 1907
Tampa, Florida 1927
Memphis, Tennessee 1909
Macon, Georgia 1912
New Orleans, Louisiana 1906
Houston, Texas 1895
Gettysburg, Pennsylvania 1913

Middle Row

Arkansas 1928
Columbia, South Carolina 1894
Charlotte, North Carolina 1929
Montgomery, Alabama 1931
Chattanooga, Tennessee 1913
Corinth, Mississippi

Bottom Row

Sumter, South Carolina 1920
Orangeburg, South Carolina 1924
Kentucky Division U.C.V. ribbon
Louisville, Kentucky 1905

Sam Padgett

"Comrades of the Battlefield"

This organization of Northern veterans of the Civil War is completely unknown to most students of the 1861-1865 period. But it was a unique and interesting group! The organization was conceived in September 1887, and apparently grew out of a jest made by George E. Dolton of St. Louis, Missouri. He originally called for the founding of an "Order of Three Months' Men", to include as members those who had served three months or more **under fire,** but the name must also have been a jibe at those whose entire term of service had been three months and who distinguished themselves principally at the meetings of the GAR. In December 1890, Dolton wrote an article stating these views that appeared in the January 1, 1891 issue of the *National Tribune* (a prominent veterans publication of that day). Letters of support were written to Dolton from around the country and in August 1891, those interested in forming such an order met in Detroit, Michigan. A constitution was written, officers elected, and an investigating committee to pass on applicants' qualifications was appointed. George Dalton was elected "General Commanding". Chapters were designated as "Battlefields" and the first, "Chickamauga", was formed in St. Louis on January 30, 1891. In Newbern, Illinois, the members formed the "Vicksburg" Battlefield. There is no information how many other chapters were formed.

Prospective members submitted a fee of $3.00 along with their application. They were required to provide proof of their combat service. Official reports, diaries, correspondence and other documentary evidence were preferred sources although sworn statements of those who actually saw the applicant under fire were accepted by the investigating committee. The committee verified these records, counted the days under fire, and, if he qualified, approved the new member. Ribbons were made available to the female members of the veteran's family, while the member himself could purchase a certificate recounting his combat days. He also received a badge which was lapel pin made of brass and partially enamelled. It consisted of a trefoil with a triangle set in the center. On the sides of the triangle were the words — "Service" — "Under" — "Fire", and in an oval in the center of the triangle the number of combat days was engraved or stamped.

Very little is known of this veterans' organization. Probably it died with the death of its founder. Dolton died in 1906. He served in Battery "M" 1st Illinois Artillery (Enlisted August 11, 1862 and discharged July 24, 1865). The war apparently had a profound effect on him and like many young men thrust into combat he seemed to be affected by the war experience for the rest of his life. He also was a member of the GAR.

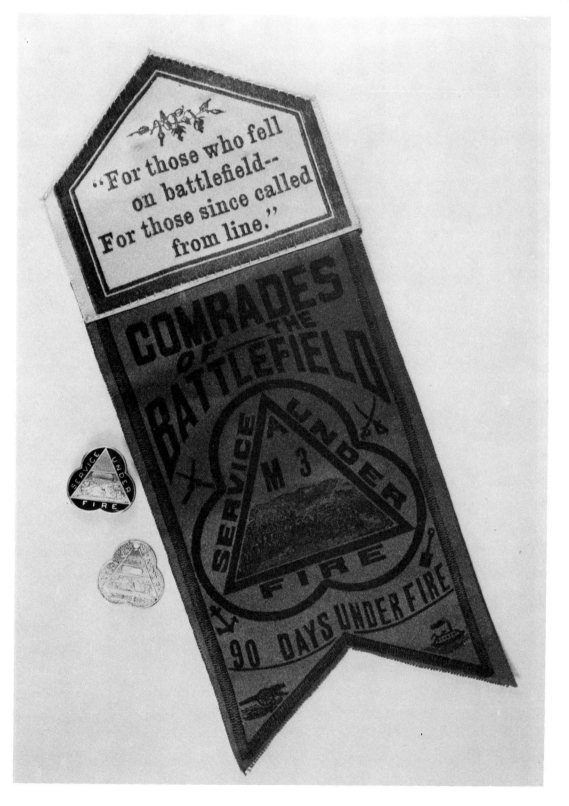

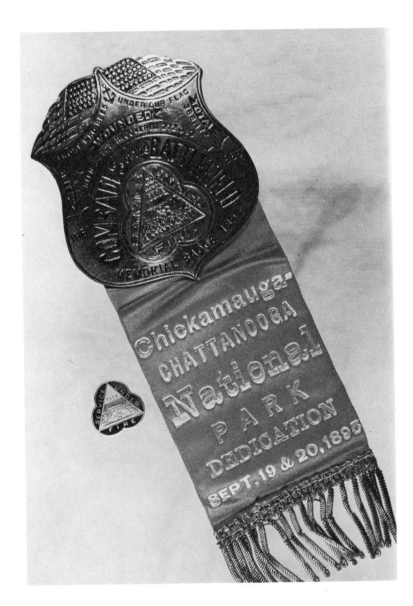

Taylorville, Ill.

A GAR badge and "Comrades of the Battlefield" badge are both wore proudly in the accompanying photograph of an unidentified member of Taylorsville, Illinois. Shown also is a group photograph of the "Vicksburg Battlefield" chapter of the Comrades of the Battlefield of Newbern, Illinois photographed May 30, 1891.

Shown also are the ribbons and badges. Apparently, there were three pieces issued each member. The lapel badge, which was to be buried with the veteran at his death was a red enamelled badge. There was also an aluminum badge, which was to be worn about the neck at all times (something like a "dog tag" of later wars) and a ribbon was of white and red silk. Also shown here is a ribbon worn at the 1895 dedication of the Chickamauga-Chattanooga National Park.

John F. Powell

After the war many Northern veterans visited the battlefields where they had fought during the 1860s. These visits were prompted by the natural curiosity to take a second look at the terrain where death was always an imminent possibility, and, in some cases, to locate the bodies of relatives and friends — either to mark the graves or to bring the bodies back home. But these visits were unorganized and usually confined to only a few individuals. It wasn't until two decades after the war that any **organized** group of veterans went South expressly for the purpose of visiting battlefields where they had fought. The originator of veterans' reunions on Southern battlefields was Francis H. Buffum, a Civil War veteran and historian. Once a household name in veterans' circles,

Buffum is now almost forgotten. Enlisting at the age of 18 in the 14th New Hampshire Infantry, he was wounded four times — his last wound being incurred while he was saving his regimental colors from capture. The historian of the 8th Vermont Infantry, in commenting on Buffum's bravery in the Battle of Winchester, Virginia (September 19, 1864) points out that the young soldier stood up while his regiment was under a terrific fire saying: "Boys, if I fall, don't forget that I did my duty." Only a **month later,** at Cedar Creek, he was shot through the body by a Confederate sharpshooter but recovered and lived to the ripe old age of 83!

During those 83 years, Buffum devoted his time and talent to perpetuating the spirit and ideals of the War. A gifted writer and public speaker he actively participated in veterans' organizations both North and South. In fact, Buffum gave more consecutive Memorial Day addresses than any speaker in the Nation — a total of 60! As a newspaper man and historian, he wrote many articles on the War, and wrote the first history of any New Hampshire regiment in the Civil War (14th New Hampshire Infantry — published in 1882). After this regimental history appeared about every other New Hampshire regimental organization came out with a history.

But Buffum's greatest contribution was his original idea of reunions between Northern and Southern veterans — in a spirit of comradeship — when they could meet together and discuss the War as citizens of a reunited country. Such a concept would have been unheard of in most countries of Europe or the rest of the world! As military editor of the prestigious *Boston Herald* in the 1880s Buffum interviewed such Confederate leaders as Beauregard and Joseph E. Johnston for his paper. From these interviews, coupled with extensive trips through the States of the late Confederacy, he came to appreciate the very deep interest in anything relating to the "late unpleasantness".

In November, 1882 Buffum laid the groundmark for the first reunion. Using the *Boston Herald* as the medium by which the veterans could be informed, he also worked closely with officials of the Baltimore and Ohio Railroad in planning details of the trip to the Southern battlefields. The veterans did go South by rail — arriving at their final destination in Winchester, Virginia where they met with veterans of such famous Confederate units as the 5th, 10th, and 52nd Virginia Infantry, and the 5th, 7th and 12th Virginia Cavalry. Many of the Confederates had been members of the immortal "Stonewall Brigade".

Buffum, as "excursion manager", was responsible for organizing and running this veterans' visit to Southern battlefields. The series of reunions (September 15-24, 1883) involved 181 Northern veterans, representing 44 different regiments, civilian guests, 4 "Sons of Veterans", and some 20 lady guests. Special guests of the 1883 reunion were Generals William H. Emory and Henry W. Birge. In addition to "campfires" for individual regimental reunions, there were several joint meetings of the Northern veterans with their former opponents of the Confederate army. Illustrative of the spirit prevalent at these joint meetings is the following as reported in the *Old Commonwealth,* a newspaper of Harrisonburg, Virginia (September 22, 1883). In his speech of welcome, the Confederate reception committee chairman said in part:

"Some nineteen years since the Federal and Confederate soldiers in the Valley of Virginia met each other in deadly conflict and received each other at the point of the bayonet — **that was war;** but today is the day of peace for all well-meaning citizens and true Americans . . . The **true** soldier of both contending armies, in April 1865, at Appomattox, signed and sealed a compact of peace and good will and that compact **they,** the true soldiers, have observed and faithfully kept and ever since then there has been peace in the land (applause) except and only except in the minds of those men who are "men of war in time of peace, and men of peace in time of war" (great laughter) . . .

At this same meeting the reception chairman pointed out that among those welcoming the Northern veterans were:

"members of the Tenth Virginia Infantry, Fifth Virginia Infantry, Fifty-second Virginia Infantry, and Twelfth, Seventh, and Fifth Virginia Cavalry, and probably of other regiments, and of the old Stonewall Brigade — men who followed the leader upon whose likeness you now look (pointing to Stonewall Jackson's picture).

It was a tremendous scene — cheer upon cheer was given and the air was filled with the waving hats of the veterans of both armies. It is questionable if ever Stonewall Jackson's memory had a grander tribute paid.

At the end of this 1883 "excursion" it was decided to draw up a permanent organization for annual reunions. These reunions were only regimental get-togethers until 1885, when veterans of both sides decided to repeat the 1883 experience. Everything was much the same except for the staging of a rifle match between the Northern and Southern veterans. Where — in all the history of past-war exchanges — would one find a well-organized and friendly contest of rifle marksmanship between veterans who some twenty years earlier had tried to kill each other! With Buffum as the captain, the Blue team won the 500-yard range, but the Greys pulled the match out with much better scoring at 200 yards. Here again, Buffum had another "first". It can be pointed out that the rifle match — using military rifles, by the way, was a forerunner of the North-South "shoots" of our day. Although future combined reunions and rifle matches were planned, they did not materialize. But the ground work had been laid for us — descendants of Northern and Southern veterans — to continue their interest in the 1861-1865 War, both in the Centennial 1960s and later on in the future.

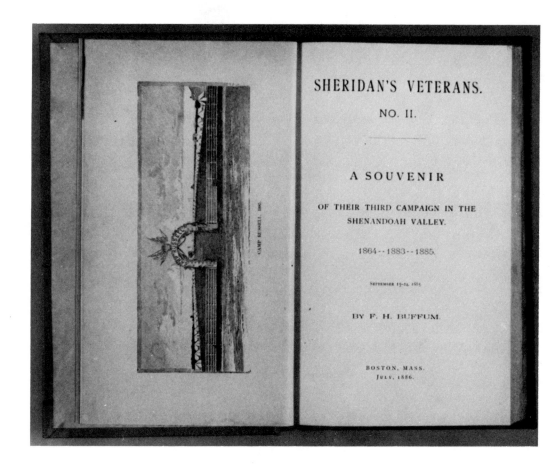

Pocket watches — of varying quality and makers — were in general use by officers and men of both contending armies. Here is another example. Worn by Edward S. Kendall of Co. "B" 15th Massachusetts Infantry. Enlisted, age 19, on July 12, 1861. He served at Balls Bluff, the Peninsular Campaign and Antietam. He was discharged for disability November 5, 1862.

Robert S. Corrette

204 WATER FILTER

This interesting example of impractical equipment was a favorite with new troops before they had seen much active service. Various types of water filters were sold to the raw recruits, usually by sutlers. We have already shown some types in Volume I (page 331) and Volume III (page 196) of the *Encyclopedia*. Shown here is the pewter tip of a water filter hose. This pewter tip came from the battlefield of Malvern Hill. Beside it in the photograph is a make-shift water filter nozzle, made by five Burnside carbine shell casings telescoped together to form a tube. The pewter tip is 1¾ inches long and ⅝ inch in diameter at the widest part.

This odd-shaped object was recently dug up on the site of a Western army post which was in existence during the Civil War. It is marked:

Wedekind's Patent
March 24th 1863

As yet it has not been identified. Any assistance from our readers will be much appreciated.

Frank A. Huntsman

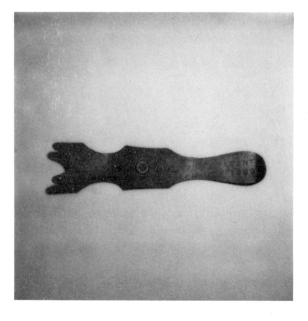 

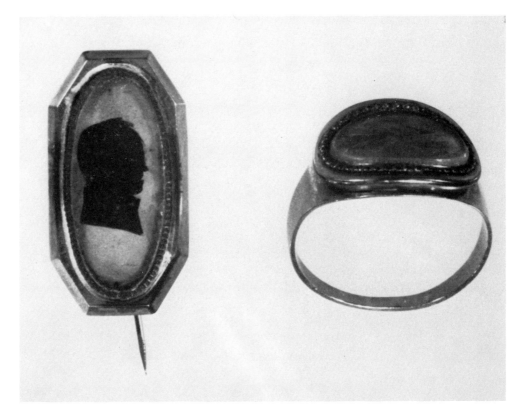

This beautiful ring and pin were from the personal belongings of Confederate General "Fighting Joe" Wheeler. The seal ring contains a lock of hair while the pin has a profile of the General. Joseph Wheeler (1836-1906) graduated from West Point in 1859. He served on the frontier fighting Indians before the war. He resigned his lieutenant's commission April 22, 1861 and went on to spend four years in the C.S. Army, rising from first lieutenant to general, and being wounded three times in the process. He served as a U.S. general in the Spanish American War and the Philippines.

There is some evidence that whistles were used by some officers during combat. If this is true, the use was extremely limited. However, whistles have been dug up on battlefields. (See page 198, Volume III of the *Encyclopedia* which shows a whistle dug up at Port Hudson, Louisiana).

Recently another whistle — different and much larger — was also recovered from Port Hudson. This, too, is of pewter.

Lee Sanzo

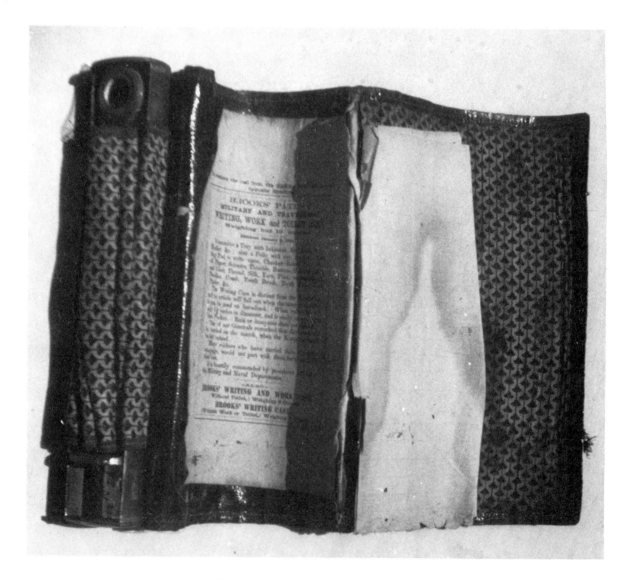

Writing Kit

When rolled up, this "Brooks Patent Writing Kit" is 8½ inches long and 2 inches in diameter. When unrolled, it is 8½ inches by 13 inches. Patented January 5, 1864.

David Corcilius

Writing Kit and candle holder

This unique outfit has a blue enamelled interior and a black leather exterior. The kit measures 3 × 2¼ × 1⅜ inches when closed. It has five functions:

    Spring covered ink well
    Small brass drawer with wax matches
    Hinged pen holder on the right side
    Hinged candle holder on the left side
    Small compartment for pen wiper

The kit still has the original candle and matches. The cover of the kit has the following stamped in gold:

               H. Trussell
               16 & 17 East St.
               Brighton

Although made in England this kit was used over here during the Civil War.

Martin J. Fowler

Pencils

(A) U. S.

Mechanical pencil used by George W. Barnes, private, Co. "H" 36th Massachusetts Infantry. He was a farmer and at age 21 he enlisted on July 21, 1862. He was discharged for disability February 5, 1863 at Alexandria, Virginia. Barnes bought this pencil in 1862.

Robert S. Corrette

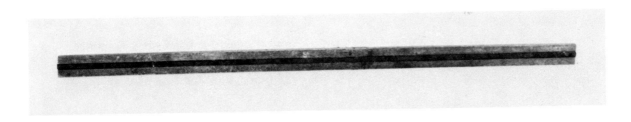

(B) C. S.

Lead pencil (showing half). 6¾ inches long. Recovered from the blockade runner *Georgiana.*

212 SELECTED BIBLIOGRAPHY AND SOURCES

I. BOOKS

ALBAUGH, WILLIAM A.,
Confederate Edged Weapons. Harper & Brothers, 1960.

ALBAUGH, WILLIAM A. AND E. N. SIMMONS
Confederate Arms. Bonanza Books, 1957.

ALBERT, ALPHAEUS H.
Record of American Uniform and Historical Buttons. Published by the author, 353 Stockton Street, Hightstown, New Jersey 08520. 1969.

GAVIN, WILLIAM G.
Accouterment Plates North and South 1861-1865, First Edition. Riling and Lentz, Philadelphia, Pa. 1963.

Accouterment Plates North and South 1861-1865, Second Edition. George Shumway Publisher, York, Pa. 1975.

GLUCKMAN, ARCADI
United States Martial Pistols and Revolvers. Bonanza Books. 1939.

United States Muskets, Rifles and Carbines. Otto Ulbrich Co. 1948.

HARDIN, ALBERT N.
The American Bayonet 1776-1964. Riling & Lentz. 1964.

KERKSIS, SIDNEY C.
Plates and Buckles of the American Military 1795-1874. Gilgal Press. 1974.

LORD, FRANCIS A.
Civil War Collector's Encyclopedia. Castle Books, Inc. 1965.

Civil War Collector's Encyclopedia, Volume II. Lord Americana & Research, Inc. 1975.

Civil War Collector's Encyclopedia, Volume III. Lord Americana & Research, Inc. 1979.

PETERSON, HAROLD L.
American Knives. Charles Scribner's Sons. 1958.

The American Sword. Ray Riling Arms Books Co. 1955.

PHILLIPS, STANLEY S.
Excavated Artifacts From Battlefields and Campsites of the Civil War. 1861-1865. Ann Arbor, Michigan. 1974.

Supplement I. Marceline, Mo. 1980.

RIPLEY, WARREN
Artillery and Ammunition of the Civil War. Promontory Press. 1970.

II. **PERIODICALS**

Military Images Magazine
Bimonthly.
706 Mickley Road
Whitehall, Pa. 18052

North South Trader
Bimonthly.
800 New Hampshire Avenue
Langley Park, Maryland 20783

III. **MUSEUMS**

ANTIETAM NATIONAL BATTLEFIELD SITE — Visitor's Center
Sharpsburg, Maryland 21782

CITADEL ARCHIVES — Museum
Charleston, South Carolina 29409

CONFEDERATE RESEARCH CENTER AND GUN MUSEUM
Hillsboro, Texas 76645

FORT SUMTER NATIONAL MONUMENT
Sullivan's Island, South Carolina 29482

GRAND ARMY OF THE REPUBLIC MEMORIAL HALL MUSEUM
Madison, Wisconsin 53702

HISTORICAL MUSEUM OF THE NORTH AND SOUTH
Acton, Massachusetts 01720

MUSEUM OF THE CONFEDERACY
Richmond, Virginia 23219

SMITHSONIAN INSTITUTION
Washington, D. C. 20560

THE UNITED STATES QUARTERMASTER CORPS MUSEUM
Fort Lee, Virginia 23801

U. S. ARMY ORDNANCE MUSEUM
Aberdeen Proving Ground, Maryland 21040

U. S. ARMY TRANSPORTATION MUSEUM
Fort Eustice, Virginia 23604

WEST POINT MUSEUM
West Point, New York 10996

CIVIL WAR COLLECTOR'S ENCYCLOPEDIA

Volume V

DEDICATION

This volume is dedicated to the members of my family who served in the Civil War.

Greatgrandfathers:

    First Lieutenant Jesse H. Lord, 2nd Conn. Inf.

    Private Jedediah Buffum, 14th N.H. Inf.

    Private Hiram E. Wetzel, 27th Pa. Inf.

GreatGrand Uncles:

    Chaplain Samuel W. McDaniel, 4th Pa. Inf.

    Pvt. Benjamin F. McDaniel, 1st Dela. Lt. Battery

    Commodore Isaiah Hanscom, U.S. Navy

Grandfather:

    Color Sergeant Francis H. Buffum, 14th N.H. Inf.

VOLUME V

FOREWORD

The author wishes to express a very special note of thanks to his wife, Marjorie, who as in preparation of former volumes, labored loyally and successfully in all phases of this book. Her contributions include layout, typing, most of the photography, and that elusive "sixth sense" about content.

ACKNOWLEDGEMENTS

ALBANESE, MICHAEL, Kendall, N.Y.
BLAINE, JAMES R., Vacaville, Cal.
BORRELL, ROBERT G., SR., Clinton, Md.
COLEMAN, BILL and SUE, Raphine, Va.
CORCILIUS, DAVE, Phelps, N.Y.
CRAWFORD, FRANK, Caledonia, Ill.
DOWNEY, J. L., Low Moor, Va.
DURHAM, ROGER S., Fort Bliss, Texas
FOWLER, MARTIN, J., Medford, N.J.
GILPIN, GEORGE, Petal, Miss.
GIRARD, EDMUND, Lynn, Mass.
HAMMERSON, MICHAEL, London, England
HOLLAND, KEITH V., Jacksonville, Fla.
JARVINEN, LARRY, Manistee, Mich.
KENT, DON, Nashville, Tenn.
KERR, JAY SCOTT, Camillus, N.Y.
LOWRY, CAROLYN, Richmond, Va.
MacDONALD, A. COLLIN, Centreville, Va.
MAGUNE, JACK, Worcester, Mass.
MARCOTTE, COMMANDER ROBERT, Lynn, Mass.
MARSHALL, WM. F., Cheektowaga, N.Y.
MATTERN, KENDALL B., Strafford, Wayne, Pa.
McBRAYER, ALAN R., Charlotte, N.C.
MERRELL, C. H., Anderson, S.C.
MEUSE, W. E., Fredericksburg, Va.
MYERS, B., Richmond, Va.
PADGETT, SAMUEL B., Lexington, S.C.
PANASUK, FRANK J., Hamburg, N.Y.
PEEK, DUFFEL, Shelbyville, Tenn.
PELADEAU, MARIUS B., Warren, Maine
REDMOND, LEO, Cayce, S.C.
REYNOLDS, ROBIN, Bloomington, Ill.
SCHREIER, KONRAD F., JR., Los Angeles, Cal.
SMARR, RAY and JEAN, Deer Park, Md.
STACEY, JOHN A., Fort Washington, Md.
STAMATELOS, JAMES, Cambridge, Mass.
STOTT, JOHN, Virginia Beach, Va.
VMI MUSEUM, (KEITH GIBSON), Lexington, Va.
WOLFER, GARY, Allentown, Pa.

INTRODUCTION

This is the last of the author's Encyclopedia series. There is no lack of material and excellent young writers of talent and enthusiasm who are capable of substantial contributions which they can make in their respective fields of specilization as they carry on.

This volume, more than any of the previous four, includes many items of a semi-military usage, e.g. mittens, non-regulation identification disc and medals, and other items not issued by the government. The "regular" items of military usage, e.g. small arms, edged weapons, etc. have been adequately covered in earlier works and by other authors as well.

Much attention has been given to variants (such as exist in identification discs) which, although already covered in other studies, can still be of assistance to the specialized collector. A few "groupings" are given to show comparisons and what a collector can do in presenting his collection.

The reader will note a certain lack of uniformity in photographs, especially in background. This is because many individuals have supplied their own items — photographed by themselves in many instances, each with a characteristic lighting technique.

Where no citation is given on a photograph it is either from the author's collection or from a contributor who wishes to remain anonymous in order to avoid theft of the article photographed.

The whole problem of non-regulation items used by the Civil War serviceman has only been treated in general terms. There were practically no catalogs for the period and price lists were few and far between. Most of the details of these soldier supplies are found in advertisements which appeared in current newspapers and periodicals. Stan Phillips used some in his excellent works on excavated relics. Konrad F. Schreier, Jr., by careful search in Harper's Weekly issues of 1864, shows what commendable research instinct and historical awareness can accomplish in one periodical for a restricted period of time. His seven types of soldiers' goods are given here in alphabetical order:

1. **ELECTION BADGES (1864):** In the U.S. presidential election of 1864, the soldiers of the Union Army returned "their Mr. Lincoln" to office. This ad is from Harper's Weekly in 1864 for one of the many campaign badges for that election. These badges were sold to soldiers, and it is to be assumed that they wore them.

Like many political items, these badges are not unusual and they are very collectible. As with many election badges they come in many variations.

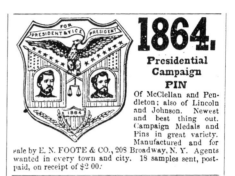

2. **FIELD GLASSES and TELESCOPES:** Despite a wide need for optical observation equipment, field glasses and telescopes were not officially issued in substantial numbers during the Civil War. Most of them went to the artillery, to headquarters officers from division level up, and to ships of the navy. They were also used for flag and semaphore communications on land and sea.

Despite the slim issue, field glasses and telescopes were widely distributed and used in the Civil War. They were privately purchased by most field grade officers who were not issued them, by many company grade officers who wanted them, and by non-commissioned officers and men who could afford them.

Most of these field glasses and telescopes were imported from France. Many were sold by dealers and sutlers, and many more by "mail" order through ads such as these from Harper's Weekly in 1864.

Notice the wide price range: from $3.50 to $25.00. The latter amount was a small fortune at the time of the Civil War.

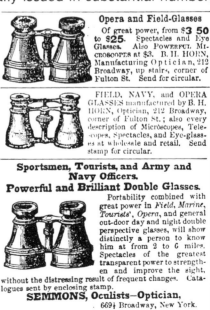

3. PHOTOGRAPHS: Today it is easy to get the impression that the collecting of Civil War "images" is something new. Nothing could be further from the truth. The soldiers collected them as well as the home folks.

Albums for the Army.
Our New Pocket Album,
holding sixteen pictures, and sold at
Seventy-five Cents,
is the cheapest and best Pocket Album ever offered to the public.
Sent by mail to any address, post-paid, on receipt of Seventy-five Cents.
SAMUEL BOWLES & COMPANY,
Photograph Album Manufacturers,
Springfield, Mass.

Good News for the Army.

Hereafter we will send, *post-paid*, any of our PHOTO-GRAPHIC ALBUMS ordered by soldiers for themselves or friends, giving an Album of the full value of the money sent.

Our Albums have the reputation of being *superior to all others in beauty and durability*, and range in price from 50 cts. to $50.

Our catalogue of
CARD PHOTOGRAPHS
now embraces about 5000 officers, army and navy, statesmen, actors, copies of works of art, &c. Catalogue sent on receipt of stamp.

Stereoscopes and Stereoscopic Views.

Our assortment of these is very extensive, including a great variety of views of the present war.
Catalogue sent on receipt of stamp.
F. & H. T. ANTHONY & CO,
501 Broadway, New York.
Manufacturers of Photographic Materials.

Union Playing Cards.

Colonel for King, Goddess of Liberty for Queen, and Major for Jack. 52 enameled cards to the pack. Eagles, Shields, Stars, and Flags are the suits, and you can play all the usual games. Two packs, in cases, mailed free on receipt of $1. The usual discount to the trade. Send for a Circular. Address **AMERICAN CARD COMPANY,**
455 Broadway, N. Y., or 165 William Street, N. Y.

Photographs were one of the few things from home a Civil War serviceman could carry with him. Although the art of photography was only some fifteen years old when the Civil War broke out, photographs were very popular during and after the war as these ads from Harper's Weekly in 1864 attest. And if they had not been collected back then, they would not be around to be collected today.

Photography first became an important business during the Civil War. Prints and everything to go with them were made in large quantities, and surprising numbers of them have survived. Of course, a good photographic print, if it is made properly and given decent care, will last a long time.

4. PLAYING CARDS: A standard Civil War recreation of both armies was card playing during long periods of camp life. Many decks of cards used have survived, but these Union Playing Cards advertised in Harper's Weekly in 1864 are a rarity. The regular suit symbols on them have been replaced by those appropriate to the Union Army. The firm making them still exists.

PLAYING CARDS.
The American Card Company's New Union Playing Cards, National Emblems.

They are the prettiest card made, and suit the popular idea. The suits are EAGLES, SHIELDS, STARS, and FLAGS. COLONEL in place of King, GODDESS OF LIBERTY for Queen, and MAJOR for Jack.

All the games can be played as readily as with cards bearing foreign emblems. Each pack is put up in an elegant card-case, and then in dozen boxes for the trade.

In order that all dealers may have an opportunity to sell these cards, a sample box of twelve packs will be sent, post-paid, on receipt of Five Dollars. Address
AMERICAN CARD COMPANY,
No. 14 Chambers Street, New York.

5. SERVICE MEDALS: The "fruit salad" citation and service ribbons and medals so familiar on today's U.S. Armed Services uniforms did not exist at the time of the Civil War. It wasn't until the middle of that war that troops regularly wore even unit identification insignia.

When large numbers of "three year volunteers" began leaving the Union Army in 1864, they had a problem: There was no stigma attached to their having left after three years' service, or even less, in fact having served at all was considered highly commendable. There was, however, a stigma attached for not having served, so those who did serve wanted a way of showing their patriotism.

The answer was found in the unofficial medals and badges shown in these ads. The advertising for them begins in 1863, and when the ads shown here appeared in Harper's Weekly in 1864, they had become widely distributed and worn. As can be seen, these "medals" came in a wide variety, and yet they are rather unfamiliar today.

The reason for their rarity would appear to be that the medals of the Grand Army of the Republic (G.A.R.) replaced them after the end of the war. With the more "official" G.A.R. medals and badges in use, these were discarded, and that made them a rarity today.

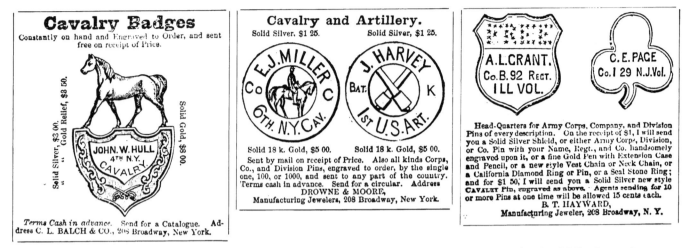

6. **SMOKING CASES:** The use of tobacco has been a habit common in the U.S. Armed Forces since their inception. During the Civil War cigars, cigarettes and chewing tobacco were used, but the smoking pipe was probably the most common way to use the "weed" on land and sea.

There were many gadgets offered for the care of pipes and tobacco, and this Ridgewood Patent Smoking Case is a typical example. It was advertised in Harper's Weekly in 1864.

These devices were widely used, and probably were pretty handy. Unfortunately they were mostly worn out, used up, and then discarded, and they are quite rare today.

7. **WATCHES:** Although they were not an "item of issue," watches were commonly carried by officers and enlisted men during the Civil War. There are several reasons for this. First, was the fact that inexpensive, mass-produced pocket watches which soldiers could afford had been introduced a decade or so prior to the war. Their price was a direct reflection of their quality, but many of them were quite reliable and accurate. Only pocket watches were used as the wristwatch was not invented until after the war. Second, Americans love gadgets, and watches were a most useful one. By the end of the Civil War scheduling operations which required the use of "time pieces" had become very important and effective.

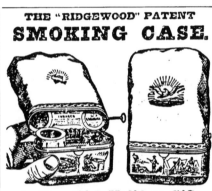

THE "RIDGEWOOD" PATENT
SMOKING CASE.

A Beautiful Holiday Gift.

Most ingenious in its combination of the *Metallic Case,* containing *Pipe* and *Stem,* Matches and Pipe Cleaner, with a handsome *Tobacco Pouch* attached, filling the Pipe by a valve, without use of the fingers or waste of Tobacco, the whole securing freedom from all odor, and *portable as a Cigar Case.* It is made for service, of various styles, at $1 50, $2 00, $2 25, $2 50, and $3 00 to $3 75 and $5 00; the two latter *richly plated and engraved.* Nothing can excel its *Comfort, Utility,* and *Economy* for all Smokers, at Home or Abroad, in the Army and Navy. As a *Present* to Friends, as a *Gift from the Ladies,* nothing could be more acceptable. FOR THE SOLDIER OF ALL RANKS, in *Camp* or *on the March,* IT IS INVALUABLE. *Large Orders,* with commendation from all points IN THE Army, daily attest this fact. **SKATERS** *will appreciate this Case.*

Also, **The Ridgewood Smoking Tobacco,**

Of *superior quality and flavor,* in packages to fill the pouch (about a week's smoking, $2 25 per doz.), and larger sizes for the General Trade. SMOKERS, DEALERS, and SUTLERS invited to call and examine these Goods. Circulars sent on order. A LIBERAL DISCOUNT to Dealers. *Single Cases* sent by mail. paid, on receipt of price and 25 cents. Also half-pound Package of this *fine Tobacco,* full weight, sent (carefully put up) *by mail,* paid, on receipt of $1 25. *All Orders* receive prompt attention.
RIDGEWOOD MANUFACTURING CO.,
OFFICE **429** BROADWAY, cor. Howard Street, N. Y.

These ads for "army" and "soldiers" pocket watches appeared in Harper's Weekly during 1864, and the ads offer the goods for sale by mail. As far as can be determined none of the dealers or the brands offered exist today.

American Watches
For Soldiers
AT REDUCED PRICES.

American Watches for Americans!

The AMERICAN WATCH COMPANY give notice that they have lately issued a new style of Watch, expressly designed for Soldiers and others who desire a good watch at a moderate price. These watches are intended to displace the worthless, cheap watches of British and Swiss manufacture with which the country is flooded, and which were never expected to keep time when they were made, being refuse manufactures sent to this country because unsalable at home, and used here only for *jockeying* and *swindling* purposes.

We offer to sell our Watch, which is of THE MOST SUBSTANTIAL MANUFACTURE, AN ACCURATE AND DURABLE TIME-KEEPER, and in Sterling Silver Cases, Hunting pattern, at nearly as low a price as is asked for the fancy-named *Ancres* and *Lepines* of foreign make, already referred to.

We have named the new series of Watches, WM. ELLERY, Boston, Mass., which name will be found on the plate of every watch of this manufacture, and is one of our trade-marks.

Sold by all respectable watch dealers in the loyal states.

Wholesale orders should be addressed to

ROBBINS & APPLETON,

Agents of the American Watch Company,

182 BROADWAY, N. Y.

NEW ARMY WATCHES.

Magic Railway Time-Keeper.

Gold or Silver composite Hunting cases, with Patent Time Indicator, just invented for the Army. Very handsome, and of sterling quality. Sent free by mail for $15. If remitted in advance, a stylish Chain, valued at $5, will be sent gratis.

From numerous notices of the press we select the following which appeared in the editorial columns of the *Scottish American Journal* of New York, February 6th, 1864:

"It is not often that we go out of our way to notice any of the numerous trade advertisements which appear in our columns, but we feel constrained to call attention to the new system of business adopted by the enterprising and respectable firm of ARRANDALE & Co. of this city, and which, we think, might be adopted with advantage by other houses. The new system we speak of consists in sending Watches and other Jewelry to any Express Office in the United States and Canada, there to be inspected by the buyer before being paid for. This is equitable and fair between buyer and seller; and as it removes the one great difficulty experienced by country buyers in ordering goods from city houses previously unknown to them, we can not doubt it will be extensively appreciated.

"We have lately inspected, among other novelties produced by this spirited firm, two watches which seem to us a great improvement on ordinary watches, and especially adapted for the use of soldiers. The one, an elegant silver Composite Watch, which we believe is warranted not to change its color, fitted with an ingenious arrangement, termed a Time Indicator, consisting of a circular opening in the upper case, combined with a second and small dial. By this contrivance the crystal is fully protected from injury, whilst the time can be readily ascertained without the trouble of opening the case. Every one knows how many positions occur where a soldier finds the opening of his watch case an inconvenient operation, and hence the the great value of this watch in the army.

"The other novelty to which we refer seems to combine all the advantages usually sought for in a watch. It is a handsome Duplex Watch, containing two distinct times, Washington and London, with patent adjusted stop.

"This watch will be, we should think, of great value to artillerists, and others in the army, wherever it is needful to mark time. It is also very useful in timing horses, etc., having what is termed sweep second hand and all the recent improvements. This watch is likely to be a great favorite in the army."

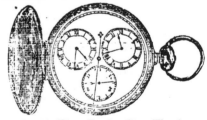

Double-Time Duplex Stop-Watch,
With Washington and London time,
FOR ARTILLERISTS,

Sportsmen, and all desiring a beautiful and accurate Timepiece. This watch has the Silver Hunting Cases, beautifully engraved Works in 15 jeweled actions. Gold balance. Sweep Seconds Hand. Patent adjusted Stop; and is in all respects a first-class watch.

EVERY OFFICER SHOULD HAVE IT.

Sent free by mail for $45 00. If remitted in advance, a handsome and fashionable chain, valued at $7 00, will be put in gratis.

All Watches are sent out in good working order, properly regulated, mailed free to any address, and warranted for twelve months.

AGENTS WANTED in every County and every Regiment, on very liberal terms. Money in registered letters may be sent at our risk, if properly sealed.

☞ Watches sent for inspection, before payment.

ARRANDALE & CO., 212 Broadway, 8 doors from Barnum's Museum, New York.

ALARM BELLS: My research so far has yielded almost nothing on the use of alarm bells in the Civil War. However, the location of some with reference to a known defensive position, e.g. Port Hudson, establishes without doubt that bells were used to sound an

alarm. Several items have come to the attention of the author. A variety of these were discussed in Vol. II of the *Encyclopedia* and IV, p. 17.) Here are some more which have come to my attention since those volumes were written.

Shown here are three cow bells, all found in defensive lines, and from three combat lines.

The largest is of bronze, 4½" tall, with an iron clapper. It was found in the 12th Corps position at Loudon Heights, Maryland, in the remains of a hut. The medium size cow bell is iron, 3⅞" tall, with a clapper made of twisted wire. The smallest cow bell is only 3" tall, made of iron with an iron ball for a clapper. This came from a hospital site at Gaines Mill, Virginia (battle fought there June 27, 1862.)

AMBROTYPE: This ambrotype is of a navy veteran — Milton B. Cushing, brother of the famous William B. Cushing. Milton was a paymaster in the U. S. Navy who entered the service August 20, 1864. Born April 20, 1837 he died New Year's Day 1886.

Martin J. Fowler

AMPUTEE CUTLERY: This knife-fork combination surely must be "one of a kind." It was used by one-armed soldiers. This grisly relic is 8″ long and 1″ wide at the widest part. It has an ivory (or possibly bone) handle and the steel blade has three tines. Marked in an oval on the blade is:

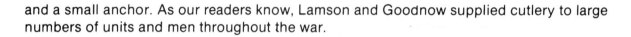

Lamson & Goodnow
Mfg. Co

and a small anchor. As our readers know, Lamson and Goodnow supplied cutlery to large numbers of units and men throughout the war.

Bill and Sue Coleman

ARMY ALLOTMENT VOUCHER: During the Civil War soldiers helped their families by sending money home. The safest way to insure its arrival was by the allotment system. The soldier using this system stated the amount of his pay to be sent home or he could accumulate the amount he wanted his family to receive before it was forwarded. He then signed a voucher as shown here. This specimen is 7½″ long and 3″ wide. Against a background of the words

A Army
Allotment

is the date, a picture of Secretary of War Stanton, a female Liberty figure holding the U.S. flag and the words:

Assistant Treasurer
of the
United States

and   Pay to   on order
dollars

Bill and Sue Coleman

ARMY REGULATIONS (C.S.):

This impressive titled book is:
A. W. Hammond's Edition,
Army Regulations, Articles of
War, Confederate States

The book, published in 1861 by Gaulding and Whitaker, is 201 pages in length. It was carried during the war by:

Samuel D. Walker
Co. "B" 3rd Battalion
Alabama Legion

Samuel B. Padgett

ARTILLERY MOBILITY: (no picture). The lack of macadam roads in most of the war's campaigns made the problem of moving heavy cannon an ever-present challenge. Often the terrain itself was marshy or the roads a sea of sticky mud or clinging clay. Diaries and journals are full of descriptions of slow advances due to execrable roads. The most famous of these marches is Burnside's "mud march" after Fredericksburg. Pieces of artillery which ordinarily were drawn by four to six horses found difficulty in making progress with double the number and finally the horses and mules were unhitched entirely from the cannon they had been struggling with. In their place, large numbers of men, sometimes nearly an entire regiment, pulled on each one of the several ropes attached to the gun. The mud at times would be almost up to the muzzle of the gun. Wagons continued to be drawn by horses and mules, but with great difficulty. If a horse or mule dropped in its harness, it was quickly cut loose and the wagons which followed passed over the body, crushing out the remnant of life.

Marshy ground likewise presented problems in the moving of heavy artillery pieces. At Fort Pulaski, the Federals used mortars weighing 8½ tons, each. These monsters had to be moved over swampy terrain, with mud about twelve feet deep. The mortars were moved by sling carts whose wheels were ten feet in diameter, and were pulled by 250 men using ropes attached to the front wheels.

Histories of the 7th Connecticut and
146th New York Infantry Regiments

10 AXLE GREASE

AXLE GREASE: This can of grease is similar to others seen by the author. The grease was issued for use in the field by artillery and wagon trains. Officially called "Carriage Lubricant" the grease is in a tin container marked "2" and has a cover to keep the grease from drying out. But due to the lapse of time, the grease has solidified. This specimen was found on Kennesaw Mountain.

Bill and Sue Coleman

AXLE GREASE CONTAINER. Although the grease itself is gone this tin axle grease container is of interest because it is marked: U.S.A.
17 Corp [s]

and the arrow which was the corps badge for the 17th Army Corps. Inside the top cover is marked:

1863

The tin container is 4½″ long, 3¼″ wide and 1½″ deep.

CORPS BADGE (3rd Army Corps): This nice corps badge, well engraved, belonged to James B. Wheeler. The badge is engraved:

J. B.
Wheeler
Battery D
1st
New York
Artillery

Wheeler enlisted at the age of 18 in Co. "I" 16th Massachusetts Infantry on August 15, 1861. He was wounded at Fredericksburg, Virginia, December 14, 1862. On May 4, 1863 he was detached to the 1st N.Y. Light Artillery. On July 11, 1864 he was transferred to the 11th Massachusetts Infantry and was discharged the same day.

Robert G. Borrell, Sr.

CORPS BADGE: This unique 2nd Corps badge was worn by a New York artillery unit. The badge is made of sheet silver with a pair of miniature brass crossed cannons as worn by enlisted men superimposed over the corps badge.

CORPS BADGE (2nd Army Corps): A fine metallic corps badge of the 2nd Corps.

It is engraved: Michael McGrath
Co. G 1 Mass
Hvy Artly

McGrath enlisted as a private, age 20, November 16, 1863, in Co. G, 1st Massachusetts Heavy Artillery. He was wounded at Petersburg, Va. June 16, 1864. On February 12, 1865 he was transferred to the 19th Regiment, Veteran Reserve Corps, and discharged August 7, 1865.

Robert G. Borrell, Sr.

CORPS BADGE: This beautiful 5th Corps badge belonged to Lieutenant Gustave Schimmel, 15th New York Heavy Artillery. He enlisted July 18, 1863 as First Sergeant; promoted 2nd Lieutenant September 21, 1863; 1st Lieutenant August 15, 1864; and Captain March 7, 1865. Schimmel was wounded August 18, 1864 near Weldon Railroad. He was mustered out August 22, 1865. The Badge has a "15" in the center and is also marked: G. Schimmel
Lieut
New York
Artillery

Robert G. Borrell, Sr.

CORPS BADGE: (5th Army Corps): This officers corps badge is in beautiful condition considering it is made of cloth. It is dark blue wool with gold embroidery enclosing red cloth thus indicating First Division of the Corps. The workmanship is exceptionally fine. The entire insignia is 1¼" square; the Maltese cross is an inch wide and an inch tall.

CORPS BADGE (6th Army Corps): A beautiful little corps badge which was worn by an artilleryman who won the Congressional Medal of Honor.

The badge is engraved:

Js A. Barber
Co. G 1
R.I.
Light
Art.

Barber enlisted in Battery "G" on August 25, 1861. He was wounded at Fredericksburg, Virginia, May 3, 1863. On April 2, 1865, he won the Medal of Honor at Petersburg, Virginia when he "was one of 20 picked artillerymen who voluntarily accompanied an Inf. assaulting party, and who turned upon the enemy the guns captured in the assault."

Robert G. Borrell, Sr.

CORPS BADGE (6th Army Corps): An ornate and expensive corps badge of silver and gold which belonged to a Massachusetts artilleryman. The Greek cross is engraved: ALBERT D. MORSE. The Cross is suspended from a crossed cannon device with the exploding bomb of the Ordnance Department between the muzzles of the two crossed cannon. A circle over the cannon is engraved:

Battery A
Mass Lgt Arty

Morse, a butter dealer, enlisted from Cambridge at age 23 on August 5, 1862. He was discharged the 19th of October 1864. This badge incorporated the badge of the 1st Massachusetts Light Artillery with the badge of the 6th Army Corps.

Robert G. Borrell, Sr.

CORPS BADGE (14th Army Corps): This unique 14th Corps badge is of stamped brass. On the back is a spot of solder where an attachment was fixed. The acorn and its stem are imposed on a maple leaf; it is 1¼″ leaf tip to leaf tip in width and 1⅜″ from tip of acorn stem to pointed leaf tip. This badge was dug just off and paralleling the Goldsboro road where Carlin's division of the 14th Corps was attacked on the morning of March 19, 1865 at the battle of Bentonville, North Carolina.

CORPS BADGE (22nd Army Corps): This 22nd Corps badge was worn by Sebra L. Blake who served in Co. "A" Coast Guard, Maine Infantry. This company served during the Civil War at Port Washington, Maryland (1864-1865). Blake enlisted February 26, 1864 and was mustered out May 25, 1865. He died on Christmas Eve, 1907.

Robert G. Borrell, Sr.

BAGGAGE CHECK (C.S.): A brass disc 1⅛" in diameter has a hole punched at the top to secure baggage item. One side is blank with only a beaded band encircling the rim. The other side is clearly stamped:

A. L. Co. 1770
Richmond

This probably refers to the "Atlantic Lines," a small railroad that connected Richmond to White House Landing along the Chickahominy River and then down the eastern side of the peninsula on the interior of the York River to Yorktown. It was a small spur line of the Richmond and York River Railroad, used to transport cotton and tobacco to Yorktown. The baggage check was dug in a C.S. gun position guarding the York River, near the approaches to Yorktown, Virginia.

BAGGAGE SEAL (MILITARY): (No picture.) Recently a military baggage seal was recovered from a Civil War site. This seal is of lead with an impressed military shield on one side and an indecipherable motto on the other. The letters which can be made out are: ". . . Uvian . . . Guac . . ." This item is identified as a baggage seal rather than a coin or identification disc because there is a line impression showing that the baggage seal was pressed over wire strapping. It was found on a stretch of Grant's military railroad which ran from City Point to Petersburg. The seal is ⅞" in diameter.

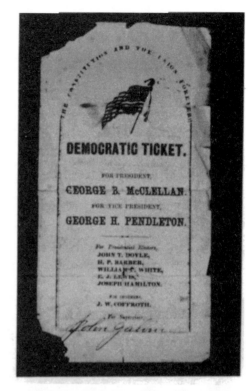

PRESIDENTIAL BALLOT, US.S. DEMOCRATIC PARTY. In 1864, Lincoln ran for re-election as President. His opponent was General George B. McClellan, the choice of the Democrats at their convention in Chicago. The "peace Democrats" were not for peace at any price, they insisted that reunion was necessary as well. But the assumption that the Confederacy would surrender its demands plus substantial Federal military and naval victories combined to bring about Lincoln's re-election.

The ticket shown here is 7¾" by 4⅛". Note the American Flag and the motto "The Constitution and the Union Forever." In addition to the candidates for President, Vice President and Presidential Electors (printed on the ballot) the name of John Galvin is written in as a candidate for supervisor.

CONFEDERATE PRESIDENTIAL BALLOT: Extremely rare ballot for President and Vice President of the Confederate States of America used at Montgomery, Alabama, February 9, 1861. The ballot shown here was for Virginia delegates. Printed on one side only the ballot is 7¾" by 4½".

BARRACKS LAMP

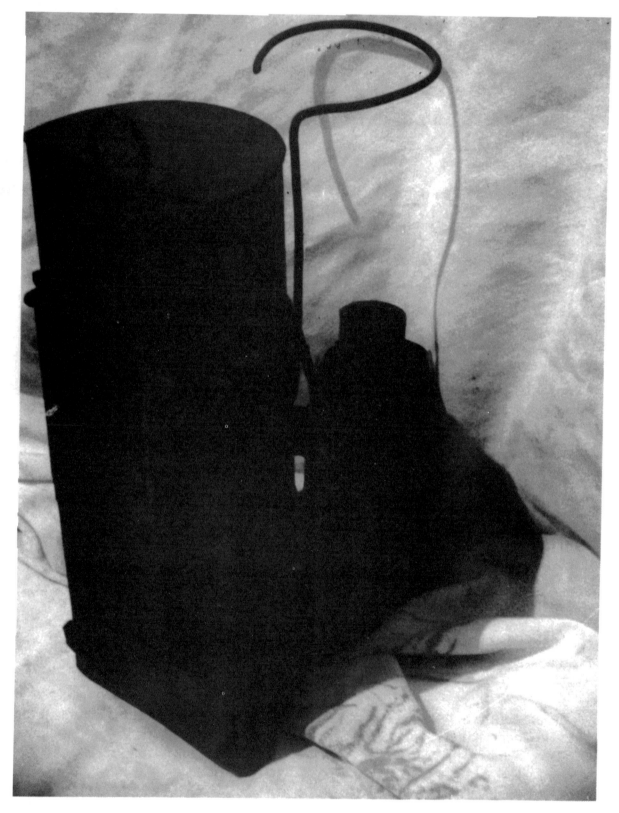

BARRACKS LAMP: This unique accessory is made of heavy tin and is soldered together in sections. The lamp is 13⅜″ tall, 3½″ wide at the back and 6″ deep from front to back. The number 3 is affixed to the top and number 37 is affixed to the bottom.

Dave Corcilius

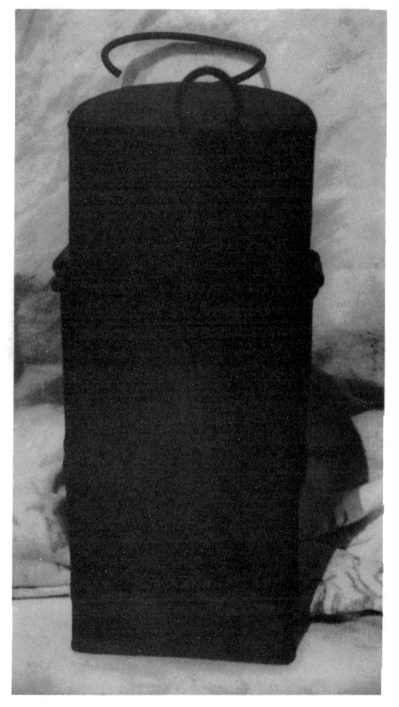

BIBLE, U.S. NAVY: This ship's Bible was issued by a Bible Society to the U.S.S. SHOCKOKON in 1863. This is the cabin Bible. The SHOCKOKON was a 700 ton sidewheel steamer. It had a crew of 112 with 6 guns. The Bible is signed by the naval hero, W. B. Cushing, and his staff. The ship saw action at Turkey Bend (James River) July 26, 1864, and also on the Pamunkey River engagement earlier, June 21, 1864. Shown in the accompanying photograph is the Bible issued May 12, 1863, by the New York Bible Society. Also shown are two Brady "cartes de visite" of Cushing who is famous for his destruction of the Confederate ship ALBEMARLE in October 1864.

Martin J. Fowler

BLACKJACK: Found at Andersonville Prison, Georgia, where it was used by the group called the "regulators" — a self-proclaimed police force made up of prisoners who defended the inmate population against marauding prisoners. The club is made of a tree root weighted with lead at the wide end. Length of club is 11". The club has a braided rope lanyard and is inscribed in ink:

Picked up at Andersonville
After the liberation

James Stamatelos

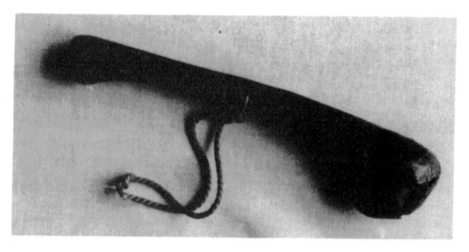

BLOCKADE RUNNER'S CABIN DOOR HANDLE: This cabin door handle is brass, recovered from the wreck of the blockade runner CONDOR. The Confederate spy Rose O'Neal Greenhow was among the passengers on the ship's last cruise from England. On the night of September 30, 1864, the CONDOR ran aground at the mouth of the Cape Fear River off Wilmington, North Carolina. Rose Greenhow drowned while attempting to escape from the stranded ship.

Michael Hammerson

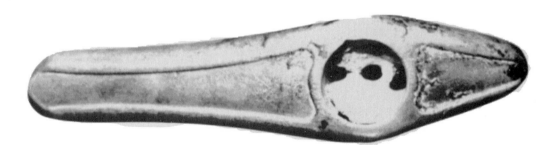

BOMBPROOF (no picture): One of the transitions to military science contributed by the Civil War was that of trench warfare. Earlier signs of this transition from purely "open warfare" was evident in the siege of Sevastopol in the Crimean War in the mid 1850s. But the 1861-1865 war was destined to show extensive trench systems — sometimes stretching for miles as at Petersburg in 1864. Artillery firing by both sides was continuous for hours on end and shelter for the men became a primary consideration — especially protection from heavy artillery and mortar projectiles. Out of this need came the "bombproof." These became very elaborate in some areas. For example, a bombproof shelter at Fort Wagner, South Carolina, was capable of holding 1500-1600 men. It remained practically intact during the 1863 siege. At Petersburg the Federal breastworks were from 10 to 12 feet thick. Under these breastworks were bombproofs for shelter against enemy mortar fire. Special bombproofs were constructed for the officers. Construction of a bombproof progressed from a hole dug in the ground much as a cellar for a house, four feet deep and 8-10 feet square. Blocks, a foot thick, were cut from pine trees and placed upright at the corners of the hole; upon these blocks were placed pine logs, completely covering the hole. Dirt was then thrown atop and packed down until there was a covering of several feet of solid earth. In like manner thousands of bombproofs were built along the whole line of both armies. They were much cooler than tents and sheltered the men not only from enemy shells but from the heat of the summer, (much as our "earth-sheltered" home designs today).

> Histories of the 7th Connecticut and
> 146th New York Infantry Regiments.

BOOT HOOKS. These were used to pull on cavalry boots by means of loops attached to the inside of the boots, themselves. The hooks were somewhat of a luxury as most men managed without using them. The larger of the two shown here is made of hand-wrought iron and is 7" long. The wooden handle is 4" long. It was Confederate — used and came from Jonesboro, Tennessee. The antecedents of the small hook are unknown. It is 5½" long and has a wood handle 2¾" in length.

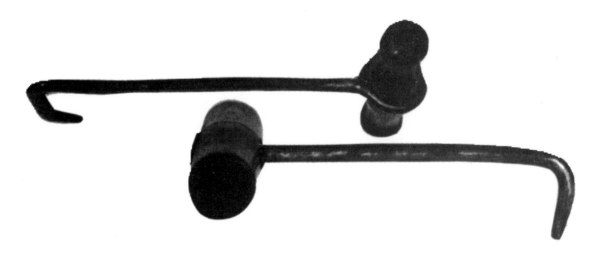

BOOTJACK: Finely made and obviously for use in the field as it is compact for travel and well designed — not a soldier's carving — equipped with brass hinges. It is 10½" long and when closed is 1¾" wide. When open the jack tapers from 4" down to 2¾". The wood appears to be oak.

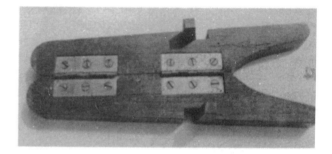

BOTTLES, LIQUOR: One of the sutlers' principal items for sale was liquor. With weeks and even months of inactivity — to say nothing of the need of many to face combat — it is small wonder that drinking was a common way of enduring nasty weather, boredom or the very real dangers of battle. The comparatively large number of whiskey flasks (some of them presentation types) as well as the eloquent story inherent in the large number of bottles being found in camp sites — all attest to the drinking habits of many officers and men. When the 5th New Hampshire Infantry broke camp for the last time on leaving the Peninsula in August 1862, dozens of bottles were found under some of the officers' beds. Similar "discoveries" were made throughout the war in other units and other places. The evidence is disturbingly irrefutable that some officers at all levels of rank were drunk while commanding units in combat as well as in camp.

BEER and SODA BOTTLES: The bottle at the left is a typical two-tone bottle — a type used extensively all through the war. This specimen is 8½" tall and 3" at base diameter. It was found in the camp of the 17th New York Infantry on Miner's Hill, Washington, D.C.

The bottle at the right is 7½" tall and 2⅜" in base diameter. It was found at Fort Pulaski and is marked with the following encircled lettering:

Jas Ray
Savannah
Ga.

The base is
marked:
C&4

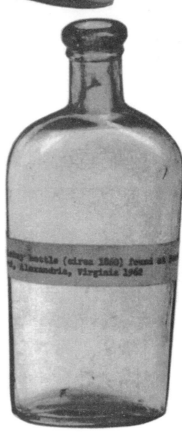

WHISKEY BOTTLES: The larger of the two is 11″ tall and 3¾″ base diameter. On one side in raised letters is:

G. G. Cornwell & Son
Washington

Cornwell was a dealer in sutler supplies in 1864. The bottle was found in Upperville, Virginia in 1965.

The whiskey flask is 6⅜″ tall and 2½″ wide at the base. It is marked Warranted Flask in raised letters and was found at Fort Ward, Defenses of Washington. This type of bottle was an inexpensive substitute for the silver liquor flasks which could only be purchased by the affluent officer or soldier.

WINE BOTTLES: These two bottles are typical of the myriads of liquor bottles of the Civil War period. Many bottles were found at Port Hudson. It was a long siege; this champagne bottle came from that siege and is 12" tall and 3¼" in diameter at the base. Color, dark green.

The light-colored, slender bottle was found on the Chancellorsville battlefield. It is 9¼" tall and only 2" in base diameter.

BOTTLE CORKER: Due to the extensive use of bottled liquids — both medicinal and otherwise — this peculiar-looking contraption had a useful purpose. It was used to put corks into bottles after filling in the field and was very probably used by a sutler. It is of hard wood, 11" long and 1⅞" in diameter at the lower end. The plunger is 9¾" long and is tipped with metal at the point where the plunger strikes the cork.

BROWNELL, FRANK: This is a rare albumen (an early photographic technique) of Frank Brownell who accompanied Ellsworth down the hotel stairs after he (Ellsworth) had taken down the Confederate flag on the hotel in Alexandria, Virginia. After Ellsworth was killed, Brownell, in turn, shot down Ellsworth's killer. For this he was awarded a Medal of Honor. This albumen was the property of his sister Mrs. Jennie Brownell Leed.

Martin J. Fowler

BELT AND BUCKLE GROUPING: These items are shown here mainly for purposes of comparison. All these items have appeared in various publications. The top belt is white buff with its original small U.S. buckle and original brown leather cap box. Both belt and cap box have JOEL STRAVISE 1860 inked on their backs.

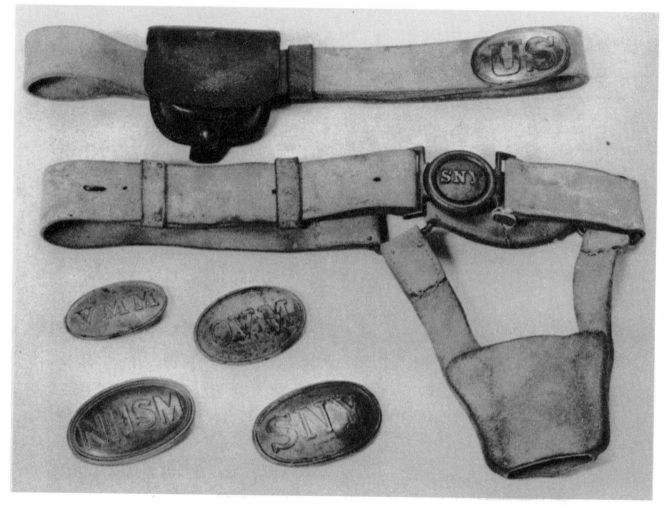

The two-piece interlocking SNY buckle is on its original white buff 1836 artillery short sword belt. Marked on the underside is

J. I. PITTMAN
MAKER

The buckles in this grouping are well known to our readers (see p. 61 of the first volume of the *Encyclopedia* series.

Gary Wolfer

Photograph by Glenn Riegel, Andy D'Angelo Photography, Reading, Pa.

MILITIA BUCKLE: As all collectors know, the variety and number of these Civil War buckles seem to be endless. This specimen is of heavy brass, 2⅝" long and 1⅞" wide. The unit ADC is not identified.

MILITIA BUCKLE: This buckle is of brass with silver letters. The buckle is 2¾" long and 2" wide. Each letter is 1" high. Although the letters WC have not been identified, it is possible they stood for Westchester Chasseurs. This unit was known officially as the 17th New York Infantry, serving for two years in the Army of the Potomac. This buckle has seen hard service.

BUCKLE (C.S.): This early type buckle was worn by one of the defenders of Columbia, South Carolina, in the February 1865 defense of the city against Sherman's advancing troops. It was found in the C.S. trench position defending the Congaree River bridge. It is brass, 2¾" long and 1⅝" wide at the widest part. It is similar in appearance to the buckle shown on p. 238 of Kerksis' book on plates and buckles.

BUCKLE (LOUISIANA): Shown here are the belt buckle and a section of a shoulder sling.

Kendall B. Mattern

BELT BUCKLE (LOUISIANA): This "Pelican buckle" is 80 by 49 mm in size. It was found in a camp near Fredericksburg, Virginia.

C. H. Merrell

BELT BUCKLE (NORTH CAROLINA): Made of brass with clipped corners, this buckle was found in a N.C. camp near Dumfries, Virginia. The initials J.T. are scratched on the front of the buckle.

C. H. Merrell

BUGLE (C.S.): Made of heavy copper, this bugle was used by a North Carolina cavalryman. The mouthpiece is a replacement and was found in a C.S. camp at Shreveport, La. The bugle is 10¾" long overall, with a 4" horn diameter. No markings.

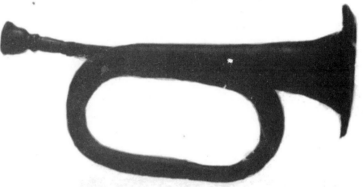

BUGLE: An extremely interesting bugle because of its association with a soldier who served in the West. The brass bugle is 16" long with a bell 4½" in diameter. Engraved on the side is: 58th Illinois, Kane Co. Out in 61—Returned in 65.

The bugle was carried by A. B. Melton, Co. "E", 59th Illinois Infantry. Melton enlisted July 4, 1863 and deserted October 1, 1863. The regiment was organized in December 1861, and it may well be that someone other than Melton also carried this bugle in the war. The regiment was a good one; it was prominent in the engagement at Yellow Bayou, Louisiana on May 18, 1864. Casualties in the war included 83 killed in action and 215 who died from other causes.

Bill and Sue Coleman

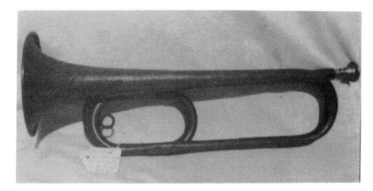

BUGLE: This is an identified specimen and therefore of interest to collectors who wish to authenticate their own musical instrument. It is brass and is inscribed: 4th N.H. Inf. 1861.

Michael Hammerson

BUGLE, U.S.: The use of this bugle in the Civil War has not been established. But its unusual shape and the eagle motif are interesting. It is 16½″ long with a bell width of approximately 4½″. As can be seen it is marked with a spread eagle and:

347
Mfg by Lyon & Healy Chicago

Scott Kerr

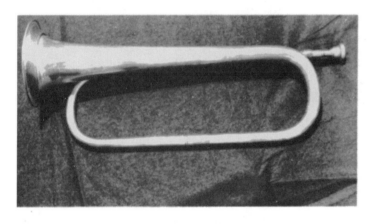

BUGLE MOUTHPIECE: These items are found with some frequency on battle and camp sites. The one shown here is of brass, 42mm long and was found at Bermuda Hundred, Virginia.

C. H. Merrell

BUTTON (no picture): U.S. Patent No. 41,292. Regulation U.S. Eagle buttons have been recovered with the back marked:

P.W.G. Pat, Jany 19th 1864

The PWG letters refer to Philip William Gengembre of Boston who secured a patent as above, stating:

"The button is secured to the cloth by means of a catch which passes through the button, the inner end of the catch terminating in a device, by turning which the button is fastened. The shank of the catch is surmounted by a tube of India-rubber which acts as a spring to tighten the locking device. CLAIM — the combination of the tubular spring D with the button body A and a locking catch or mechanism made and applied to the button, substantially in manner and so as to operate as specified."

BUTTON BOARDS: The Civil War was in too many cases, a "spit and polish" war for the troops. Uniform buttons had to be kept shiny and the sutlers did a thriving trade in the sale of polishing materials. This handy gadget would be slipped over the buttons to be polished thus protecting the uniform cloth from staining. Shown here are two types. The smaller is heavy brass, 3¾" by 2 3/16", with a 1½" diameter hole. No marking.

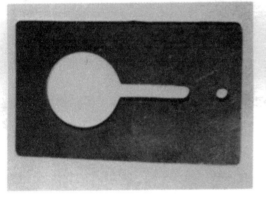 

The larger button board is brass, 6¾" long and 1⅝" wide. It is stamped at the top as follows:

Dodill Parker & Co.
Limited Manufacturers and Contractors
Birmingham

overstamped with:

31 L 97
896

Official British connection with the Parker company is evidenced by the broad arrow and "W.D." on the reverse side of this button board. Therefore, it is obviously an import.

Jack Magune

CALENDAR: This is the second metallic pocket calendar that the author has encountered. One previously described in Vol. II, p. 21, was also circular, made of brass and 1¾" in diameter. The one shown here is much different. The design differs, is made of pewter, and is marked:

Copyright secured 1855
A. J. Tipping & A. J. Smith
proprieters
Winchester, Va.

Carolyn D. Lowry

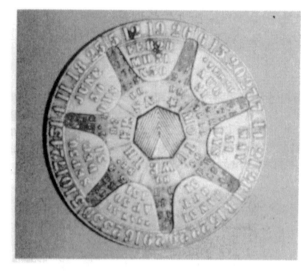
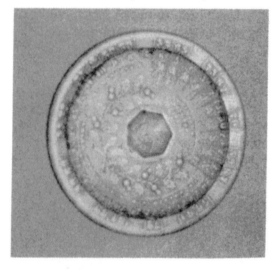

CANTEEN: This is a fine example of a Confederate wooden canteen. The canteen is made of cedar; it is 7⅛" in diameter and 2¼" deep. There are three metal guides for the carrying strap. The old faded tag reads:

Confederate Canteen
Battle of Williamsburg, Va.

Samuel B. Padgett

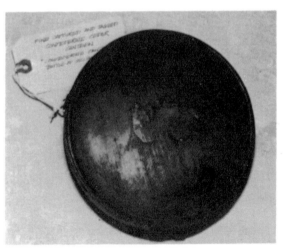

CANTEEN (C.S.): On July 6, 1863, Battery "K" 1st U. S. Artillery crossed the Potomac River at Williamsport, Maryland, in pursuit of Lee's army after the battle of Gettysburg. It is believed that this canteen was picked up by a member of Battery "K" and marked to remember that date and place.

Robert G. Borrell, Sr.

SAILOR'S CAP: First introduced in 1852 for wear at sea, the "thick blue cloth caps, without visors" were made the standard cap for sailors in 1866. The crown shows a touch of personal adornment common in the Navy in the Civil War period. The back is laced closed to permit adjustment for head size.

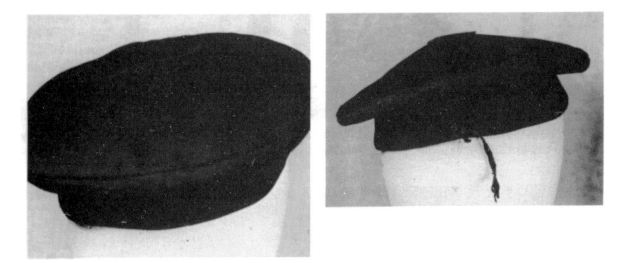

CAPTURED BY MOSBY: This 8" × 8" report must have been typical of many rendered by Federal cavalrymen serving in the Shenandoah Valley in 1864. The reason was to be found in the activities of the "Grey Ghost" Colonel John S. Mosby. The letter itself is self-explanatory:

> Personally appeared before me George W. Hunt, Priv. Co. A 1st Conn. Cav. who being sworn says, that while with a detachment going from dismounted camp to Virginia their command at or near Harrisonburg, Va. Sept. 25th 1864, he with Sergt. Lyman A. Adams of Co. A 1st Conn. Cav. were getting water from a spring a short distance from the road and that while there were captured with their horses, arms and equipments, the property of the U.S. for [which] Capt. J. B. Rogers is responsible by a squad of Mosby's guerrillas and that said Geo W. Hunt afterward escaped and reached the Federal lines. The following is a list of the stores so captured.
>
> (2) Two cavalry horses
>
> Sworn and subscribed to me this ____ day of _____ 1864.

Sergeant Adams was released from captivity March 10, 1865.

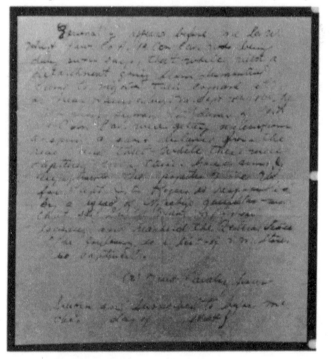

CARBINE TUBE: This rare item is a Sharps carbine tube. It holds 26 percussion wafers separated by wooden plugs. The tube is 5.1 cm. × .6 cm.

Frank Crawford

CARTE DE VISITE VIEWER: This unique apparatus was used by the soldiers to examine in detail their CARTES DE VISITE sent from home by friends and relatives. The magnification glass, an integral part of the lid, permitted the viewer to see the details in the CARTE not possible with the naked eye. This one is finely made of hard wood, perhaps mahogany, and is 5¼" long, 3⅛" wide and 1" deep. A sliding slot of wood in the bottom of the case enables the viewer to set the CARTE at the best distance for viewing as one would prop a picture up on an easel.

CARVINGS: In addition to carving items merely for pleasure soldiers also carved out items of practical use as well. One of these was the nipple protector for the musket. While the Enfield musket and carbine came equipped with nipple protectors the Springfield and contract muskets had no such advantage. It is true that the U.S. Patent Office issued a patent for a nipple protector as early as May 27, 1862, but apparently nothing came of it. Throughout the entire war the standard infantry and cavalry weapons, i.e. muskets and carbines, had nothing to protect the nipple on top of the barrel. Accordingly, the common soldier had to do the best he could to compensate for the strange lapse of his Government. He did what American soldiers have been doing since colonial days — he improvised. He carved his own protector out of the simplest item handy — the soft lead bullet in his cartridge box. Incidentally, many of his southern counterparts — not armed with the Enfield — did the same thing.

CARVED BULLETS: There are more than 100 carved items in this display. As one would expect, most are merely carving to pass the time of day. But it is interesting that a significant proportion of them was done to supply an equipment deficiency. The top row is entirely nipple protectors and cartridge or cap box finials. Number 11 in the fourth row (reading left to right) is a bottle stopper; the second row has several "sinkers" for fishing, while a lead pencil is at the bottom of the display. These carved bullets were found at many different campsites and battlefields in all theaters of the war. This display is an example of what one collector could do with a narrowly based collection of a single item.

CARVINGS (MISCELLANEOUS): Most of the items shown here are carved bullets and not unique in any way. But the fourth row has several carved items of interest. Left to right:

1. Pendulum weight from Virginia.
2. Attachment (?) Port Hudson.
3. Pencil, 3rd Massachusetts Cavalry camp — Louisiana.
4. Tooth, 3rd Massachusetts Cavalry.
5. Saber belt attachment, 3rd Massachusetts Cavalry
6. Canteen stopper, Vicksburg.

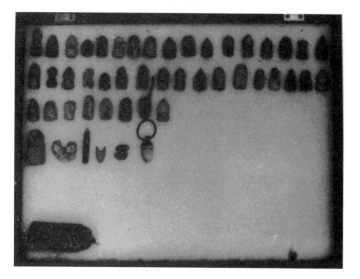

CARVING, WOOD: This unique carving is a coffin with a removable "corpse." All made of pine wood by a Maine soldier. The coffin has a hinged lid on which is carved:

Jonny
Reb

The coffin is 3¼" long, 1⅝" wide at the widest part, and ¾" deep.

Bill and Sue Coleman

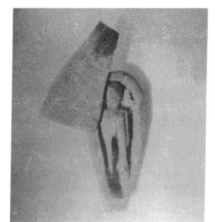

CHAPLAIN'S CROSS AND RING: This polished bone cross is 1⅛" tall and is equipped with a small brass eyelet at the top to suspend from a cord. Faintly inscribed on the cross arm, in old English script, are the initials "G.G.J." The horn ring has the same initials in old English script. They were worn by Chaplain George G. Jones, 13th New Hampshire Infantry. He was 39 years old at the time of enlistment. Appointed chaplain September 3, 1862, resigned May 9, 1865.

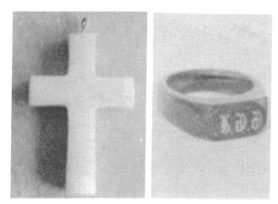

CHAPLAIN'S BUCKLE (C.S.): This unusual chaplain's buckle was found on Allegheny Mountain in West Virginia. It came from a Confederate camp.

Kendall B. Mattern

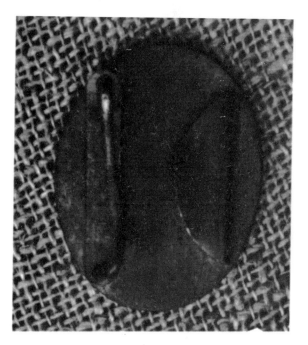

CLEANING KIT, LEATHER: This kit was made for field use to clean leather equipment, including boots and shoes. Obviously made for officers, the kit came in a japanned tin box 6½" long, 4" wide and 2" deep. Marked on the cover is:

Tiffany & Co.

Contents include saddle soap, chamois cloth, various brushes, including a clothes brush with a leather cover marked with a crown and:

Superior
Warranted

This is an unusual and very fine kit, indeed.

Bill and Sue Coleman

CLOTHESPINS: The soldier scorned the need for clothespins in the field but they were useful in permanent camps, hospitals and other installations of a settled nature. The one shown here is much like some still in use today but a bit more crude. This one is 4½" long and fashioned out of hard wood. The other made by a soldier, is most ingenious. The soldier took a small branch of a hard ash tree, peeled off the bark to the bare wood, and cut it to a length of 6¼". He cut a short "V" at one end. Then he split the piece of wood almost to its full length, up to within ¾" from the top end. This gave it some tension. Then he took a zinc band 5/16" wide and secured the band with a small pin through it and into the wood. This is another example of a soldier's ingenuity supplying a need not met by the government.

COAT HOOK FOR THE TENT: This device consists of a 2" wide leather strap 6½" long with a 5" outer strap and buckle to wrap around the center pole of a tent. The 5 brass coat hooks are individually riveted to a strap at 1½" intervals. The hooks are 2" deep. This has an old museum tag which reads:

Carried by Major Elliot C. Pierce
13th Mass Volunteers

Elliot began his service as sergeant major and ended his service as major. He was wounded at Second Bull Run and Spotsylvania.

James Stamatelos

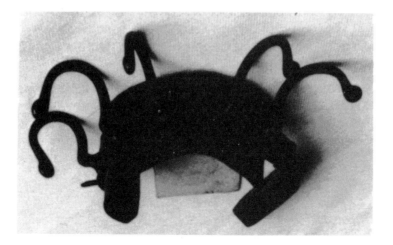

COFFIN PLATE: Care of deceased comrades was much better in the early months of the War than in later years when the number of casualties was overwhelming in both armies. Shown here is an ornate coffin plate measuring 9" by 4¾", made of copper which is heavily silver-plated. The inscription reads:

Henry L. Wyatt
Co. K. 1st N.C. Vol.
1861

Wyatt was from Edgecome County, North Carolina and was killed at the battle of Big Bethel, June 10, 1861. He is believed to be the first soldier to die for the Confederacy.

Frank J. Panasuk

COLLECTING: Collecting relics of the war began during the war itself and continued on a somewhat modest scale after 1865. As a result of renewed interest in military matters generated by the two world wars, and possibly by a nostalgic demand for a return to the "glamor" of bright uniforms and inspiring band music, there was a great surge in Civil War collecting in the post-World War II era. This urge expanded to a "craze" during the centennial years of 1961-1965. The author was fortunate to be among the pioneers of this period, associating in close friendship and interchange of information with such men as Harold Peterson, Bill Albaugh, Bill Gavin, Fred Todd, Tom Dickey, and others. Most of the pioneers are now gone. However, the author believes that the principles and ethics of the dedicated collector are still valid.

It is suggested that a beginning collector decide what particular time period and type of artifact he would like to concentrate his time (and money) on. Covering the waterfront is no longer feasible unless one is extremely wealthy and has extensive display area. Having a goal is a must to prevent one from dissipating both his energies and money leading to wide detours. There is no positive gain in constantly comparing your collection with someone who has spent a lifetime collecting his.

Label and keep a record of prices as you acquire each item. Get as much data as you can on the original owner or user of the item. Never fabricate a story to make an item seem more interesting. Do not deal with anyone who fabricates stories or alters the markings on an original item. Do not replace parts with newer parts to make your item seem more appealing. I once knew a well-known Confederate collector "make" a fine C.S. musket by "cannibalizing" four other muskets. What he ended up with was a fine musket which never really existed.

Do not encourage the wide-spread sale of replicas — and insist on all replicas being designated as such. In passing relics on to other collectors be truthful and honest in all details. If you adhere to these standards of complete honesty both you and all other collectors will prosper and your collections will always be of a very real value to you and your descendants or posterity.

A word is in order about looking for relics on non-government land. Relic hunting on this land is forbidden and infractions bring heavy punishment. So far as civilian property is concerned, it is wise, and good manners, to get permission before looking for your relics. Close all gates behind you and fill all the holes you dig. Cattle can break their legs in the holes or they can get out through open gates. For good relations — now and in the future (you might want to go back to that location) take time to chat with the owner of the land. Sharing what you found is always appreciated. For safety sake it is very sensible to take someone with you, especially in wild or unfamiliar terrain. The author well remembers this hard lesson learned early in his collecting career.

While teaching in Mississippi in 1950 he decided to visit the Jefferson Davis plantation on an island in the Mississippi River. No boats were available so a friend flew him in a cub plane. The island was deserted except for one lone family; the vegetation resembled a jungle. The tenant advised the use of one of his horses in getting around but in youthful eagerness to get started he did not want to wait to round up the horse so started off on foot. As he rounded a curve in the trail leading along the island, a very large bull with immense horns pawed the ground while giving the evil red eye. Then he charged. Luckily the author was unencumbered with heavy equipment for digging and having long legs was able to swing up into a tree as the bull roared by underneath. And there they confronted each other. All afternoon the collector sat in that tree while the bull constantly circled underneath or butted it with his shoulder trying to shake out his adversary. It was only about sundown when the man finally decided to find out why the collector had not returned. Moseying down the trail leading an extra saddled horse came the rescuer. In hindsight, the author realized he should have indeed taken the proffered horse in the first place. Having a small camera slung around his neck he took one clear picture of that bull to prove this is not just a tall tale.

Lastly, do not fool around with Civil War projectiles. They can still be lethal. Many amusing and some tragic experiences can be cited in support of this admonition. Contact a bomb disposal expert instead of trying to defuse the projectile yourself. If the projectile has or had a fuse, it is dangerous. Of course, if it is solid shot there is little danger.

NEW SOURCE OF CIVIL WAR ARTIFACTS

Most Civil War collectors are now very aware of the great scarcity of all Civil War items on the open market. Increasingly, the dealers in military items are giving up in their search for relics of the 1861-1865 period because of this and are turning their attention to other periods of our history. The Civil War camp sites and battlefields now only grudgingly yield up an occasional bullet or battered axe head; increasingly they are off limits to private collectors. More and more collections are being built up through trading between collectors.

But, amazingly, a new and unexpected source of artifacts has been discovered. Recovery of artifacts from the Federal ship MAPLE LEAF, sunk by a Confederate mine while en route to Jacksonville, Florida, on April 1, 1864 has begun. This steamer was carrying some 400 tons of cargo, consisting mainly of the camp and personal baggage of the brigade headquarters of Generals Robert S. Foster and Adlebert Ames and three infantry regiments. The regiments, 112th, 169th New York and 13th Indiana, all had sutlers and substantial sutler supplies were also on the MAPLE LEAF.

Under the inspirational but practical direction and driving zeal of Dr. Keith Holland, ably assisted by such dedicated research personnel as Mark Shaw and Lee Manley, the MAPLE LEAF is giving up its cargo on a well-developed and executed recovery plan. The complete removal of the cargo from the ship may take up to ten years, but it will be well worth the effort. Recovered items will be sold to defray the cost of this long-term salvage operation. The artifacts thus far recovered are very well preserved. Moreover, the MAPLE LEAF'S cargo included unusual items of great historic interest as evidenced by the nature of the items recovered so far. With some 400 tons of Civil War artifacts, indisputably authentic the prospect is dazzling.

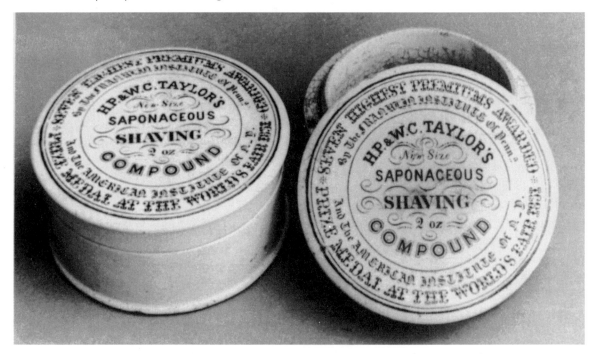

COMMEMORATION POETRY: Some time ago the author had the honor and pleasure of working with Bell Wiley on a project in the Civil War history. The author of such excellent books as *The Life of Johnny Reb* and *The Life of Billy Yank* told me that an incredible outpouring of drivel, euphemistically labelled "poetry", appeared during the Civil War. Although this is very true, yet there is a poignancy in some of the verses, especially in those written in sorrow at the death of a loved one. Here is just such an example. It appeared during the war and presumably in memory of two Wisconsin soldiers who died within a week of each other but in different theaters of war.

COMPASS (Probably presentation): This is a beautiful item and rare. Brass compass belonged to Harvey Church who enlisted as private in Co. "H" 5th New York Heavy Artillery on August 7, 1862. Promoted to corporal September 17, 1862; sergeant November 25, 1862; second lieutenant (Co. "A") January 26, 1864; first lieutenant February 7, 1865 (Co. "H"). He was discharged February 10, 1865 at Harpers Ferry, West Virginia. The lid to the compass is engraved with a cannon and the legend:

Sergt
HARVEY CHURCH
5th
N.Y. Vol. Arty.

Robert G. Borrell, Sr.

COMPASS: Shown here are two brass compasses used in the Civil War. The larger is 2″ in diameter; the smaller is 1½″ in diameter.

Jay Scott Kerr

COUNTERSIGN: Security from infiltration and surprise attacks was of continuing concern to both armies throughout the war. The situation was greatly complicated by the divided loyalties present in many of the active areas of campaigning and the fact that both sides spoke the same language and, to a large extent, were of the same ethnic background. For better security the sentinels and units on outpost duty were provided with countersigns which functioned for recognition and were changed daily. The one shown here was signed on January 15, 1863 by the "officer of the Day" Captain A. S. Tourison, 147th Pa. Infantry. The countersign on that day was: BUNKER HILL.

Kendall B. Mattern

COLLAPSIBLE CUP CONTAINER: Made of tole tin this container held the folding or collapsible drinking cup. The container is 2⅝" diameter and marked on the cover:

S.H.M. & Co.
Collapsion Cup
Wallingford, Conn.

Jack Magune

CUPS, COLLAPSIBLE: Folding cups of the Civil War era are, in themselves, not rare enough to warrant special attention. But the one shown here is interesting to the collector because of the markings on the cover. The cup container is of japanned tin, 1⅜" deep and 2¾" in diameter. In white letters on the cover is the following:

Pocket
Drinking Cup
Meriden
Britannia
Co.
Meriden
Conn.

This collapsible or folding cup is of hard rubber and is marked on the cover:

Niles Drinking Cup
Patented June 5th 1860

On the bottom of the cup are the initials F.N.P. The cup belonged to private Francis N. Prevost of Pittsford, Vermont. Prevost enlisted January 15, 1862 in Co. "B" 7th Vermont Infantry. He re-enlisted February 24, 1864 as a musician and was discharged August 5, 1865 for disability.

Marius B. Peladeau

CUP: It is quite obvious that metal cups were much more likely to survive the war than china specimens. Here is an interesting cup used in the famous Cooper Union Shop Saloon in Philadelphia where thousands of federal volunteer regiments were fed en route to the front.

Kendall B. Mattern

CUP: As one would expect crockery of any kind was not likely to survive in unbroken condition from the ravages of war or from the impetuosity of men wielding metal detectors. Here is a pleasant exception, a cup from Grant's headquarters at City Point, Virginia. The handle is missing, quite probably blown off in the explosion resulting from excellent saboteur activity by the Confederates August 9, 1864. The cup is fluted, 3″ tall, 3⅝″ in diameter at the top and 1½″ at the bottom.

CUTLASS, (C.S.): An extremely rare Confederate cutlass — probably a pattern type for possible contract sales to the Confederate government. The cutlass is marked *C.S. Armoury;* there was no official affiliation with the C. S. Government. Possibly this cutlass was made at the C. S. armory factory at Wilmington or Kenansville, North Carolina. Another possible source for this cutlass was some English manufacturer like Mole, etc. No definitive answer is available to the owner of this fine specimen. The cutlass is 24½" long overall with a 19¼" blade. The blade is stamped C.S. Armoury and the front of the guard is stamped No. 1.

William F. Marshall

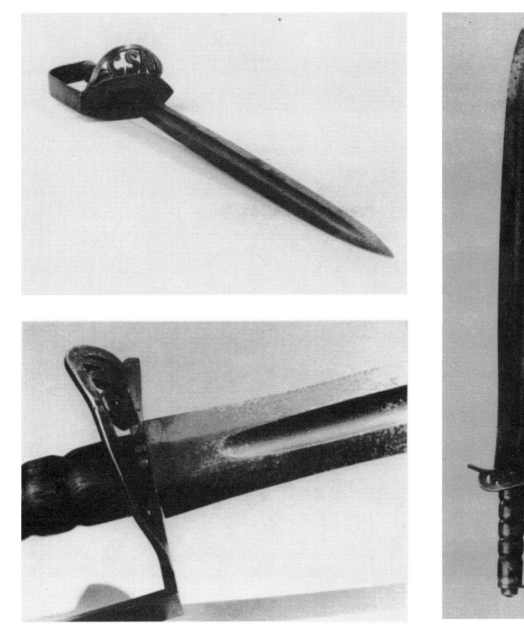

DENTURES: This has to be one of the rarest of dug Civil War artifacts! These sterling silver dentures were recently recovered from the Spotsylvania battlefield. The bullet was found very close to the dentures; of course there is not necessarily any connection between the two. Note the porcelain tooth.

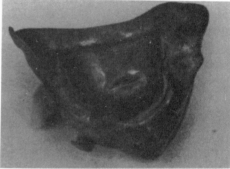

LAP-DESK: Consists of roll top — oak slats with linen flaps. The desk rolls neatly into a tube. There are tin and pewter compartments for pens, etc. marked:

C. P. Merrill
Co. K 50th Mass.

The desk is stamped:

A. P. Griffin
Patented Feb. 4, 1862

Martin J. Fowler

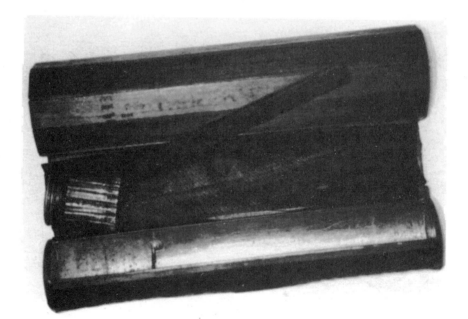

DIARY: This diary and stencil belonged to John R. Maybury, a corporal in Co. "L", 10th New York Cavalry. He enlisted in Solon, New York on October 12, 1862. Maybury was wounded at Ground Squirrel Bridge, Virginia, May 11, 1864 and again at Stoney Creek, Virginia, December 1, 1864. He was mustered out June 26, 1865 at Alexandria, Virginia.

Michael Albanese

DISPATCH CASE: Another Confederate rarity! This C. S. dispatch case is the only one of its type which the author has seen. Both front and rear views are shown here.

Frank Crawford

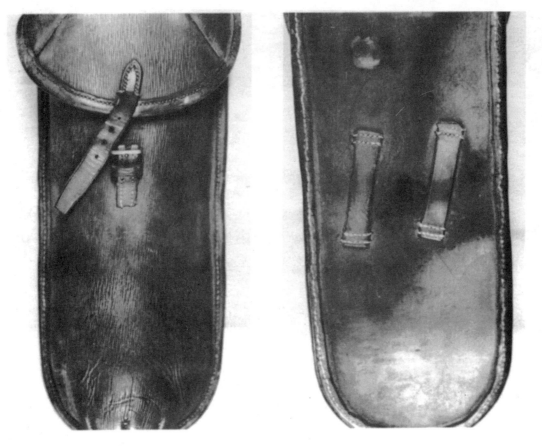

50 DITTY BAG

DITTY BAG - U.S. NAVY: The ditty bag was used to carry one's personal effects, e.g. shaving equipment, etc. This one is of muslin, light brown in color and is 5½" in diameter. The base is reinforced. It closed with a drawstring. The bag is regulation Navy issue, with an eagle with spread wings and an anchor. The bag is also stenciled U.S.N. as shown.

Martin J. Fowler

DOCUMENTS — MONTHLY DUTY REPORT (C.S.): All Confederate documents are scarce and all are interesting. This particular one was never filled in presumably because of the Confederate retreat after the battle of Fisher's Hill, September 22, 1864, where this document was picked up. Both sides of the paper are shown here. It is 18¼″ by 12¼″ in size.

Scott Kerr

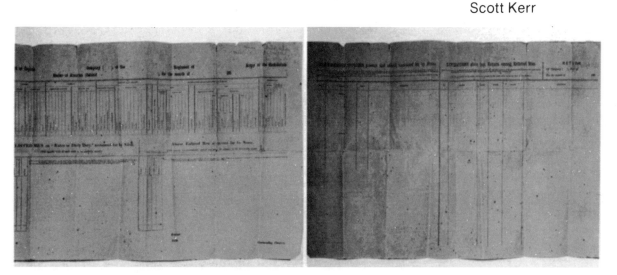

FURLOUGH EXTENSION (C.S.): This certificate recommending an extension of furlough is 7½″ by 6″ in size. It was issued to:

Private L. C. Cummings
Co. "F" 45th North Carolina Infantry

(The regiment was in Grimes' brigade). Cummings was granted a furlough June 1, 1864 in Richmond, Virginia by a medical examining board. He suffered from a gun shot wound in his right breast. The surgeon signing the certificate was Surgeon W. H. Monro, C.S.A. The Assistant Surgeon was S. B. Simmons. (C.S.A.)

Scott Kerr

DRAFT EXEMPTION: By the conscription act of March 3, 1863, the United States provided that all able-bodied male citizens between 20 and 45 years of age were liable for military service. Among the various exemptions were those drafted personnel who could furnish an acceptable substitute or could pay the sum of $300.00. Shown here is a receipt for the money by a New Jersey resident. It might be noted that the Confederate government had similar provisions for exemption in its conscription law enacted in 1862.

Kendall B. Mattern

DOCUMENTS 53

HOSPITAL PASSES: These rare documents were used at the Overton General Hospital in Memphis, Tennessee. They are green in color and, as can be seen, have stipulated both 5 p.m. and 11 p.m. as times which the recipient patients had to be back.

Frank Crawford

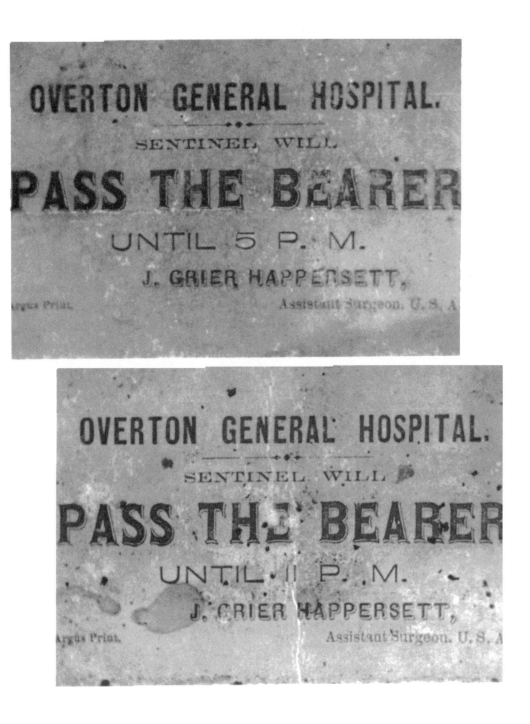

PACKET DECK TICKET: Much of the travel by troops throughout the war was by ocean or river transport. The "Deck Ticket" shown here was by the St. Louis and New Orleans packet. It was good for "Deck Passage" for Private Frank Lampert, Co. "H", 15th Illinois Infantry, from White River to Vicksburg, Mississippi. The *Empress* was later sunk by C.S. General N. E. Forrest.

Frank Crawford

DRUM: This snare drum is typical of many non-regulation drums used during the war. It is 8¾" deep and 16½" in diameter.

Stamped on the top of drum head is:

C.M.S.
1863

The drum was carried in the war by musician Charles M. Stephens, Co. "A" 1st Michigan Sharpshooters. He enlisted at Dearborn, Michigan at the age of 16 on April 18, 1863 and was mustered out July 28, 1865. He was still living in 1917 and attended the 39th annual Encampment of Michigan's department of the Grand Army of the Republic.

BATON (Drum Major's): This baton is made of hard wood with a natural oil finish. It is 38" long with a 3¾" wood ball at the top. The ball shows numerous traces of gilt. The tip is capped with nickel-plated steel. An intertwined braided blue and white cotton cord, with tassels at the end, covers the length of the shaft. This baton is marked:

Pat. 1846
5
MS
Inf

The baton was used by the 5th Mass. Infantry during the Civil War.

Frank J. Panasuk

ELLSWORTH'S HAIR: Ellsworth was killed in Alexandria, Virginia as he descended the stairs of a hotel after taking down a Confederate flag which had been flying from a flagpole on the roof of the building. One lock of his hair is neatly braided and tied with a blue ribbon — possibly dating from the time he was a baby. The four locks of hair are at the corners of the poem.

Martin J. Fowler

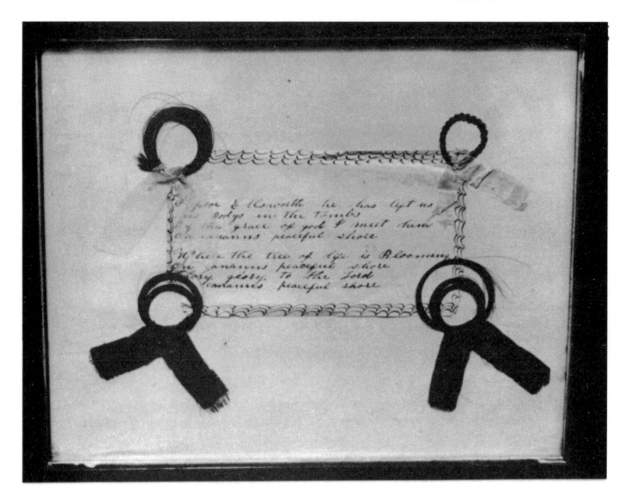

ENLISTMENT CERTIFICATE: In the early months of the war many men were enlisted first in the service of their local military company and later this company would become part of the national military forces. Such is the case here. The document is a certificate that Thomas F. Stroup enlisted in the service of the State of Pennsylvania on June 1, 1861 and is signed by the captain commanding the infantry company (in Philadelphia). The signing was witnessed by the orderly sergeant (first sergeant) of the company.

Thomas F. Stroup was one of five brothers who served in the war. He is number 2 in the back row in the accompanying picture.

Kendall B. Mattern

ENLISTMENT OF A MINOR: Thousands upon thousands of soldiers on both sides enlisted in their teens. Therefore it was necessary for these youngsters to get their parents' permission to enter the service. Often a young man would leave home and enlist without the required parental permission. Early in the war — when volunteers were plentiful — the young man could be returned to his family — discharged without serving his country. But as the war wore on, and casualties mounted these same young men were accepted in later regiments.

Martin J. Fowler

CARTRIDGE BOX: This is the U.S. Model 1839, caliber .69 cartridge box, equipped with a white buff shoulder sling. The box contains the original double pair of tins. All the plates have been removed. This example is marked as made by:

R. Dingee, N. York

On the rear of the shoulder sling are the initials "E.E." just above where the breast plate was fastened. On the curve of the outer flap (rear of cartridge box) the box has been cut square to indicate C.S. service. This and another example which was missing its sling were found in a barn at Gettysburg, Pennsylvania.

The rear view of another cartridge box shows the rounded end of the outer flap. This example is of enameled leather with a large script "N.G." plate on front. This box contains original double tins. There are no maker's or inspector's markings on this box.

Shown in the accompanying photograph are rear views of the two boxes found at Gettysburg. Both of these cartridge boxes were made by R. Dingee of New York.

Butch Myers

CARTRIDGE BOX (Volunteer Militia of Maine): A russet leather caliber .58 cartridge box with the original Volunteer Militia of Maine box plate attached. This is an extremely rare cartridge box with the type of box plate shown here. Probably this was for militia use because of the non-regulation features of the box, especially the lack of belt loops for attaching the box to the belt. There never was any such provision but only loops on the back of the box to serve as guides for the sling. No maker's marks.

Shown also in this grouping are a Federal cap, canteen, and tintype. The cap is the type called "bummer's cap". The canteen is Federal regulation. The cloth covering is brown. The carrying sling has inspector's marks while the pewter spout is marked:

C.H. Johnson & Co.
1865

The tintype is probably that of a Confederate officer. The gray kepi has a cloth insignia consisting of a wreath surrounding the letters "R.R." The tintype on top is stamped:

Melaino Plage
Forneff's Pat. Feb. 56.

(Photographed by Glenn Riegel, Andy D'Angelo Photography, Reading, Pa.)

Gary Wolfer

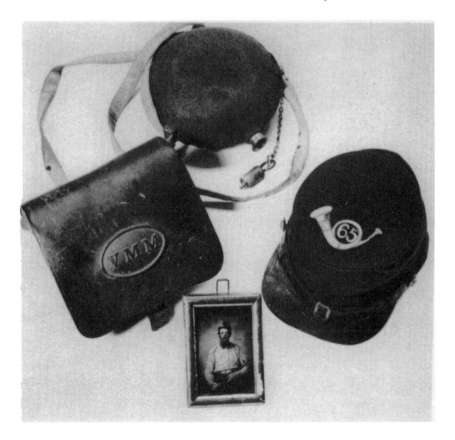

MVM CARTRIDGE BOX: This type of cartridge box was used in the early months of the war by some militia units called into service by Lincoln's call of April 15, 1861. Similar types are shown on pp. 110-111 of Volume III of the Civil War Collector's *Encyclopedia*). The box shown here is 7½" long, 5" wide and 1¾" deep. It is of black leather with the initials "MVM" (Massachusetts Volunteer Militia) on the cover. The liner is of tin. In bold lettering on the inside of the box are the initials M.W.W. Research indicates that the box may have been carried by Private Myron W. Whitney, Co. "I" 45th M.V.M. He enlisted September 17, 1862 and was discharged July 7, 1863. The owner — whoever he was — had decorated the inside of the cartridge box flag with two U.S. flags in color.

CARTRIDGE BOX PLATE (battlefield relic): This oval U.S. cartridge box plate was struck almost exactly in the middle by a Confederate bullet. Found on the battlefield of Chickamauga.

James Stamatelos

CAP BOX and BAYONET SCABBARD. C.S.: The cap box and bayonet scabbard shown here are of special interest. They are examples of Confederate repair of original U.S. equipments. The cap box was possibly a U.S. Model 1850 but for some unknown reason the entire outer flap/back and the inner flap were removed. A new back/outer flap of two pieces of "split leather" were sewn together and the body was then sewn to this with a single belt loop thus resulting. The original holes were not followed as some exist on the body. In its rebuilt condition the box does not have an inner flap or a place for a vent pick. It does have a small piece of wool glued in place. There are no markings on this box although some sort of pin may have been attached to the front. This cap box was purchased in Richmond, Virginia.

The bayonet scabbard was originally a U.S. Model 1842 specimen, but has been altered to fit a caliber .58 bayonet. No maker's or user's marks are on the piece which was from Winchester, Virginia. This repair probably took place in Richmond arsenal. In this specimen the entire throg has been replaced; only the original brass tip was retained.

Butch Myers

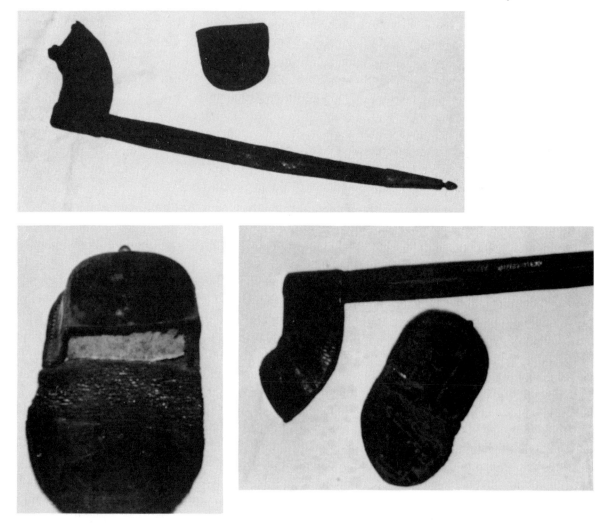

EQUIPMENTS, (C.S.): As all readers are aware, authentic Confederate equipments are rare indeed. Shown here, however, are a C.S. cap box and an embossed C.S. caliber .58 cartridge box.

The cap box is similar to the U.S. Model 1850 (shield front) having no copper rivets as reinforcement on the belt loops. The original wool fleece and vent pick are missing. The specimen shown here is of blackened leather, sewn with flax at 7-9 stitches per inch. The outer flap is held with a brass finial. There are no maker's or user's marks. The stitching matches that of the cartridge box shown here. The cap box and cartridge box came together.

The cartridge box is black leather and constructed similar to that of the U.S. Model 1855 cartridge box. Embossed on the flap is C.S. in an oval border. The buckles and belt loops are not reinforced with rivets. The original sling and tins are missing. Brass finial. Note the square cut of the outer flap at sling loops. The box has no maker's marks. The set was purchased at an estate sale in Greensboro, North Carolina. Photographs show both front and rear views of this set.

Butch Myers

EYEGLASSES: This type of double glasses was invented in 1797 by J. Richardson of England. These "double glasses" were originally designed to limit the amount of light reaching the eyes of a person whose eyesight had been damaged by measles. Both specimens shown here measure 4½" across the front. The octagonally framed pair have blue lenses on both front and sides; the oval lensed pair have blue sides and clear lens fronts.

Alan R. McBrayer

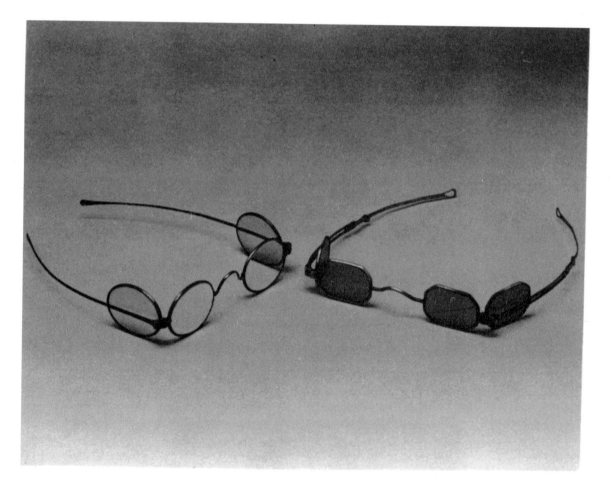

FIFE MOUTHPIECE: This specimen measures 1⅝″ in overall length. It fits a fife ⅞″ in diameter. Marked:

Rogers Impr'mt

Alan R. McBrayer

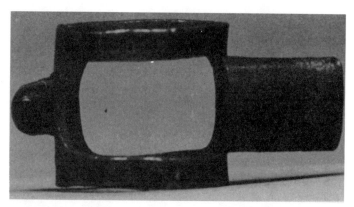

FISHING GIG: Here is another example of the Civil War soldier's improvisation in the field. This fishing gig was found at a Federal camp near Keyser, West Virginia. It was fashioned from a pike. The overall length is 13″; each tine is 2″ wide; the socket itself is 1″ in diameter, tapering to ¼″.

Ray and Jean Smarr

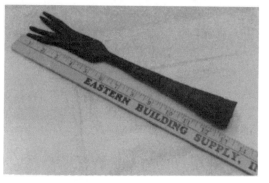

FLAG FRAGMENT - (C.S.): Shown here is a common type of pocket New Testament as supplied by the American Bible Society in New York, This Testament is dated 1862, and very probably was taken from a captured or dead Federal soldier. It was taken home at the close of the war by a Confederate officer. This officer also tore off a small piece of his unit's flag at the time of surrender. The Testament has the small piece of flag with the inscription in the front:

Our Flag
1865
Capt. Harris
Charleston, S.C.

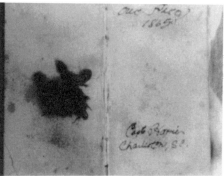

FLAG FRAGMENT: Identified piece of a flag which was sent by a David Mitchel to Mrs. Eliza Crawford. The accompanying note states that this is a piece of the flag which Ellsworth put up to replace the C.S. flag he tore down just before he was killed.

Martin J. Fowler

FLASK (Presentation): The whiskey flask here is typical of the flasks of the Civil War period. It is especially interesting in the extent and quality of the engraving. The front of the flask cup is engraved:

2nd Lieut.
E. P. Newkirk

The profile of a cannon and pile of cannon balls is also depicted.

The other side of the flask cup is engraved:

Battery H
First New York
Artillery
2 April 1863

Newkirk enlisted as a sergeant September 12, 1861; promoted second lieutenant (Battery "H") June 6, 1863; First lieutenant April 18, 1864; captain by brevet March 13, 1865; discharged June 23, 1865, at Elmira, N.Y.

FLASK: This beautifully made whiskey flask is 5 5/16″ high. The pewter cup is 2 1/16″ high. The woven cover is made with side loops to accommodate a shoulder sling. This flask is marked:

F.D. & P.B.
Brevetes S.G.D.G.

Alan R. McBrayer

COFFEE WAGON: Photographs of the reconstructed "coffee wagon" discussed in the second volume of the *Encyclopedia* (pp 59, 62) give the reader a better idea of that interesting Civil War vehicle. The Park Historian, W. E. Meuse, National Park Service, has kindly furnished this information. In a letter along with the two photographs shown here, Mr. Meuse wrote in part:

> "The Chase and Sanborn Coffee Company has presented the National Park Service with a meticulously detailed reproduction of the coffee wagon used during the Civil War by the U.S. Christian Commission — [this wagon was] nicknamed 'The Christian Light Artillery' by the soldiers."

W. E. Meuse
National Park Service
Fredericksburg and
Spotsylvania National
Military Park

FORT SUMTER'S FLAG RAISING. On April 14, 1865, elaborate ceremonies were held at Fort Sumter where General Robert Anderson raised again the original flag which had been lowered exactly four years before, in 1861. The author's maternal grandfather, color sergeant of the 14th New Hampshire Infantry, took six flags of his brigade to the flag-raising ceremony. As he wrote later "it was a notable event; and when, as the battle-scarred ensign touched the peak, the flags waved, the score of bands struck up patriotic airs, the shouts of the assembled thousands welled up from within those battered walls, and the thunders of more than one hundred cannon from forts, batteries, and men-of-war shook the very harbor . . . [all combined to emphasize] the triumph of the Union."

Shown here is the front page of the program for this historic event. The label "1124" is probably the seat allocation number for the ceremony.

Michael Hammerson

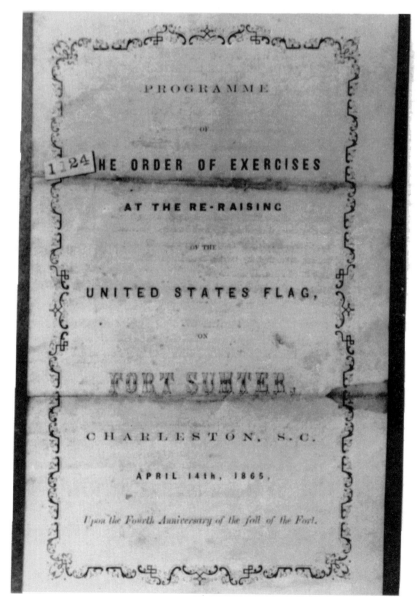

CARD GAME: This game, entitled *The Commanders of our Forces,* was put out by E. C. Eastman of Concord, New Hampshire in 1863. It contains 80 cards of which 62 are of battles and other events, while the remaining 18 are of generals, admirals, and other leaders. The game belonged to Edvardus L. King of Vergennes, Vermont. He served as private in Co. "F" 5th Vermont Infantry, enlisting August 30, 1861. He was wounded June 5, 1863 and again on May 5, 1864. King deserted November 14, 1864 but returned to his regiment on January 26, 1865 and was mustered out June 29, 1865.

Marius B. Peladeau

CARD GAME: Shown here is the cover to the Civil War card game entitled *The Commanders of our Forces.* The box is multi-colored showing marching Zouaves and ironclads. It is marked as being patented in 1863. "A game for old and young."

Martin J. Fowler

"AUTHORS" CARD GAME: The game of *Authors* is still being played today. Here is the Civil War version. The box measured 3⅞" by 2 11/16" and each card is 3½" by 2¼". This set was "published" by John H. Tingley of New York in 1863. Note, early games were published like books rather than being manufactured. There are 46 cards in the deck. The authors selected for the game are American and British, mainly from the first half of the 19th century, e.g. Hawthorne, Irving, Scott, Dickens, etc.

Alan R. McBrayer

PLAYING CARDS: Civil War deck of playing cards. Marked:

A. Dougherty
26 Beckman St.
Manufacturer
N.Y.

Jay Scott Kerr

DOMINOES. The game of dominoes was popular with men in barracks and in the field. Many soldiers who found chess too boring or too difficult did enjoy playing dominoes — a game which did not need a board for playing and thus was more easily carried in the field. This set is interesting because each piece is decorated with the American flag, in color. The flag has 7 stripes (red and white) and 13 little white stars on a blue field. Each domino is 1¾" long and ⅞" wide.

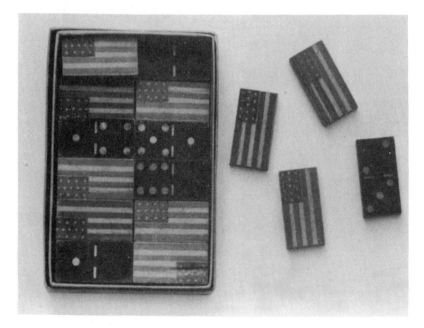

GAME: This unique game was played on heavy cardboard which folds in half like a checkerboard. Opened it measures 12¼" by 12"; closed it measures 12¼" by 6". The opened board has an entire black surface on which there are 1¼" squares, such as a checkerboard, 81 squares in all, each square lined in gold paint. The center square has a fancy design in its four corners, with another design in center that may be meant to resemble a bastion or fortification. On the 32 squares around the outer edges of the board there is a 5-pointed gold print star in each. This may have been a "spinner" game, where an arrow or indicator was spun to determine the moves.

In clear print on the outside "fold" in black and red lettering is:

> The splendid new game
> of Freedom's contest or
> The battle for the Union,
> by the Federal and Rebel
> armies.

In smaller print is: Published by D. P.Ives & Co.
Boston, H.P. Ives, Salem

And in the very small print at the very bottom is:

> Entered according to
> Act of Congress, in year
> 1863, by S.B.Ives, in
> Clerk's Office District
> of Massachusetts.

On the back (outside cover) of the "fold" is printed a long list of "New and Popular Games" published and for sale by Henry P. Ives, Salem & D.P. Ives & Co., Boston, No "spinner" if there ever was one, nor "men" or "pieces" were found with this game board.

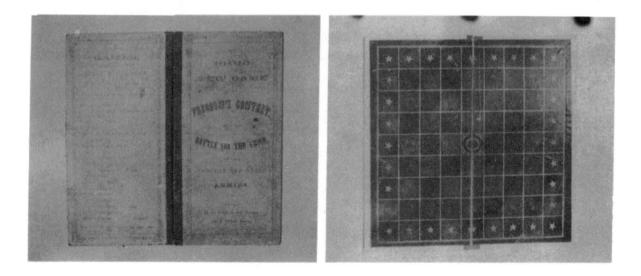

CHECKERBOARD: This checkerboard was sent from home to a Confederate soldier serving in the field. It measures 14¾″ by 13⅝″ open and 7⅜″ by 13⅝″ closed. It is red throughout except for the black squares. Marked in script on one side is:

Robt Side
Harlin City
State of S.C.

CHESS SET: This chess set was carved at Libby Prison, Richmond, Virginia, by Private Jackson Webster, 10th Wisconsin Infantry. Webster was captured at the Battle of Chickamauga.

Frank Crawford

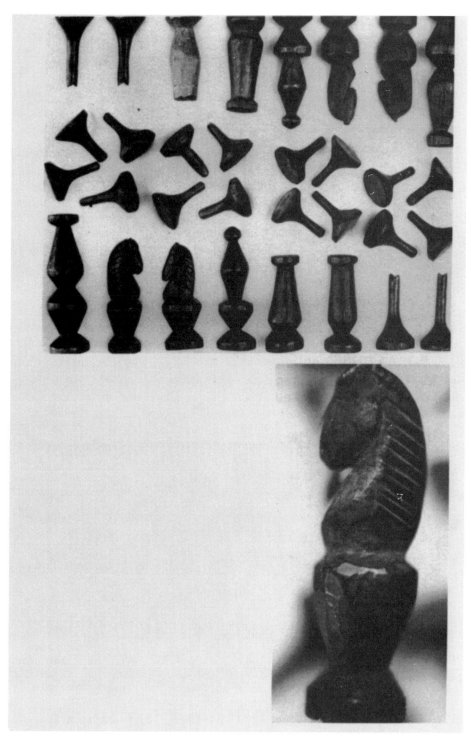

PICK-UP-STICKS. The unique little game popular with children was adapted to the interest in military events of the Civil War. The game consists of ten carved items, including a musket, bow, shovel, etc. The pieces range in length from 3¼″ to 3½″ and are numbered 10 to 100.

Bill and Sue Coleman

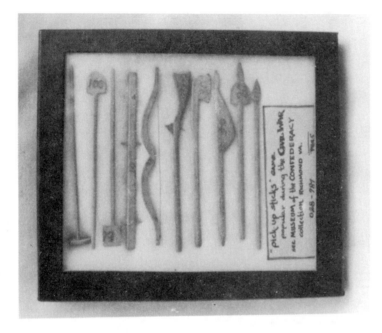

POKER CHIPS: Although poker chips have been described in earlier volumes of the *Encyclopedia* the accompanying photograph shows several variations of the types of chips used in poker and other Civil War games.

Bill and Sue Coleman

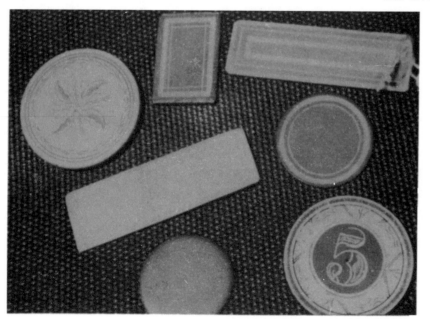

"GRANT'S PETERSBURG PROGRESS": This newspaper was printed by Union Soldiers after the occupation of Petersburg, Virginia, in April 1865. Shown here is Issue No. 4, April 10, 1865, giving news of the surrender of Lee's army the previous day. Information is not available to the author as to how many more issues came out or how many issues 1-4 were printed. The reverse side is also printed.

Michael Hammerson

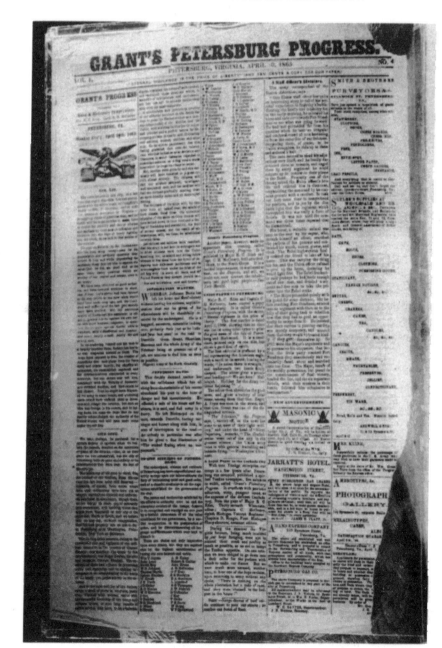

GUIDON: This South Carolina battery guidon was carried by T. F. Ferguson's battery at Charleston, S.C. and in the western theater. Ferguson himself was wounded just outside Jackson, Mississippi. The guidon is blue with a crude star in the center; the lettering is painted in gold. This guidon is 19½″ tall and 17¼″ long.

Samuel B. Padgett

GUN TOOLS

CLEANING ROD: Shown here is a pistol cleaning rod which was recovered from the Wilderness battlefield. The rod is brass, 5¼″ long and ⅛″ in diameter.

C. H. Merrell

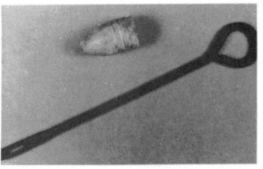

SHOT SCOOP: This gauge is of brass. It was found on the Wilderness battlefield. The scoop is 2¾″ long and ⅝″ in diameter.

C. H. Merrell

HANDKERCHIEF: This patriotic handkerchief is decorated with such military objects as revolvers and crossed sabers. It is 13¾″ by 11¾″ in size and has a song with chorus. The song itself was one of the most popular of the war period in the Federal armies — "The Battle Cry of Freedom." It was written by George Frederick Root.

Kendall B. Mattern

HARDTACK: One of the basic foods issued to troops during the war was hardtack. This hard biscuit came in various sizes. The largest was about six inches square. It generally was eaten after softening in water. Many soldiers added salt pork — another basic food issued to the troops — and the hardtack and pork would be fried together in a frying pan or half canteen. Often sugar would be added or even salt and pepper for flavor. The resulting dish received a designation "unsuited to ears polite" according to a veteran of the 1st Massachusetts Cavalry.

HARDTACK: Hardtack was actually a saltless biscuit — very hard until softended in liquid. It was nutritious but tasteless; it became a basic food element in armies both East and West.

Along with the hardtack went coffee — usually issued in the bean form. If a soldier had a coffee mill or grinder, rarely was such the case, he would grind his beans. But usually he pounded them in his cup. That some soldiers or officers *did* have coffee grinders is attested to by the fact that grinders have been found fairly frequently on Civil War camp sites.

In reading diaries and letters of Civil War soldiers it becomes clear that "hardtack and coffee" made up the entire menu for many Yanks and Johnny Rebs. These two pieces of hardtack were found in an old haversack 122 years after the war. Both pieces have shrunk from their original size. The larger one is 3" by 2¾" and the smaller is 3" by 2½".

HARDTACK: Although hardtack was one of the basic food items in the Civil War, very few specimens have survived to the present time. This is especially true of complete biscuits in unbroken condition. And of those which have survived, most of them were brought home by the soldiers. (See p. 113 of Volume I of the *Civil War Collector's Encyclopedia.*) The specimen shown here was recovered from the 1862-1863 Federal winter camp at Falmouth, Virginia. This biscuit measures 3" by 2⅞".

HARDTACK (identified): The old label on this piece of hardtack is an error so far as the battle site is concerned. Actually, the battle was Fredericksburg (December 13, 1862). The 23rd New York Infantry was organized at Elmira, New York, to serve two years. The companies composing it were raised in the counties of Chemung, Cortland, Allegany, Schuyler, Steuben, and Tioga. It was mustered into service July 6, 1861, and mustered out May 23, 1863. It fought at Rappahannock Station, South Mountain, Antietam and Fredericksburg.

Michael Albanese

C.S. SLOUCH HAT: Rarest of the rare! This hat is of a felt material and is brownish-gray in color. It measures 16″ from front to back and is 15″ in width with both sides down. The crown is a little over 5″ tall. The hat cord is black in color and is made of cotton. The star which is affixed to the front is composed of metallic thread and silver sequins.

Samuel B. Padgett

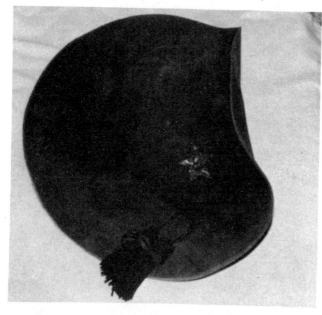

HAVERSACK (C.S.): Authenticated Confederate haversacks are rare indeed! Here is one which came from a GAR post in the North. The haversack is of cloth with a leather cover. Inscribed on the cover flap is:

J.A.B. Co. H 25th G.V.

The haversack is 15¾″ tall and 13½″ wide. It has three leather belt loops on the back.

Samuel B. Padgett

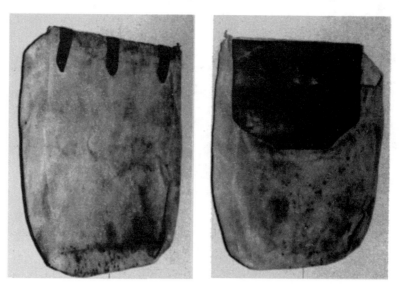

HOOF CLEANERS: Thousands of horses for cavalry, artillery and wagon trains were used during the war. Keeping them in good shape for active service involved among other maintenance, good feet and this meant clean hooves. Several types of hoof cleaners have been seen in private collections and museums. Both of the two shown here were adequate for their purpose but are crudely made and quite different in appearance. The T-shaped cleaner was found at Port Hudson and is 5½" long while the L-shape cleaner is 5¾" long and came from Macon, Georgia. Both were used by Confederate troops.

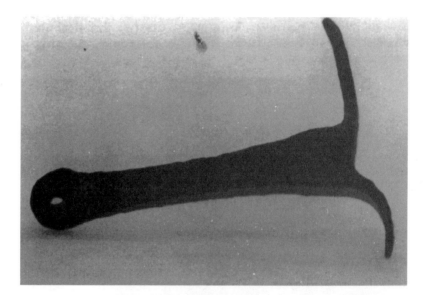

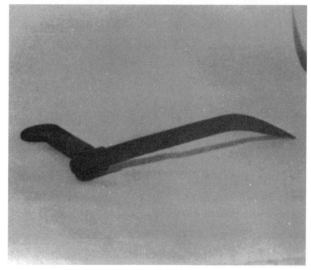

IDENTIFICATION DISC: Although identification discs have been discussed in earlier volumes of the *Encyclopedia* and elsewhere, the one shown here is rare enough to merit inclusion. The Lincoln motif is one of the rarer designs of identification discs. Much more common are discs with the eagle motif. As can be seen by the accompanying photograph, the disc was worn by A. P. Bismore. This soldier, whose name was Andrew, was a cooper and enlisted as private in Co. "A" 41st Massachusetts Infantry on August 20, 1862. (Incidentally, he was the only Bismore from the State of Massachusetts in the War.) The first service of the regiment was in the Department of the Gulf. Early in 1863 the regiment became mounted troops and on June 17, 1863, was officially designated the 3rd Massachusetts Cavalry. As cavalry troops, the regiment served in the siege of Port Hudson, Mississippi. Private Bismore apparently became sick during the winter of 1863-64 and was discharged March 28, 1864 at New Orleans, Louisiana.

McCLELLAN IDENTIFICATION DISC: (Left) This is an exceptionally small identification disc. It is about the size of a modern penny — it is only ¾" in diameter. The bust of General George B. McClellan shows the general in uniform and is encircled by the words:

> Maj. Gen. G. B. McClellan
> Peninsular Campaign

Since the Peninsular Campaign ended in mid-1862 it is probable that the disc was made sometime between July and September 1862 (McClellan's great battle of Antietam, September 17, 1862, is not on the disc). The reverse side of the disc is blank — purposely left so that the wearer of the disc could have his name, regiment and hometown stamped on it.

IDENTIFICATION DISC. (Right) A typical "dog tag" as worn during the war. This particular specimen was worn by Corporal T. J. Wallace who served in Company "M" 2nd New York Heavy Artillery.

Robert G. Borrell, Sr.

IDENTIFICATION DISC: These unusual identification discs are obviously for wear by artillerymen. The one carried by an officer is engraved:

1st Lieut. Eugene McGrath
Co. E 5th N.Y. Art.

McGrath enlisted as a Second Lieutenant in Co. "F" 5th N.Y. Heavy Artillery on August 1, 1862. Only 6 weeks later he surrendered with the garrison at Harpers Ferry (September 15, 1862). He was paroled by the enemy. He was commissioned First Lieutenant of Co. "E" of the Regiment January 28, 1864, and was dismissed April 6, 1865.

The other disc is like the McGrath disc but is engraved:

·J. R. Bean
I N.H.L.A.

John R. Bean enlisted as private in the 1st New Hampshire Light Artillery on August 27, 1861. He was 29 years old and came from Biddeford, Maine. He was appointed Corporal, then Sergeant, and Second Lieutenant, December 3, 1864. He was discharged June 9, 1865. He died April 23, 1886.

IDENTIFICATION DISC (Pewter): (Left) As is well known, the great majority of discs are brass. However, the one shown here is of pewter. It was worn by 2nd Lieutenant James A. Pray of Captain E. B. Dow's Battery, Maine Artillery. Pray was born in 1840 in Gardner, Maine. He enlisted February 19, 1862, at Augusta, Maine in the 6th Battery, 1st Batallion, Maine Light Artillery. He later was commissioned a Second Lieutenant and was killed in action at Petersburg, Virginia, June 18, 1864.

Robert G. Borrell, Sr.

Two unidentified Civil War artillerymen wearing the identification discs described on p. 85 are shown here.

Robert G. Borrell, Sr.

IDENTIFICATION DISC: This tag belonged to Corporal Walter S. Rogers, Co. "D" 14th Massachusetts Infantry, which was changed to an artillery regiment early in 1862. (The new designation was 1st Massachusetts Heavy Artillery.) Rogers, at age 22, enlisted July 5, 1861. He was a shoemaker by trade. Promoted Corporal January 9, 1862, he was wounded at Spotsylvania May 19, 1864. He was discharged July 8, 1864.

Robert G. Borrell, Sr.

IDENTIFICATION DISC: This disc belonged to Mathias Bitner who served in Battery "H" 2nd Pennsylvania Artillery. As can be seen from the photograph he was from Green Castle, Franklin County, Pennsylvania.

IDENTIFICATION DISC: This is one of the rarer identification discs in that battles in which the wearer had participated are also stamped on the disc. This disc was dug. On the tag is the name: J. W. Nutting as well as his home town, Decatur, Michigan. Nutting's unit, Battery "G" 1st New York Artillery is shown and also:

Battles

Malvern Hill

Antietam

Fair Oaks

Robert G. Borrell, Sr.

IDENTIFICATION DISCS: These discs are of New York soldiers and are of interest in showing the effects of adverse soil conditions on the metal which had been in the ground for over a century. This particular disc belonged to William Barey, who, at age 28, enlisted on September 29, 1862 in Co. "H" 13th New York Infantry. On June 24, 1863 he was transferred to Co. "K" 140th New York Infantry. Barey was wounded in action at the Wilderness May 5, 1864 and captured March 31, 1865 at White Oak Ridge, Virginia. He was released May 16, 1865.

The disc on the left was worn by Sergeant S. H. Cotton, Co. "I" 74th New York Infantry. He enlisted at age 21 and died of wounds September 7, 1862 at Eckington Hospital in Washington, D.C.

IDENTIFICATION DISC: The 74th served with Pope during the Second Bull Run campaign. The disc on the left belonged to Corporal E. S. Turchi, Co. "E" 40th New York Infantry. He also served in the 30th and 55th New York Infantry regiments. After all his service he came through alright and was mustered out August 28, 1864. On the back of this disc is inscribed the battles in which Turchi participated:

Yorktown, Williamsburg
Fair Oaks, Seven Days Battles,
Fredericksburg, Chancellorsville
Gettysburg, Kellys Ford
Mine Run.

Note the unusual placement of the hole at the top of the disc for the carrying chain.

Michael Albanese

CONFEDERATE IDENTIFICATION DISC: (Above Right) Generally speaking, all Civil War identification discs and badges are rare. Confederate "dog tags" are almost unheard of. But here is one which was dug up on the Cold Harbor battlefield. It was made of a dime. beaten flat by a hammer, and, with a punch, was inscribed:

D. B. Cox
1861
CSA

The disc is about ¾" in diameter. There were several men with the name D. B. Cox who served in the Confederate Army. But the only one who could have been present at Cold Harbor in June 1864 was Bedford B. Cox who used D. B. Cox as his name on military records. He served in the 38th Virginia Infantry. He fought at Cold Harbor but was not a casualty; he must have lost his dog tag during the battle. His unit was subsequently returned to the Petersburg defenses and Cox was wounded just before the end of the war in Lee's retreat from Petersburg.

IDENTIFICATION BADGE (ENGINEERS): This badge consists of a shield with the Engineer's "castle" at the top. The badge measures 1″ wide and 1¾″ tall. The center of the shield is divided into 3 sections on which is engraved:

Co. B
U.S Engineers
M. S. Fickett

James Stamatelos

Fickett is here shown in uniform and wearing his Engineers badge, Mariner S. Fickett enlisted in Boston at age 20 on December 11, 1861. He served as Sergeant of Co. "B" until discharged on May 10, 1867.

STICK PIN?: This unique pin was made from an 1853 quarter and belonged to Clement Lavaly who served in the 12th Independent Battery, Ohio Light Artillery. Lavaly was born February 23, 1844 in Pulaski, New York. He enlisted August 14, 1862 at Columbus, Ohio and was mustered out July 11, 1865 at Camp Chase, Ohio. He died January 15, 1923. The back of this 1853 quarter was smoothed off to permit the engraving as follows:

C. Lavaly
12th Ohio Ind.
Battery

Robert G. Borrell, Sr.

IDENTIFICATION BADGE: More attractive, and therefore more expensive, were the various identification badges offered for sale by dealers and sutlers. Often these silver badges were in the shape of a shield. This one is engraved with the word UNION at the top and the following around the border:

P. H. Work
24th O. V. L. A

The badge belonged to Corporal Philip H. Work, who enlisted October 23, 1861 in the 60th Ohio Infantry. On August 16, 1863 he again enlisted in the 24th Independent Battery of Ohio Artillery. He was discharged June 24, 1865. Work died January 13, 1905.

An unidentified artillery sergeant is shown here wearing the silver identification shield.

Robert G. Borrell, Sr.

IDENTIFICATION BADGE: Another of the shield-shaped badges which were so popular with many of the soldiers this one is marked:

O. C. Benton
17th
N. Y. A.

Sergeant O. C. Benton enlisted August 21, 1862 in the 17th Independent Battery of New York Light Artillery. He was discharged in Richmond, Virginia on June 12, 1865.

Robert G. Borrell, Sr.

IDENTIFICATION BADGE: Here is a simple, practical identification badge of silver as worn by an artificer of artillery. "Artificers" were workmen in the Artillery, i.e. carpenters, joiners, wagon-makers, harness-makers, etc. There were two per company or battery. This badge belonged to Artificer Cyrus W. Remington, Light Battery "C", Rhode Island Artillery, which became Co. "C" 3rd Rhode Island Heavy Artillery. Remington enlisted August 22, 1861, discharged June 9, 1865, and died March 10, 1926. As can be seen from the photograph it is engraved:

Cyrus W. Remington
Co. C
3d R. I. Artillery

Robert G. Borrell, Sr.

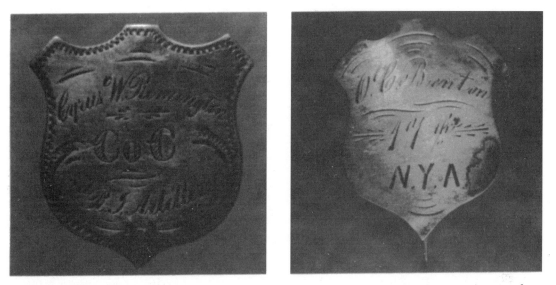

IDENTIFICATION BADGE: Silver Signal Corps identification badge in the shape of a shield with enamelled Signal Corps flag in the center. The badge is lettered with SIGNAL CORPS USA above the flag and the soldier's name George M. Robinson inscribed in an arc below the flag pole. The badge is approximately 1½" square.

James Stamatelos

IDENTIFICATION TAG: These tags were issued by the U. S. Christian Commission to soldiers before going into combat. The "Christian Commission" was a civilian agency, no official connection with the United States government or state agencies, and was composed of religious and philanthropic members dedicated to assist the fighting men of the Federal armed forces. The tag is 2¾" long and 1¾" wide. Inscribed on the tag's front:

AZRA MILLS
Co. F 9th Regiment Maine Vols
3d Brigade
2d Division
10th Corps

Inscribed on the obverse:

Martha Mills [his wife]
Corinna, Maine

James Stamatelos

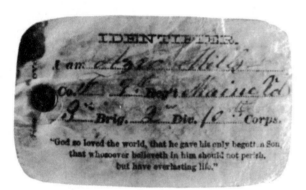

The Latin word "impedimenta" applies generally to things that impede, such as baggage and supplies. Today the term has come to be used loosely to indicate items both necessary and unnecessary which are carried by soldiers in the field. And much unnecessary impedimenta was carried by many Civil War soldiers. This was especially true of the Federal infantry men, one of whom here describes what he saw as men of this regiment left for the front:

It must force a smile into the face of every old veteran . . . as he recalls the loading up . . . process, preparatory to his leaving his State for the front . . . He thinks it certain he shall need a pair of slippers to rest his aching feet . . . Two or three changes of underwear are, of course, indispensable, and also as many pairs of socks, gloves, necties (sic), suspenders . . . Now come the tourniquet. He has his choice to carry that or bleed to death . . . Then the havelock . . . to protect the back part of the head and neck from sun and dust as well as against sudden colds from wind and rain. Next comes the half-dozen or more of patent medicines and appliances . . . the bullet-proof, steel vest lining, a "sponge-cap-pad" to keep the head cool, bottles of Jamaica ginger, anti-scorbutic mixture, tooth ache drops, a "medicated abdominal supporter" and a "buckskin lung protector". Especially important is the "soldier's drinking tube" consisting of a 3 foot rubber tube, having at one end a pewter mouthpiece and attached at the other end to an "automatic duplex water-filter." The knife-fork-spoon combination was very popular as well as a toilet kit holding brushes for hair and teeth, comb, looking glass. The soldier also "needed" a pair of buckram leggings, a portable inkstand and writing portfolio (holding paper, pens, pencils), revolver, and a dirk-knife with which to fight the Black Horse Cavalry and Louisiana Tigers.

Captain A. W. Bartlett
Co. "C" 12th N. H. Inf.

INPEDIMENTA, (C.S.): Contemporary accounts of Confederates in the field indicate that in some cases at least, they had many of the superfluous items sarcastically assumed by many Southern writers as being characteristic of the Yankee invaders. Shortly after the Confederates abandoned their winter camp site at Centreville, Virginia, the following description appeared in the British weekly journal *All The Year Round* (No. 160, May 1862, "Conducted by Charles Dickens"). This unknown reporter told of finding hundreds of well-built cabins, each with a fireplace, where the Confederates spent the winter of 1861-1862. Here at Centreville, Virginia, the Federals looked with envy at the numerous empty brandy and whiskey bottles left by the enemy. At the railroad station at Manassas, Virginia, the souvenir hunters had a field day. "There lay in confusion property of all kinds that the Confederate soldiers in the hurry of departure had not time to pack and carry with them. Trousers, coats, shirts, drawers in abundance; old iron and brass; bottles and tin boxes, trunks, valises, knapsacks and boots, barrels of provisions, bacon and hams, flour and cracknels; bowie knives, swords, guns, cars and carriages, blankets and horse covers, books and papers . . . The books were chiefly Bibles, prayer books, sermons, and books of sacred music. There was a sprinkling, also, of very moral novels . . . I found a letter which illustrated the volunteer spirit. It was from a civilian to his brother who was serving in a South Carolina volunteer regiment. The civilian "has his heart with the men who volunteer." As no punctuation marks were included the reader must supply them as he sees fit.

IMPROVISATIONS

U.S. IMPROVISATIONS AT VICKSBURG (no picture): During the siege of Vicksburg, General A. E. G. Ransom used "Mantlets" to protect his artillery gun crews. This was a temporary protection for artillery, engineer, or infantry troops in the embrasures of defensive or offensive positions. The mantlet can be of metal but more often is of oak planking. At Sevastopol, the Russians used plaited rope. In the Vicksburg siege General Ransom had a battery so close to the Confederate lines that he used mantlets at the gun embrasures. A gun would be loaded and pointed, and then fired just as the mantlet was removed. The first time a gun was fired from it a storm of rifle bullets poured in but a gunner jumped on the gun and shouted, "too late."

Other improvisations were employed. When the working parties carried the saps to the base of the defensive works, the besieged would light the fuses of 6-pound shells and toss the shells over the parapet. These shells would roll down among the working parties and explode, occasionally doing serious damage.

A young soldier named Friend, Co. "C", 20th Ohio Inf., on detached service in the division pioneer corps, devised wooden mortars which proved quite effective. A very small charge of powder in one of these would be just powerful enough to lift a shell over the enemy's parapet and drop it on the enemy. The shells caused much annoyance among the defenders. After the surrender, the garrison troops were very curious to see how these mortars were made.

INSIGNIA: Brigadier General Rufus Saxton, Jr. was a well-known figure during the Civil War. After graduation from West Point in 1849 he served in Indian campaigns until 1861. He served in various staff positions until appointed brigadier general on April 15, 1862. Most of his service was in South Carolina. Earlier he had so bravely defended Harpers Ferry, May 1862, that he later (in 1893) was awarded the Congressional Medal of Honor. He was breveted Major General on January 12, 1865. He died in 1908. His photograph is shown here, along with his autograph, shoulder straps, and hat insignia which is 2¾" long and 1¾" wide at the widest part.

MILITIA. SHAKO WREATH: Truly beautiful and unusual. This type is not found very often. It is of fairly heavy brass, 4" wide at the bottom and 3¼" tall. Original unit is unknown to the writer.

DRAGOON HELMET INSIGNIA: This silvered brass eagle was originally part of the 1833 dragoon helmet insignia along with a half-sunburst background for the eagle. It is possible that some militia unit adopted the eagle insignia itself for use on the headgear. Dimensions: 2¼" wide, 2⅝" high.

ARTILLERY INSIGNIA: An unusual artillery insignia 2⅜″ long. The gold braid wire oval encircles crossed cannons with a bull's eye center. This rare insignia is on red felt.

PALMETTO INSIGNIA: The Palmetto tree grows abundantly in South Carolina, especially along the coast and was the main motif on the State seal since April 2, 1776. The heavy brass South Carolina insignia shown here is 2″ tall. It has wire fasteners in the back for attachment to the uniform. This specimen was found in Charleston, South Carolina.

C.S. LIEUTENANT'S INSIGNIA: A "Lieutenant Sim" wore these insignia during the war. They were shown at veterans meetings in the post-war period. The insignia, still sewn on the original uniform cloth, are gold in color and 1⅜″ in length.

PALMETTO GUARDS HAT WREATH: This South Carolina unit identified itself as from Charleston, being present at Fort Sumter where the 67-year old Edmund Ruffin was permitted by the Palmetto Guards the honor of firing the opening shot of the war. This silver insignia came from Charleston. It is 1⅞″ long, 1¼″ tall at the highest place, and the letters are each ⅜″ in height. No markings.

CAP INSIGNIA — NAVAL SURGEONS AND ASSISTANT SURGEONS 1862-1864:
The device of live oak leaves and acorns was adopted for officers of the Medical Corps in 1862. The wreath pattern, nearly closed at the top is typical of this period compared with a larger, open wreath of the pre-1862 period.

John A. Stacey

CAP INSIGNIA — NAVAL ENGINEERS AND ASSISTANT ENGINEERS 1864-1866:
The device of four oak leaves formed in a cross was adopted for officers of the Engineer Corps in 1861. The wreath pattern is more open than the 1862-64 pattern but is smaller than the open wreath pattern of the pre-1862 period.

John A. Stacey

HARPS: Left: Corcoran's Irish Legion (brass, pin back). Right: silver Irish Harp, pin back.

HARP AND BUTTON: An Irish harp and Massachusetts Volunteer militia button. Both were found together in a 2nd Corps camp in Culpepper, Virginia.

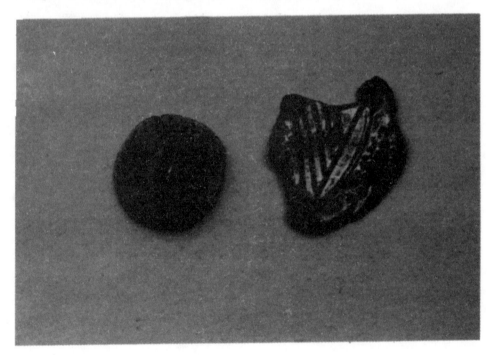

BUTTONS: Left: 69th New York Infantry buttons. Right: Finian buttons used very late in the war.

Also used after the war.

A. Collin MacDonald

NAVAL PETTY OFFICER'S RATING BADGE 1841-1866: The eagle and anchor device as an insignia for petty officers was adopted in 1841. The shield embroidered on the eagle's breast is a personal touch common to the period as the insignia was hand embroidered over a pattern issued to the petty officer.

John A. Stacey

INTRENCHING TOOLS: The Civil War is especially significant in the many firsts during 1861-65. Among these "firsts" in military science, weaponry, and tactics was the practice of "digging in" whenever time permitted either army. The imperative need for hasty intrenching was necessitated by the tremendous improvement in fire power, both small arm and artillery. It became obvious to the common soldier — if not to his commanders! — that survival was due to intrenching as fast and as completely as possible. Although Lee was derisively called the "king of spades" for his insistence on intrenching in 1861, by 1864 both sides were using intrenchments very extensively. On September 8, 1864, Corporal William Boston, Co. "H" 20th Michigan Infantry wrote in his diary:

> "Talk about MacClellan digging — Grant has done more of that in this campaign than has been done before in the whole war."

Perhaps Grant did learn something from Cold Harbor! Since "digging in" was a way of life, both East and West, it is greatly to the discredit of the responsible parties that they did not develop an intrenching tool for the foot soldier. At Chancellorsville the greater part of the Army of the Potomac did not even have spades and axes. The men were forced to use their bayonets, tin plates, pieces of boards and their bare hands. (See p. 91 of *Soldiers True* — 111th Pennsylvania Infantry, John Boyle.) A few regiments, like the 126th New York Infantry, were fortunate that a "little spade" was part of the men's accounterments. But except for the crude intrenching tool shown here, extreme left, no adequate tool of light weight was provided so far as is known to the writer. A "trowel bayonet" was issued after the war as part of the 1874 infantry equipments. But one must wonder how long the Sioux or Cheyenne warriors hung around to permit their white adversaries to "dig in".

Intrenching tools have been discussed in earlier volumes of the *Encyclopedia* **series** (Vol. 1, pp. 143-145; Vol. II, pp. 90-92, and Vol. IV pp. 104-106.) Shown here are three interesting types. The tool on the left is of heavy steel, 7" long with a blade 4¼" wide. It could well have been cut down from a large spade for military use. It was dug in a C.S. position on the battlefield of Cedar Mountain. The center tool is but 5½" long with a blade 2¾" wide at the widest part. This specimen was hand forged by a blacksmith and was found in a Federal camp site.

The unique tool on the right is the only specimen of this type ever encountered by the author. Since it was found at Fort Donelson and therefore dates from early 1862, it may well be one of a type found impractical for field use after that date. It is 9" long overall and 4½" wide at the widest part. Each "tooth" is 6" in length.

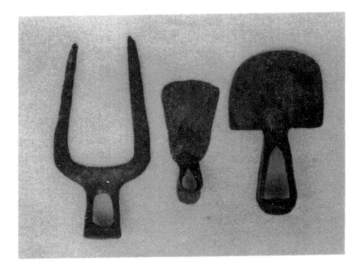

INTRENCHING TOOL: The intrenching tool shown here is a variant type used by some Federal soldiers in 1862. (See p. 143 of the first volume of this *Encyclopedia* series.) This specimen was dug up on Bolivar Heights, outside of Harper's Ferry, in the Federal trenches that faced Stonewall Jackson's troops before the fall of the town, September 15, 1862. Marius Peladeau, owner of this intrenching tool, has a very interesting theory about these tools. He thinks that the locking ring was taken off because it would only have raised cuts and blisters on the hands of anyone using the tool. His theory is that "some enterprising Yankee manufacturer" with some iron working machinery purchased real cheap some rejected bayonets (the blades having failed the government inspection, etc.) and turned the shanks and ground down the blades into entrenching tools to make quick dollars on the inexperienced young soldier going off to war.

Marius B. Peladeau

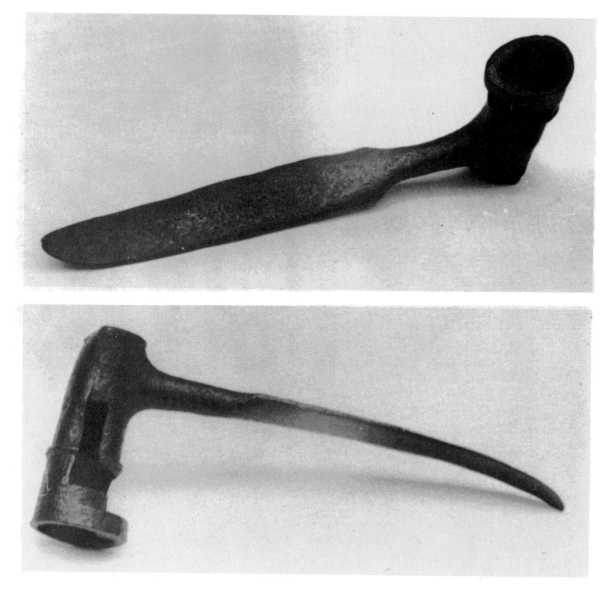

SPADE (Ames): Camp or Infantry spades were issued to troops in the field. This type of square-bladed spade saw extensive use through the war as evidenced by the many specimens recovered from battlefields, intrenched positions, and camp sites — East and West. This specimen is 30″ long and is marked:

O. Ames

Dave Corcilius

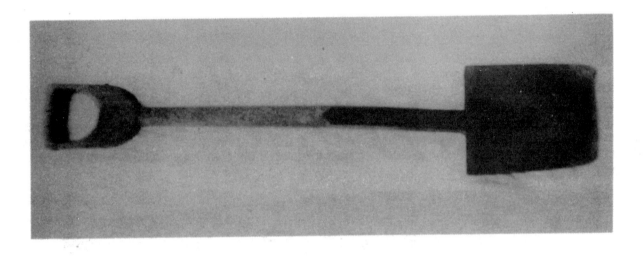

SPADE CARRIER: This is a very rare item; usually the men carried their shovels and spades themselves or loaded them on wagons. This carrier is of black leather 9¾″ by 8¼″ in size and with an attached carrying strap about 5 feet long which can be adjusted to the soldier's size by a buckle.

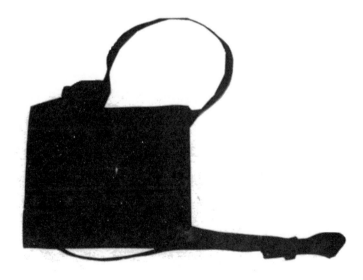

IRISH BRIGADE MEMORABILIA

IRISH BRIGADE MEMORABILIA: Certain brigades on both sides in the war stood out as excellent fighting units. In the Federal Army one of the most famous of these was the Irish Brigade. This unit served in the 2nd Army Corps under the redoubtable Hancock. The brigade was composed of 63rd, 69th, 88th New York Infantry regiments; along with the 28th Massachusetts and 116th Pennsylvania Infantry regiments. The brigade lost over 4,000 men in killed and wounded; this was more men than ever belonged to the brigade at any one time! And, with the exception of the 28th Massachusetts, the regiments were small — each with about 800 men as compared with 1,000 men in most infantry regiments. During its service it was led by five different commanders and of these there were three killed in action. Shown here through the courtesy of A. Collin MacDonald are items connected with the war-time service of the Irish Brigade.

FLAGS:

(a) Shown here is a section of the 4th regiment (28th Mass. Inf.), of the Irish Brigade. The lettering "4 Regt Irish Brigade" can be seen at the top of the flag. The 28th Regiment was known as "FAUGH-A-BALLAGHS" (Gaelic for Clear the way). This flag was carried by the Irish Brigade at Marye's Heights (Fredericksburg) December 13, 1862. It was also carried at Chancellorsville and Gettysburg. The bottom half of the flag is missing. This was red ribbon and carried the Gaelic motto translated as "Never retreat from the clash of spears."

(b) Flag with substantial section "filled in." This was the first Irish flag presented to the 28th Massachusetts Infantry. Presented January 18, 1862 it was used until November 23, 1862 when the 28th Regiment formally joined the famous Irish Brigade.

(c) Regimental flag of the 28th Regiment. The regiment left Boston January 20, 1862. It first served with the 9th Army Corps and then with Hancock's 2nd Corps, Army of the Potomac. It has the sky blue field with gold stars. The "Old Glory Blue" was a very common color for regiments from Massachusetts. Half the flag is gone due to wear and tear during the war. All these flags are currently being restored by the State of Massachusetts and are in the State House Capitol, Boston.

JACKET, CONFEDERATE: This home-made butternut shell jacket was worn by Private Andrew J. Duncan, Co. "K", 21st Mississippi Infantry. He subsequently served in Co. "D" 7th Mississippi Cavalry. The trousers which went with the jacket have a waist tightening buckle marked: Patent 1856

Michael Hammerson

JEWELRY: Women occasionally visited their men folk in the army during active operations and frequently did so when the troops were in camp for extended periods of time. This was especially true for the winter months when active operations were at a minimum. While visiting their men the wives, sisters and daughters naturally wanted to look their best. On such occasions they wore jewelry like that represented in the display shown here. All objects in this display were recovered from the Confederate lines at Petersburg.

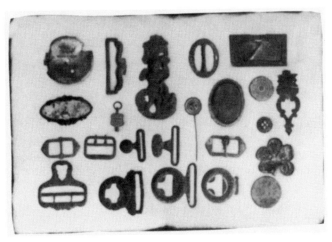

RINGS: Shown here are two rings both done by Federal prisoners of war. The handcarved bone ring is approximately 9/16″ by ⅞″ and has a scrimshaw design of the American flag with blue and red inks added for color.

The wooden ring is carved in the shape of an infantryman's equipments: U.S. buckle, cartridge box, cap box, bayonet scabbard. The belt encircles the finger. The cartridge box is ½″ by ¾″.

KNIFE, BOWIE: This soldier's Bowie knife was made by Buck Brothers of Worcester, Massachusetts. It is shown here with the original leather scabbard. The knife has a flat-sided rosewood handle with fluting for the finger grip. Three circular silver pieces are inlaid in the handle. At the base of the handle is a German silver ferrule. On the brass cross guard is:

John M. Lamb
25th Reg. Mass

The blade is 6½" long and the handle measures 4½" in length.

James Stamatelos

BOWIE KNIFE (C.S.): This is a massive bowie-type side knife with original leather scabbard. The knife is 18" long overall and weighs 40 ounces. It is of blacksmith construction. The right side of the blade is deeply marked:

Death to Abolition

The leather scabbard is hand sewn and shows much use and wear.

Frank J. Panasuk

KNIFE: This specimen is typical of the knives imported from England by soldiers of both sides. Marked:

G. Wostenholm & Son
Washington Works
Sheffield

The knife was carried in the war by a M. DARE.

Kendall B. Mattern

KNIFE, C.S.: This fine knife was taken home by a Maine soldier. The knife is 13½" long overall and has an 8" blade. There are no markings but the knife is of superior workmanship.

BOOT KNIFE, CONFEDERATE: The most-publicized non-military weapon of the Confederate soldier was probably the bowie knife. Specimens of this weapon shown here — a boot knife — are comparatively rare. This knife is 9″ long with a wooden, hand-made sheath. There are no markings.

Scott Kerr

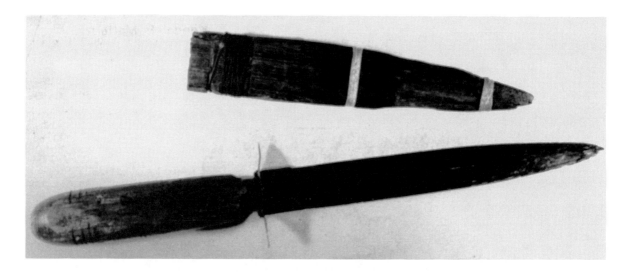

KNIFE: This fancy pocket knife, with its brass and bone handle, is 4½″ long. It is decorated with an eagle and shield and was found in a C.S. trench at Mine Run, Virginia.

C. H. Merrell

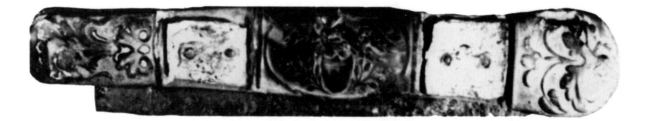

POCKET KNIVES: Identified. One of the most commonly encountered personal items which the campsite or battlefield yields to the relic hunter is the pocket knife. These handy items functioned as table cutlery, intrenching tool, and also as the tool which produced so many varied carvings by soldiers of both sides. Shown here are two different types.

The knife with the various tool attachments is a farrier's knife and was used by a trooper in the 1st Maine Cavalry. It is 3¾" long with 2 blades. The longer blade is 2¾" long and the shorter blade is marked:

James Muxlow
Sheffield

This knife has bone handles which strongly resemble ivory. It has a corkscrew, a hoof pick for cleaning the horse's hooves and an awl for punching holes in leather.

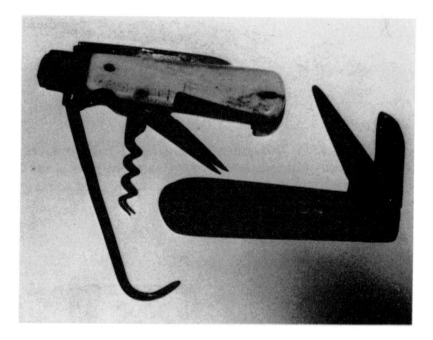

The other knife is a common jack-knife, 3½" long, with two blades, and bone handles. It was carried by EDWARD J. HOON, Co. "H" 13th Pennsylvania Infantry, and was in his pocket when he was wounded at Winchester, Virginia, September 19, 1864. It is interesting to note that jack-knives made up a substantial percentage of the items included among the effects of the Federal dead at Gettysburg. (For other types of pocket knives see p. 142 of Vol. II of the *Encyclopedia*.)

FRUIT KNIFE: An excellent example of the fruit knife in use during the war. Length when closed is 3¼". It has a blade and a "pick" and is made of sterling silver. In an oval on one side of the knife are the initials (in script) F. H. These letters stand for Frederick Hardy, who was Captain of Co. "K" 6th New Hampshire Infantry. Hardy enlisted as a private at age 20 on October 29, 1861. He rose through all the enlisted ranks to captain on January 8, 1865. Mustered out July 17, 1865.

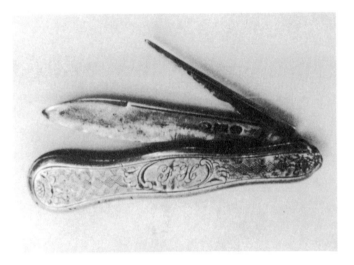

DIRK, NAVAL: Although this dirk dates from the first quarter of the Nineteenth Century, some of its type were still in use by the time of the Civil War. This particular dirk has a double eagle motif for a guard, is etched, and has a gold-filled blade with an ivory handle.

Marius B. Peladeau

LEATHER POLISH

LEATHER POLISH: Very rarely did a container like this survive! It originally contained polish for boots, shoes, and other leather items. The container is of tole tin, 3½" in diameter, with the original label which reads:

William R. Warner's
Union Oil Polish
47 & 48 N. Market St.
Boston, Mass.

Under a military eagle on the label is:

Apply it thin and polish at once

Entered Act of Congress 1861
. . . District of Massachusetts

Jack Magune

LIGHTING EQUIPMENT

CANDLE HOLDER: Some enterprising soldier used a condensed milk can to fashion this candle holder. The can is 4¾" tall and 2½" in diameter at the bottom. The can is a condensed milk tin as shown in Phillips *Supplement,* page 178, and in his first book on page 152. The maker of this candle holder very neatly and cleanly soldered an inverted funnel for the top and a handle on the side. Used by a Maine soldier.

CANDLESTICK: A very unique and rare little candlestick for use in the field. It is small enough to be carried easily in the pocket. It is equipped with a small hook for carrying. The candlestick on the back is marked.

Patent

Marius B. Peladeau

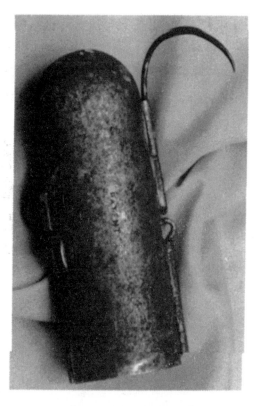 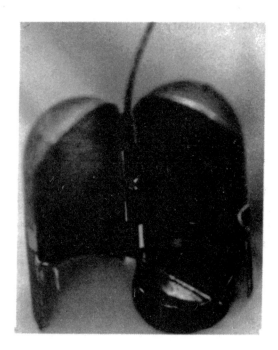

"UNION" CANDLE HOLDER: Very unusual. Made of heavy paper it is 6¼" in diameter and 11" when fully open. Has a cardboard bottom with a tin holder for the candle and a cardboard top with a wire handle for hanging. Red, white and blue motif with stars, eagle, and UNION on the sides.

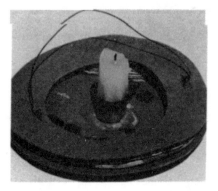 

TRAVELLING CANDLESTICKS: These were known as the "doughnut" candlesticks, obviously because of their shape. The ones shown here are of officer-grade. They are of olive wood, British made, and were in current use by British officers at the time of the Civil War. They were probably first seen by American observers during the Crimean War. Examples were brought to the United States where, in brass, their descendents became a common Civil War item.

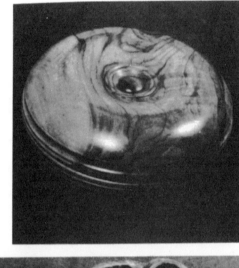

CANDLESTICK, Patented: Iron and pewter candlesticks of this type are relatively common. But this one is of particular interest as it is marked:

PAT. Nov. 1861

It is 1½″ in diameter and 2½″ tall overall. From Harrison's Landing, Virginia. (No picture of this candlestick is shown in this volume.) It is similar in appearance to the one shown on page 99 of Volume II of the *Encyclopedia*, i.e. the third candlestick from the left in the second row.

Bill and Sue Coleman

CANDLE SNUFFER, (NAVY USED): This candle snuffer came from the U.S.S. TULIP which sank in 1864 when her boilers exploded at the mouth of the Potomac River in the Chesapeake Bay. Forty-eight Union soldiers were killed in the accident. The candle snuffer was recovered by a husband-wife dive team from Virginia in 1985. The brass candle snuffer is 6¼″ long. No markings.

OIL LAMP: A primitive oil lamp which may go as far back as the Revolutionary War. This lamp was operated by placing oil in the bowl and lighting it. Of very crude manufacture, it was made by riveting a heavy iron hasp to a round iron "bowl." This very early lamp was found in Glade Springs, Virginia and probably saw Confederate use.

SHIP'S LAMP: Made of heavy tin and constructed so as to not slant with the motion of the ship. The rim around the lamp is 6¼" in diameter while the lamp proper is 4¾" in diameter. This lamp used a wick and some kind of oil, possibly whale oil, for illumination. The lamp hung in a suspended position only since the bottom of the lamp is rounded and would not have stayed upright on a flat surface.

LOVE TOKEN, CONFEDERATE: This is a "remembrance, love token" presented by a Southern girl to her soldier as he left for the War. It is a 1857 half dime, with seated Liberty and date on one side. The other side has been "cleared" of all markings and the name IDA with a scalloped border has been engraved on the smoothed surface. Two punched holes permitted the owner to wear it on his wrist. Rare and a fine love token dug in General Fitzhugh Lee's North Carolina Cavalry camp near Five Forks, Virginia.

MAP OF A REGIMENTAL CAMP SITE: This 9¼" by 7" map was drawn by a Federal sergeant and sent home by regimental mail. Since all this was done when the regiment was at the front performing picket duty it is all too clear how the sergeant violated a basic principle of military security.

On December 21, 1862, the 14th New Hampshire Infantry, a new regiment, marched into Poolesville, Maryland, where it performed picket duty through the winter of 1862-1863 (the map is misdated; it should be Dec. 29, 1862). The map was the work of Sergeant John W. Sturtevant of Company "G". This careless sergeant rose to the rank of captain by the end of the war.

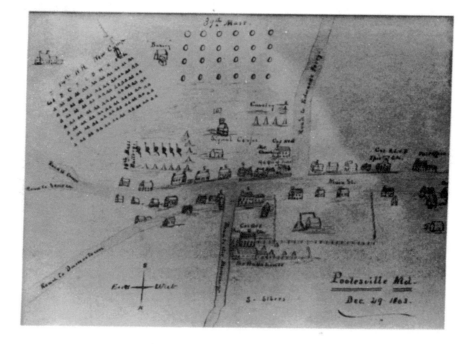

MAP READING INSTRUMENT: This is an extremely rare and interesting item. It was custom-made for use in the field. Such an instrument of the Civil War period was completely unknown to the author until he saw this one (apparently there is at least one other known to its owner). This instrument was used in the planning of marches in major military moves. By its use the commander could decide on the speed of the movement, when to start, how far to go, and the time of arrival at the destination.

The instrument is made of medium weight sheet brass. The distance between the points on the instrument represent the distance on a map covered by a specific group (infantry, cavalry, artillery) of a moving unit. The instrument is 7½" long at the longest part and 5¼" wide at the widest part.

Duffel Peek
(Photo by Overcast Productions, Ltd)

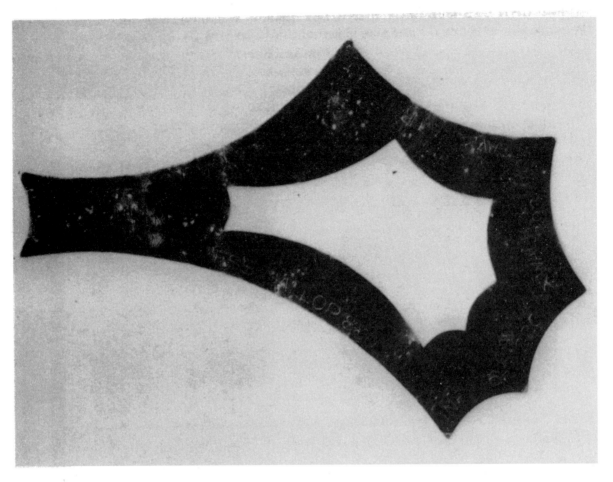

MATCH BOX: This match box was used during the War; in fact it still contains several Civil War matches. The box opens at both ends. Made of hard rubber and is 2¾″ by 1½″ in size. No markings.

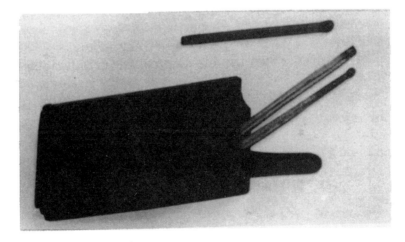

MATCH BOX: This brass match box (54mm × 37mm) was recovered from the Wilderness battlefield. On one side is written:

Milwaukee Beer
is famous
Pabst
has made it so

The other side has the following:

Pabst
Milwaukee   C. H. Merrell

MATCH BOX: The period of this box is debatable; some collectors believe it is post-Civil War. As of this date the author has not been able to definitely establish its use during 1861-1865. The box is exactly the same size as the previous one. This metal specimen is decorated with the U.S. shield, flags, and spears on one side and a wreath flanked by two eagles on the other. It opens at both ends. One end has a ribbed surface for striking the match. No markings.

OHIO: Although the ribbon to this medal is gone, the medal itself is of interest. The obverse shows a female figure holding a wreath over the uncovered head of a soldier. Below are the dates 1861-1865. On the reverse is the legend:

The State of Ohio
to
Albt. H. Mohr
veteran
Co. H 14th Regt
Ohio Volunteer
Inft.

The medal is bronze and is 1⅜″ in diameter.

SOLDIERS' MEDALS: Various types of veterans medals became popular both during and after the War. Several types are shown here.

KEARNY'S BRIGADE: The medal proper is of bronze. The red silk background has gold lettering:

Veteran of Kearny's Brigade

The bronze 6th Corps badge has the following:

First
New Jersey Brigade
Society
1862

Owner is not identified.

NEW JERSEY: An all-bronze medal marked as follows:

(obverse)
1861   1865
Ready to Die for the Honor of
our Country

There is a central motif of an infantryman standing in front of a cannon and a flag.

(Reverse)
2083
Presented by the State of
New Jersey
to
Charles L. Glazer
Veteran
of the Union Forces
in the
Civil War
1861-1865

Private Charles L. Glazer, Co. "L" 1st New Jersey Cavalry, enlisted September 19, 1861 and was wounded in the right hand at Cold Harbor and discharged September 22, 1864.

169th NEW YORK INFANTRY: The bronze medal is attached to a light blue silk ribbon. It is marked:

169 N.Y.S.V.

No identification of this medal's original owner is available. The 169th New York Infantry, as part of the 10th Army Corps, saw very heavy fighting during its term of service, September 1862 to July 1865, losing 618 men killed and wounded.

WEST VIRGINIA: This medal, unlike the Ohio veteran's medal, still has the carrying ribbon of red, white and blue. It has a bronze clasp with the lettering

Honorably discharged
W. V.

The medal proper is the same size as the Ohio medal. Interestingly enough, the motif on the obverse is similar — a female figure crowning the returning soldier. Although also dated 1861-1865, the medals otherwise differ considerably in detail, especially in the backgrounds for the central motif. On the reverse side of the medal is the legend:

Presented
by the
State
of
West Virginia

The recipient of the medal is identified by the following lettering on the medal's edge:

George G. Arnold
Co. B
2nd Vet. Inf.

COMMEMORATION MEDAL: Made of bright copper, 1⅛″ in diameter this medal was probably struck in 1862. On the obverse is depicted the naval fight between the *Monitor* and the *Merrimac* and the caption:

The First Battle Between Iron Clad
War Vessels

The reverse side of the medal has a wreath enclosing the following:

The Rebel Steamer
Merrimac
with
12 guns
Defeated by the
Union Steamer
Monitor
with
2 guns
Hampton Rds. Mar. 9, 1862

COMMEMORATION MEDAL: Like the Monitor medal, this one also is made of bright copper. To whom these medals were issued and in what numbers, is, at the moment, unknown to the writer. This particular medal is about 1″ in diameter. The obverse is decorated with a youthful figure astride an eagle, and the U.S. flag. Underneath is the caption:

Young America
1862

The reverse side has the following:

U. S. Armory
Established
by
Act of Congress
in April
1794
Springfield, Mass.

LINCOLN MEDALS: The Lincoln medals have special significance for Civil War students and collectors. The larger of the two medals shown here is 3⅛″ in diameter and is lettered on the back:

Inaugurated
President
of the
United States
March 4, 1861
Second Term
March 4, 1865
Assassinated
April 14, 1865

The smaller of the two Lincoln medals is 1⅞" in diameter and is lettered:

March 4, 1861
to
April 15, 1865
Emancipation
Proclaimed
Jan. 1, 1863

U. S. Mint
Pollack

Kendall B. Mattern

SURGICAL KITS: Both these kits were used by Ralph Baird McCleary during the War. He was a physician who enlisted as a private in the 1st Missouri Volunteer Engineers. He eventually was promoted to hospital steward, but often served as an assistant surgeon (according to his pension records).

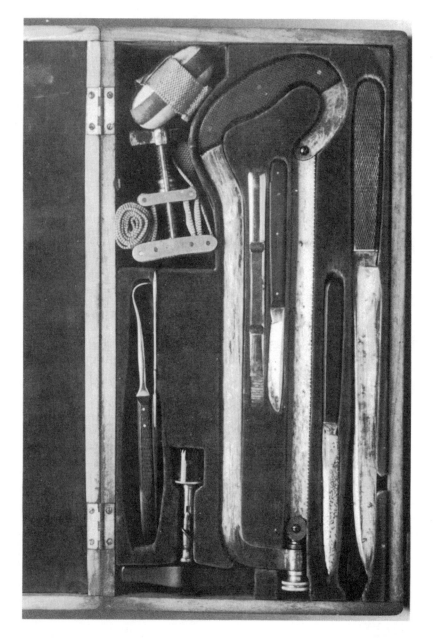

The one-layered kit measures 15½″ long, 8½″ wide and 2⅛″ deep. It is marked Goerck. No information is available to the author on this maker.

Alan R. McBrayer

The two-layered kit measures 16⅜″ long, 6″ wide and 3″ deep. It is marked as having been made by Helmold, an instrument maker at the College of Physicians in Philadelphia.

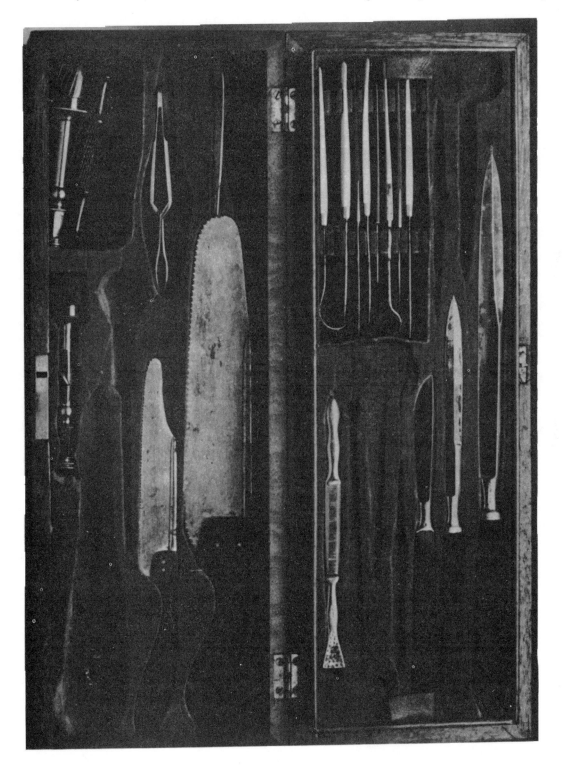

MEDICAL CANTEEN: This is a variation of the medical canteen. It is made of tinned-sheet iron throughout, including the spout. This canteen measures 9 11/16″ by 7⅛″.

Alan R. McBrayer

MEDICAL AND SURGICAL EQUIPMENT

MICROSCOPE: This is a fine brass instrument, 6″ tall, with a 1¾″ diameter base and 1″ at the top. The walnut box is marked on the inside cover:

Paul Roessler
Optician
351 Chapel St.
New Haven, Ct.

Bill and Sue Coleman

SYRINGE: This glass syringe is the type used for irrigation of cuts or wounds. It was not used for injections. The tube is clear glass and the plunger is green glass. It has a cotton pad inside and a pewter screw-on top. When extended the syringe measured 5½″; when closed it is 3¾″.

Alan R. McBrayer

TOOTH EXTRACTORS: These instruments are typical of those in use during the Civil War period. The pliers are plated steel, 7¼" long. They are marked:

F. Arnold, Balt.

The "tooth key" is a vicious instrument, designed to lever out the tooth. It measures 6⅜" long with a 3½" handle. No markings.

Alan R. McBrayer

MEDICAL AND SURGICAL EQUIPMENT

AMBULANCE WATER KEG: The wounded men of both sides needed water. Obviously, the canteens carried on the person by the soldiers were entirely insufficient in number and capacity to meet the demands of the battlefield. Accordingly in the rear of each ambulance under each seat was a water keg with the end containing a faucet situated for quick and easy dispensing of water.

This sturdy oak keg is 20″ long and 8″ in diameter at each end. To fill the keg a brass-lined hole is at the top of the keg. This hole can be closed by a brass cover which is screwed down into the hole. The keg is bound with 6 iron bands and is equipped with a carrying handle and "legs" so that the keg will remain upright on a flat surface. It has a brass faucet and is marked MED. DEPT. on one side and also on one end.

COFFEE POT: The general category of Mess Equipment has been discussed in earlier volumes of the *Encyclopedia.* Although some coffee pots have been shown it is believed that the one here is also of interest. It is quite typical of the tin mess gear which was used so extensively throughout the War. This coffee pot is of heavy tin throughout, including the pouring handle. It has seen extensive use as attested to by the many minor dents and the blackened bottom. It is a large coffee pot 11¾″ tall, 11″ in diameter at the bottom and 6″ at the top.

War mess equipment is almost endless. This cup, made of tin, has a pouring spout with a strainer for use as a coffee-maker. It also functioned as a drinking cup. It is 3⅝″ tall and 4⅛″ in diameter. As is almost invariably the case with Civil War tinware there are no markings.

COPPER CUP: This cup is very probably Confederate. The author has a copper mess plate recovered from the C.S. lines at Port Hudson. The cup shown here came from the Shenandoah Valley, near Staunton, Virginia. The cup is made of medium-weight copper, 4½" tall and the same in diameter. The handle and over-all appearance of this item exactly resembles the usual tin cups of the 1860s.

MESS KIT (U.S.): One of the many varied types of mess kits used by the early volunteers. Only a few were in evidence after the first few months of the War. This one is made of tin, a substance much in use in the mid-19th Century. This mess kit is 5⅛" in diameter and 2½" deep. The kit consists of the pail, a tin cup, and the cover which also served as a plate. The cup nestles smoothly in the pail and is 3¾" in diameter and 2⅛" deep.

MESS KNIFE (C.S.): Most of the cutlery used by the Confederate forces came from the North or from abroad. Domestically made cutlery items are rare in the Confederate South. That some were made is evidenced by this mess knife stamped:

J. Conning
Mobile

The knife is 10″ long with a wooden handle and a 5¼″ blade. It came from Blountville, Tennessee.

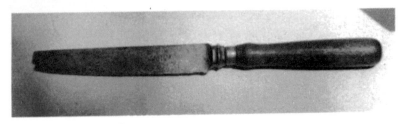

FORKS (C.S.): These two forks are excellent examples of the lack of even basic equipment in some Confederate units. The longer one is 6¼″ in length and made of wood. The shorter is 5⅛″ long and is made of bone. Each fork, home-made or not, is well made. From North Carolina.

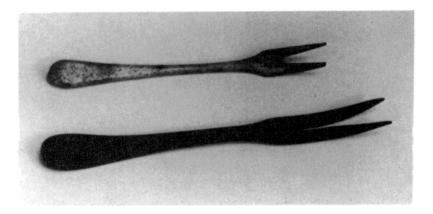

KNIFE-FORK COMBINATION: The overall length of this knife-fork combination is only 6″ when closed. The handles are constructed of "Britania", a metal similar to pewter. Fork and knife are highly polished steel. Both halves slip together to form one small unit. This combination is of high quality construction and is marked:

E. D. Wusthof

The inscription on the handle reads:

Capt. T. Maguire
2nd Reg. U.S. Lt. Art.

Frank J. Panasuk

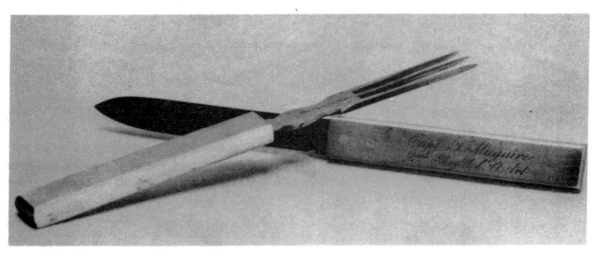

SPOON: General Grant's spoon presented to Ulysses Grant Beath by Mrs. Grant, August 9, 1900. Beath's father, National Commander of the G.A.R. wrote a history of the G.A.R. The son was born the day General Grant was in Philadelphia in 1885. Consequently, the son was named after the General.

Kendall B. Mattern

KNIFE-FORK-SPOON COMBINATIONS: Various types of these have been described in earlier volumes of the Encyclopedia. The two shown here are definitely deluxe types and fall in the category of presentation pieces.

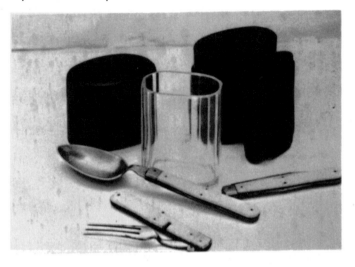

TYPE I. Black oval case 5″ tall and contains a glass liner which can be used as a drinking cup, with three cutlery items: (a) folding spoon, (b) knife, (c) fork-corkscrew combination. All handles are of ivory. Although well made there are no markings on this item.

TYPE II. Round, wooden case, 5½″ tall. The top unscrews. This set includes a silver cup and the following items:

(a) folding spoon, (b) knife, (c) folding fork (but no corkscrew). As with Type I there are no identification of maker on any of the items. However, the silver cup is etched:

Surg.
J. Josiah
22nd
Me. Inf.

This regiment was a nine-month unit, raised in October 1862 and served in the 19th Corps.

SILVER COIN: This was called a "two-bit" piece. It is 26 mm on a side and came from a U.S. camp near Falmouth, Virginia.

C. H. Merrell

CONFEDERATE MONEY LITHOGRAPH FRAGMENT: Here is a fragment from a hand-engraved lithograph stone used by Keatinge and Ball, Columbia, S. C. in printing the backs of 1864 Ten Dollar Confederate notes. This fragment was found by an arrowhead hunter along the Congaree River at Columbia, S. C. It is the only piece known to the individual who found it or to the author.

Leo Redmond

SONG BOOK: Music was very popular with the troops — it was one of the few recreations available. This was true for both instrumental and vocal music. Many types of song books appeared. They were usually small enough to be carried in the pocket. This is a copy of *Army and Navy Melodies*, with its patriotic motif. A chaplain of the 16th Massachusetts Infantry in the field during the 1862 campaign carried this.

Martin J. Fowler

SHEET MUSIC: Sheet music was in extensive use throughout the war. Shown here are examples of both North and South. The *Music of the Union* is 10½" by 13¼" in size and is a "Medley of Nat'l airs for piano arranged by Chas. Grobe." It was published by Oliver Ditson and Co., 277 Washington St., Boston, Mass. The lithographer was J. H. Bufford, of Boston.

The Confederate specimen was "Dedicated to Jefferson Davis" and is entitled Confederacy March. The music is by Alfred F. Toulmin and the photograph of Davis is by McClees of Washington, D. C. The size is 10" by 13". Published by George Willig of Baltimore in 1861.

Bill and Sue Coleman

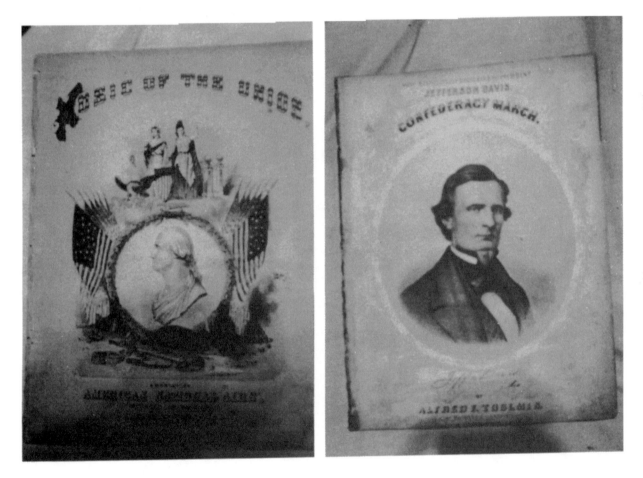

CONCERTINA: This type of accordion, is of light wood, 10¼″ long and 5½″ wide. It is marked: Universal Accordion

It was carried during the War by Justin Follis, Co. "G" 87th U.S. Colored Troops. Follis enlisted at Carrollton, Louisiana, on May 29, 1863. He was born in Louisiana, and was 27 years old at the time of his enlistment. He was 5′6″ tall and a laborer by trade. Tragedy struck this soldier. On August 23, 1865, while still in service, he accidentally fell overboard and was drowned in the Red River, Louisiana.

Bill and Sue Coleman

FIDDLE: Music, both vocal and instrumental, was a very popular source of inspiration and enjoyment in camp. Harmonicas were probably the most commonly used because they were easily carried and were not expensive. Some soldiers took violins to war and some even made their own. Here is a home-made "fiddle," probably pine wood, which was used by J. Williams, Co. "D", 1st Maine Cavalry.

Michael Hammerson

NAVY REPAIR KIT: This sailor's sail and rope repair kit was used during the War by Ordinary Seaman J. E. Adams of New Hampshire. He served in the Mississippi Flotilla on the U.S.S. *OHIO, Maria Denning* and *Benton.* The kit was stored in a small canvas bag, decorated with light and dark brown stripes. The contents consist of: a bamboo needle case with 8 iron needles; 2 pieces of beeswax to waterproof the ropes; a leather palm punch for driving needles through canvas; a collection of zinc rings which were used as sliding rings on halyards; an iron spike with a flat head for punching leather; a wooden-handled awl; and a copper spike on a thumb lanyard for splicing rope.

Michael Hammerson

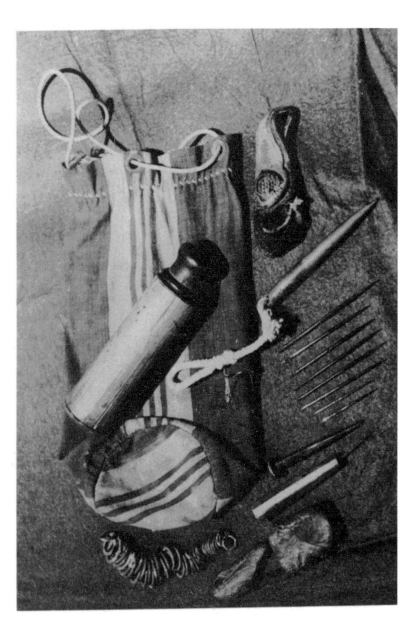

NAVY SAILMAKER'S KIT

SAILMAKER'S KIT: This is a regulation Navy sailmaker's kit, stamped U.S.N. 1860. It consists of a tube to hold needles used to repair sails and leather items. Four needles came with the tube. Also shown is a sailor's thumbstall of leather with the outline of an anchor impressed in the brass thimble.

Martin J. Fowler

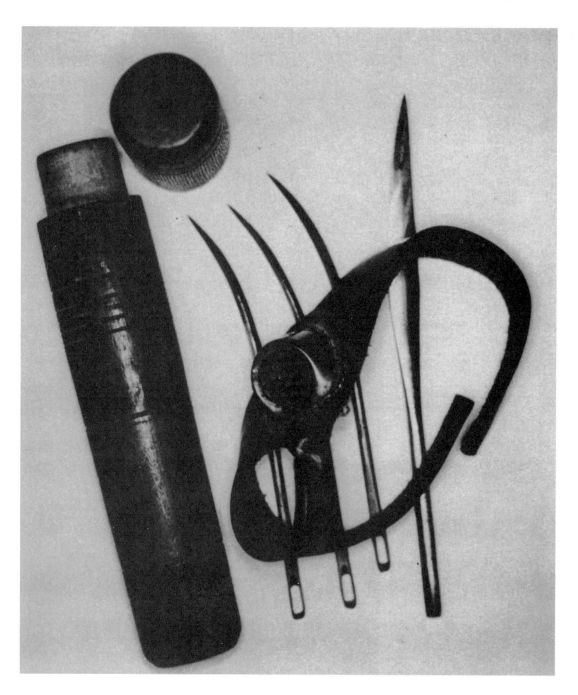

NECKTIE: Photographs of the 1861-1865 period clearly show that neckties were very commonly worn with the uniform. But apparently very few of these neckties have survived to the present day. The one shown here is the first seen by the author. It is a colorful affair, red silk with black polkadots. It is 32½″ long and 1″ wide. The ends are pointed since it was intended to be tied as a bow tie. The necktie gradually widens out from the part going around the neck to the tips.

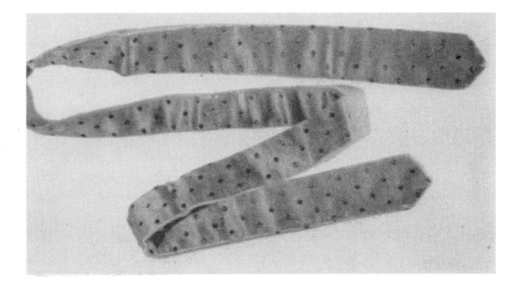

NEEDLE CASES. Not to be confused with the "housewife" these cases are for needles only. Both shown are of red leather. The larger one is 3⅛″ by 2¼″; the smaller is 2½″ by 2″ at the widest parts.

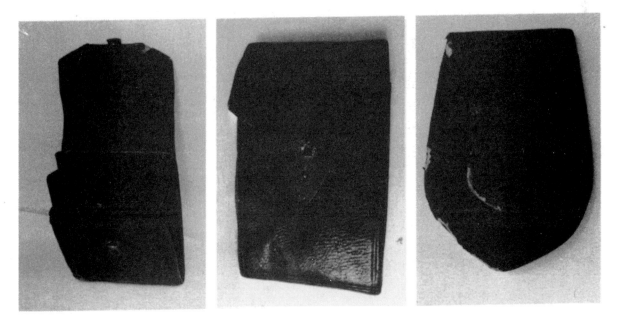

PAINT SET

PAINT SET: This watercolor paint set is a type carried in the field by soldiers and artists accompanying the troops in campaign. The case is of solid walnut, 6¼" by 2½" in size. The set includes 4 brushes with feather quill stems and small decorative cakes of varying solid colors.

Martin J. Fowler

PATRIOTIC PIN: This fine gold-plated pin was made by B. T. Heyward, Manufacturing Jeweler, 203 Broadway, New York. It is decorated with a spread eagle at the top and cannon with a stack of cannon balls at the bottom. The center is a photograph of a general surrounded by 12 oval discs, each engraved with a battle and its date. These presumably are battles in which this unidentified general participated. This is a very unusual patriotic pin.

Robert G. Borrell, Sr.

PATRIOTIC PIN: This is a sailor's commemorative pin — "Our Little Monitor." A copper token has been drilled to be attached to a standard eagle pin of the period. While the image of the U.S. ironclad vessel is upside down, the reverse has a wreath encircling the date, 1863, right side up.

John A. Stacey

PATRIOTIC PIN: This brass patriotic pin is of Kossouth (Hungarian revolutionary patriot) holding the American flag and shield. On the shield is the word UNION and on the flag the word CONSTITUTION.

James Stamatelos

PENSION LETTER: This is a 3-page pension letter from Dennis Harrington of the U.S.S. MIAMI. He was wounded by a piece of the same shell which killed Commander Charles W. Flusser of the MIAMI, April 19, 1864, in an engagement with the Confederate *Albermarle.* Shown also in the background is the U.S.S. MIAMI.

Martin J. Fowler

NON-REGULATION GROUPING: These items were carried in the field by a Federal officer. They are typical of the Civil War period and include a writing kit, large stencil, Bible, "Carte de visite" of the Federal officer, razor, etc. The original owner of these items was Augustine W. Clough, a First Lieutenant of Co. "H" 13th Maine Infantry. Clough was mustered in that rank at Augusta, Maine on December 12, 1861. He enlisted as a private at age 30 on October 14, 1861. He was promoted to Captain April 28, 1862.

Photographed by Glenn Riegel, Andy D'Angelo Photography, Reading, Pa.

Gary Wolfer

PILL BOX: This beautiful item is probably a pill box. Of special interest, of course, is the eagle motif on the cover. It is 1¼" on each side.

Scott Kerr

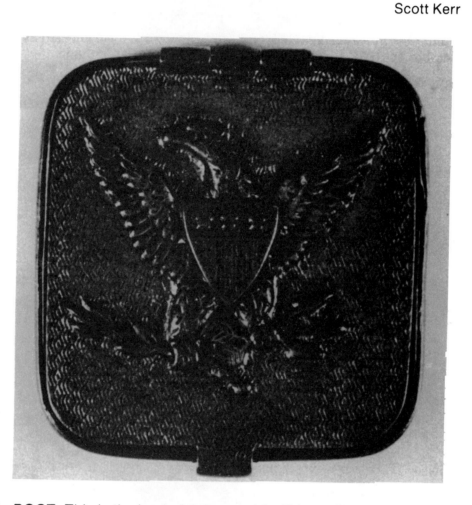

PISTOL, BOOT: This is the boot pistol carried by Private Clement Newton Bassett of the 8th Texas Cavalry (Terry's Texas Rangers). It has been stated that this unit was the most heavily engaged cavalry unit of either side during the War. "Clem" Bassett was the personal scout of General Joseph Wheeler and was voted a medal by the C. S. Congress for valor but the medal was never struck nor bestowed. Bassett was shot in the head during a battle near Aiken, S.C. in January 1865. The bullet passed through his hat; the hat itself is now in the Museum of the Confederacy in Richmond. Bassett survived his wound. The pistol is .44 caliber, smoothbore, and is marked *Anderson Texas* on top of the barrel. The grips are of ivory and are inscribed:

C. Bassett 8th Texas Cav.

and bear the Texas Ranger star and the date 1862.

Frank J. Panasuk

PROPAGANDA LEAFLETS (No picture): Since 1914 the general public has become increasingly aware of the important role of propaganda in war. The employment of aircraft to drop leaflets across the lines, often to induce enemy soldiers to surrender or desert, has become too frequent a practice to merit special attention. Certainly a pioneer in this practice was General Benjamin F. Butler during the Civil War. A war correspondent, Charles A. Page, writing a letter from the General's headquarters on July 16, 1864, told of Butler sending up kites carrying hundreds of copies of Lincoln's "Amnesty Proclamation." The kites were sent up when the wind was "right" to carry them over the enemy's lines. As a result, deserters did come into Butler's lines, induced by a "o' lot o' han' bills thet kim down from o' big kite thet scooted over whar we war." The deserters were intelligent, if illiterate, and they had decided to come over by the Amnesty Proclamation. As the war correspondent put it in his letter: [these copies of the Proclamation] . . . "like the quality of mercy which is not strained, droppeth to the Rebels like the gentle rain — droppeth not from clouds, but from kites."

DOUBLE PULLEY - NAVY (bronze hardware): This extremely rare Naval double pulley is a U.S. Navy Ordnance Department issue. It weighs 21 pounds, is bronze and dated 1862. This type was used with Dahlgren guns. It is marked.

USNYW
Ord. Dep
1862

The initials stand for the United States Navy Yard Washington.

Martin J. Fowler

DOUBLE PULLEY - NAVY (iron hardware): On page 151 is a double pulley of wood with iron hardware. It is 12″ overall. It is stamped USNYW, 1862, and an anchor. This pulley was used to run guns in and out and was used with Dahlgren and Parrott cannon on board ship.

Martin J. Fowler

RAILROAD RELIC: On August 26, 1862 the Confederates attacked the great Federal supply depot at Manassas Junction. The small Federal force was easily dispersed and the Confederates wrought havoc in the depot including wholesale destruction of railroad rolling stock and rails. The rails, themselves, were twisted to render them useless. Shown here is a section of one of the rails thus destroyed. This particular rail is the model known as the 1855 Pear Rail and was found by a Northern Railway employee one day while he was repairing track. The piece is 3⅜″ high on a 3¼″ wide base.

RECRUITING CARD: Most recruiting appeals were to be found on large posters which were of the dimensions which could be easily read. They were put up on public buildings such as town halls and recruiting depots. This notice is only 4½″ long and 3¼″ wide. The glossy white card is printed in blue and red ink. Note that it emphasizes the bounties offered as well as the names and locations of recruiting officers.

James Stamatelos

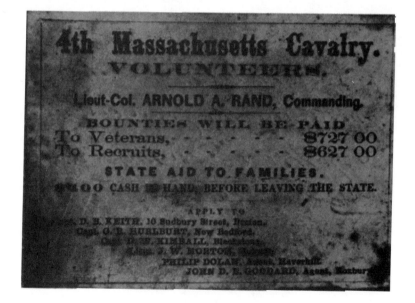

ELECTION NOTICE: This recruiting broadside is a notice of election to a regiment in 1861. Issued by the Colonel (Rush C. Hawkins), this rare broadside was for membership in the 9th New York Infantry, better known as "Hawkins Zouaves." It is 5" by 8".

Martin J. Fowler

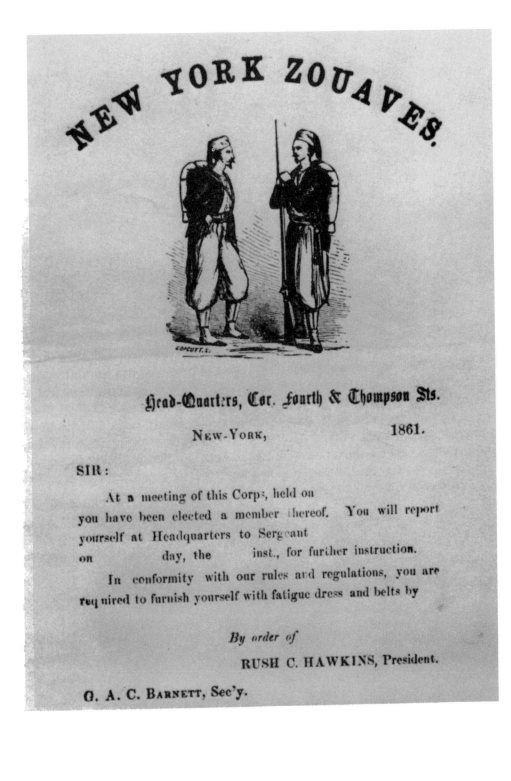

ROSARY: This Rosary, recovered on the Wilderness battlefield is in excellent shape. It has a silver cross and brass figure. The 30″ chain is of metal.

Bill and Sue Coleman

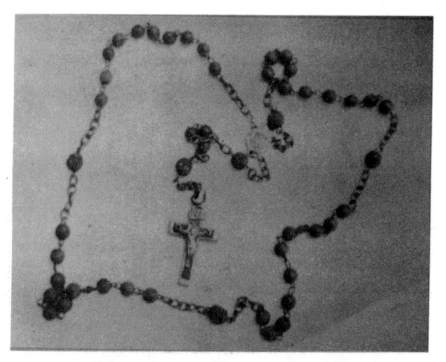

ROSETTES (Artillery): These are from the bridle of the horse ridden by Captain J. B. Hubbard, 1st Maine Battery, while serving as an aide to General Godfrey Weitzel. Hubbard was on this horse when he was killed in action at Port Hudson, Mississippi. None of the rosettes was damaged when Hubbard was hit. Each rosette is 2¼″ in diameter; each brass star is 1⅜″ wide at the widest point. The rosettes were part of a semi-military bridle purchased from a commercial harness dealer. The rosettes are comparatively rare but the author has seen a few similar specimens. The rosettes have a brass rim with the brass stars set on a red background.

ROSETTES (C.S.): These are rare and unique bridle rosettes. The author has never seen any of similar appearance and size. They are of iron and came from Augusta, Georgia. Apart from the CS their size is likewise unusual in that they are larger than most Civil War rosettes. These are 2¼″ in diameter.

ROSETTE (C.S.): A small C.S. rosette was recently found in a C.S. camp in South Carolina. The rosette is in too deteriorated condition to be shown in a photograph. However, if it is of interest in that it has C.S.A. in old English letters. The rosette is of brass and is 1⅛″ in diameter.

ROSTER POEM OF A MAINE COMPANY: This is printed on heavy paper giving a poetical version of the roll of Company "F", 10th Maine Infantry. Surely a unique item. The poem reminds one of those contributed by fraternity brothers at college functions or "inflicted" on returning alumni at a commencement or reunion. Evidently the poem was composed before the 10th Maine saw action. It fought extremely well and suffered heavy losses at Cedar Mountain. The poem closed with the promise that if "Death take some of us . . . we'll look to yonder land above . . . we'll tell their friends how brave they died . . ."

Kendall B. Mattern

SADDLE (C.S.): This Williams saddle was used by John Morrison, a courier with Mosby in the War. Morrison first enlisted at Staunton, Virginia, and served under Jackson but was wounded in the leg in the Shenandoah Valley campaign. On recovery from his wound, which was severe enough to keep him out of the infantry, he joined Mosby's rangers. At that time he was presented with this saddle by the widow of its former owner who had been killed in action serving with Jeb Stuart. Morrison gave the saddle to its present owner about 1930.

J. L. Downey

SASH BUCKLE: Due to their fragile construction, sash buckles are rarely recovered in complete condition. The author has several fragments of these buckles from Civil War sites. This one is from the battlefield of Stone's River, Tennessee, December 31, 1862-January 2, 1863. It is the typical 2-piece buckle of thin brass and measures 2¾″ when closed. The eagle-decorated center piece is 1⅛″ in diameter.

SHIRTS: These essential items of wear were of all patterns and material. Typical of such variety are the two shown here. One is of wool, 30″ long, with 20″ sleeves. The neck, sleeves and bottom are trimmed in red. The other shirt, made for an officer is thin cotton, 32″ long, with 23½″ sleeves. The shirt has no standing collar and the front is pleated.

SLIPPERS: Obviously very few of these survived the war! In fact, only a few officers bothered to take house slippers into the field. But here is a pair of "officer's camp slippers." A similar pair can be seen in the Gettysburg Visitors Center Museum.This pair is 10″ long with narrow toes. These slippers have leather soles but cloth uppers. They lace up on the sides.

TOE PLATE: This unusual toe plate was found in the path of the Yankee advance on the Confederates about 200 yards where they clashed with the enemy on Rich Mountain, Virginia, July 11, 1861. It is iron, 5″ long and 1 5/16″ high. No markings. A ridge ½″ high runs around the complete length of the toe plate.

Ray and Jean Smarr

SHOE HEEL AND TOE PLATES: Now that most of the exotic relics have been dug up on camp sites and battlefields the collector regretfully gives up on concentrating on such items as belt buckles and now looks for "new fields to conquer." One of these fields is to be found in the vast variety of heel and toe plates. Shown here are a few of the many types used.

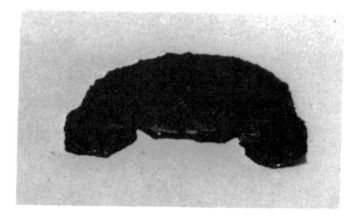

HEEL AND TOE PLATES:

(reading left to right)

Row 1 — Port Hudson | C.S. Camp Marshall Texas | Nashville | C.S. Camp Mill Springs Kentucky | Antietam

Row 2 — Nashville | Vicksburg 26th La. Inf. | Antietam | C.S. Port Hudson | Port Hudson

Row 3 — Seven Days' Battle | Atlanta | Chancellorsville | Spotsylvania | Atlanta

Row 4 — Ft. Peyton Florida | Savannah | Fredericksburg | Nashville | U.S. Camp La Grange Tennessee

Row 5 — Antietam | C.S. Marshall Texas | (3) Battle of Mansfield, La.

Row 6 — Battle of Mansfield, La. | Fredericksburg | Petersburg | Battle of Double Bridges, La., Apr. 3, 1864 | Fredericksburg

Row 7 — Pleasant Hill La. | 92nd N.Y. Inf. Ft. Anderson N.C. Mar. 14, 1863 | C.S. Arsenal Marshall, Texas | (2) Resaca, Georgia

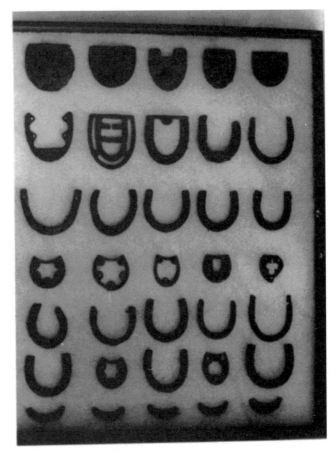

SHOULDER STRAPS (Ames): These Civil War shoulder straps are made of stamped brass and were from the effects of the Ames Manufacturing Company. The straps are ready for the cloth background and are in mint, unused condition. Each strap has 6 prongs for attaching the cloth and the coat or jacket. They are 4″ long and 1½″ wide. The brass is bright enough to look like gold.

SHOULDER STRAPS (Bent and Bush's Military Establishment): The colonel shoulder straps shown here are somewhat unique in that they are identified as to the firm which produced them. The paper label on the back of each strap reads:

From Bent and Bush's Military
Establishment/Corner of Court
and Washington Sts. Boston

This firm was located at the above address from 1850 to 1867. In 1868 it moved to 273-275 Washington Street and in 1875 it moved to 447 Washington Street. The straps themselves, have the stamped metal borders with large silver eagles. The backing material in front is a rather lush velvet-like fabric which is deep yellow in color.

James R. Blaine

SHOULDER STRAPS (Robinson's patent): Shown here is a pair of shoulder straps of "Robinson's Patent". Gideon Robinson, New York City, patented this item December 2, 1862. It consisted of a border of coiled wire upon a mandril (or spindle) of half-round shape. Both straps are marked on the back with maker and patent date. The backing material on the front side and straps is gold lace, like the straps described in the 1864 Schuyler, Hartley and Graham catalog: "gold lace centre for cavalry." The borders are of fancy gold bullion, as are the captain's bars.

James R. Blaine

INFANTRY CAPTAIN'S SHOULDER STRAPS: The straps are 5" long and 2½" wide. Light blue background denoting Infantry, with gold border and gold captain's bars. These straps are "as manufactured" and have not been cut from the surrounding border, which is a black felt-like material ½" wide on all sides.

James R. Blaine

CAVALRY MAJOR'S SHOULDER STRAPS: The straps are 4¾" long and 2⅛" wide. The background material is a lush dark yellow. The triple borders are alternating colors; the outer is silver, the middle is gold and the inner is silver. The major's leaf in each case is gold.

James R. Blaine

STAFF CAPTAIN'S SHOULDER STRAPS: These are "Smith's Patent" shoulder straps. They have heavy stamped brass borders and captain's bars. The straps are 4" long and 2" wide. The background of each strap is a lush black velvet material.

James R. Blaine

SHOULDER STRAPS (Hospital Corps?): These straps are 5" long and 2" in width. The central field of the straps is steel blue velvet, bearing Old English letters "H. C." in silver. No one has yet been able to definitely identify the significance of the letters. Possibly they stand for Hospital Corps, a civilian organization which was formed in 1862 to assist the Federal Army's medical service. However, the civilians in this "Corps" lacked the essential characteristics of honesty and sobriety and the organization was soon disbanded.

James R. Blaine

SHOULDER INSIGNIA (U. S. Navy): Shown here are both epaulettes and shoulder straps of a lieutenant. The set is unusual in that it was manufactured in England and is so marked on both epaulettes and shoulder straps. The importer's label reads:

From Wabnock & Co.
519 Broadway
New York

The japanned tin storage box measures 8⅝" wide, 6" high and 6" deep.

Alan R. McBrayer

SHOULDER STRAPS (Navy): The corps device without rank insignia represented this grade until early 1864. At that time, it was assigned to Second Assistant Engineers and later to Third Assistant Engineers as relative rank increased for Engineers.

John A. Stacey

SHOULDER STRAP - NAVAL LINE LIEUTENANT 1864-1878: Lieutenants were assigned two gold bars to show rank, along with their corps device, in 1862 and the smaller style anchor was introduced in 1864. The gold bars were replaced by silver in 1878.

John A. Stacey

SHOULDER STRAP - NAVAL PAYMASTER (UNDER 12 YEARS) 1861-1864: Paymasters with less than twelve years service held relative rank with Line Lieutenants. The Corps device of three oak leaves and acorns without rank devices represents the grade.

John A. Stacey

FULL DRESS EPAULETS - NAVAL LINE LIEUTENANT 1852-1862: The large anchor device was adopted for Line Lieutenants in 1852. These epaulets, worn by Lt. James A. Doyle, have the device in stamped metal. In 1862, the position of the anchor was changed from horizontal to vertical in the center of the pad to allow space for rank devices.

John A. Stacey

SHOULDER STRAP - NAVAL LINE LIEUTENANT 1852-1862; Naval Line Ensign 1862-1864: The rank of Ensign was introduced into the Navy in 1862 and was assigned the anchor device used by Lieutenants since 1852. The large size anchor was discontinued in 1864 in favor of a smaller style. This strap has a metal border and device on a black velvet backing.

John A. Stacey

170 SIGNAL CANNON

SIGNAL CANNON: This is the quarter deck signal cannon from the U.S.S. WABASH, flagship of Admiral Dupont during the Civil War. It weighs 70 pounds, having a 24" barrel with a bore of 1⅞". It is 28" long overall. The barrel is of cast iron; the mountings are of brass and nickle-plated brass. The carriage is of oak and is a perfect representation of a U.S. Navy marsilly carriage. The quality of the material and workmanship of this signal cannon is high; it very probably was the personal property of Admiral Dupont because of its superior quality over other Civil War signal cannons.

Frank J. Panasuk

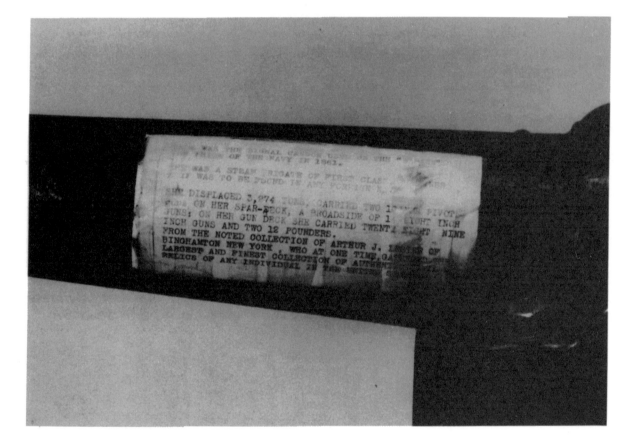

SIGNAL LANTERN: This lantern, made of tole tin, is 6½″ tall and 3½″ in diameter. Has folding wire handles and a glass lens measuring 2¾″ in diameter. Equipped to use whale oil. This lantern was carried by a Sergeant Peck, 7th Connecticut Infantry and issued to him as special equipment for the amphibious assaults at Forts Fisher and Wagner.

James Samatelos

Note: This lantern description is included in this volume because it has been identified as having been used in the field. Some doubt previously existed about the designation "Signal Lantern" as discussed on p. 73 of Vol. III of the *Encyclopedia*.

SLAVE TAG: Extremely rare today are the metal tags worn around the neck of slaves for identification purpose. The author has seen several of a similar type — heavy brass and rectangular in shape. This example is 2″ long and 1″ wide. On one side is stamped:

Moore
Plantation
Pitt, N.C.

On the other side is stamped:

36
1858
Lousia 20

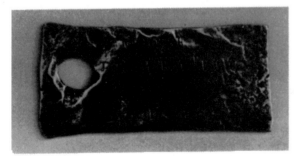

SNIPER'S RIFLE: This is a .38 caliber, heavy sniper's rifle, weighing 14 pounds. The overall length is 47″, barrel length is 31″. It is stocked in highly-figured walnut and has a back action percussion lock. The lockplate, upper tang, breech, trigger guard, and buttplate are engraved with a panoply of arms. The top of the barrel is marked:

W. Billinghurst
Rochester, N.Y.

Also on the left side of the barrel is marked:

C. E. Young. Co. S.S. 112 R.N.Y.S.V.

Frank J. Panasuk

SOUVENIRS: Americans are inveterate souvenir gatherers. It is fortunate that this was true for the Civil War soldiers of both sides for many items have survived because of eager souvenir hunters. Souvenirs fall into several categories based primarily on the method of acquisition. I. Battlefield collecting and looting: The first and most obvious category is the souvenir picked up on the battlefield or liberated from a private dwelling place or public building. It is well known that Confederate commanders picked a battlefield clean after their enemy had left the combat area. The Federals also brought in captured weapons and equipment. After Malvern Hill, Federal stragglers returned to their regiments bringing in all types of weapons. On inspection, the officers found that in the same regiments "there had been collected every caliber and pattern known in the service: the Springfield, Harper's Ferry, Sharp's, Burnside, Maynard, Enfield, Tower, Belgian, French, Richmond, Palmetto, etc. . . . men who [had] lost their own . . . [appropriated] their neighbors. When not of the caliber of the regiment, . . . [the muskets] were turned in, assorted, and re-issued. [In this way] . . . each regiment, brigade, and division, if possible . . . [was] armed alike." Needless to say, many soldiers managed to keep the weapons they personally had captured.

At Camp Jackson in St. Louis, the Federals captured 1200 "best U.S. rifled muskets . . . a magnificant arm . . . stamped U.S. 1861 . . ." probably made about March or April of that year.

Later in the War, when the Federals were well equipped with infantry weapons, commanders would occasionally order captured weapons be destroyed. For example, a company of the 123rd Ohio Infantry was ordered to destroy all the muskets left on the battlefield of Piedmont (Hunter's 1864 campaign). The regiment collected 1250 muskets and rifles, put them in piles on top of piles of fence rails, and set the whole on fire. Although repeatedly cautioned to lay the pieces so that their muzzles would all point in the same direction, the men became careless and some of them were seriously wounded by the discharge of the arms when heated by the fire.

Many souvenir hunters did their collecting by themselves. Such a man was James Burrows of Company "H" 16th Massachusetts Infantry. On the field of Spotsylvania he collected relics from various parts of the battlefield — pieces of fallen oak trees and bullets from the tree, bits of exploded shells and odd-shaped bullets, badges from caps showing the different corps involved in the battle. In the lines of the 9th Corps he saw something shining in the bed of a little brook. It proved to be the hilt of a sergeant's sword. On drawing it out of the mud and removing the scabbard, the blade proved to be clean and shiny.

Sometimes relics were returned to interested parties of the other side. For instance, a button cut by a Confederate soldier on the battlefield of Second Bull Run, August 31, 1862, from the coat of Colonel Fletcher Webster, 12th Massachusetts Infantry, was presented to the Fletcher Webster GAR Post 13 of Brockton, Massachusetts, March 29, 1883. Colonel Webster was found dying by Jesse Burley, Company "H" 19th Virginia Infantry. Burley cared for the Colonel, and in return for his kindness, the dying officer gave him a ring from his finger — an old family keepsake. This ring was returned to Webster's widow after the War. Burley also donated the button to Post 13.

The fine action of Burley was comparatively rare. More common was looting and stealing. Late in 1864 Federal 5th Corps headquarters took possession of a fine house one night and Headquarters personnel took three haversack loads of books from the fine library in the house. One soldier took a 7-volume edition of Josephus' works, Homer and Herodotus in Greek, a Greek grammar, an edition of Cabell's *History of Races in Man*, and three or four other books.

While on transports, men of the 128th New York Infantry visited the wrecks of the CUMBERLAND and the CONGRESS. This visit was on September 12, 1862, some months after the sinking of these obsolete ships by the ironclad MERRIMAC. The men got many small trophies, including spikes, pieces of sails and even flags.

Earlier, in June 1862, the 51st Pennsylvania Infantry was assigned the duty of guarding the tomb of a Revolutionary War officer — a General Speight. Despite a vigilant guard detail the tomb was destroyed by relic hunters. The handsome marble slab that covered the coffin, and contained the birth, death and military service of the deceased, was broken into fragments and carried off, leaving the coffin exposed to full view.

Even more macabre was the action of relic hunters involving a Confederate spy hanged on the outskirts of Frederick, Maryland, just after Gettysburg. The spy's body was still hanging from the tree when the 149th New York Infantry marched by in pursuit of Lee's retreating army. Every one of the 149th wanted a souvenir from this C.S. spy. By the time the unit had passed, the clothes had been removed from the dead man, piece by piece, except a small portion of his shirt around his neck. The tree on which he had been hanged had also commenced to disappear. The knees of the dead spy were drawn up; portions of the body were badly swollen and putrefied. "The sight was loathsome, disgusting and sufficient for a lifetime."

2. Exchanging or "Swapping": A second major source of souvenirs was exchanges between Federals and Confederates. Sometimes this was done between captor and captured. The day after the battle of Williamsburg, May 5, 1862, Lieutenant Samuel L. Hughes and Sergeant Richard G. Rogers, Co. "C" 93rd Pennsylvania Infantry visited a hospital for wounded Confederate prisoners in Williamsburg and exchanged some of their buttons for Virginia buttons and other relics which they thought might please the folks at home. Sometimes captured swords were returned. At the battle of Ball's Bluff, October 21, 1861, Lieutenant J. Evarts Greene of the 15th Massachusetts Infantry surrendered to Captain O. R. Singleton of the 13th Mississippi Infantry. At the same time the Lieutenant turned over his sword to Singleton. After the War Singleton returned the sword to Greene as a token of good will.

But it was on the picket line that most exchanges took place. Picket lines were established to prevent communication with the enemy and especially to give advance warning of an attack. A front picket line was supported by a rear line, composed of sentinels working in pairs, prepared to assist the front line in case of emergency. In the rear of this second line was a reserve force. Each sentinel remained on guard two hours and then was relieved. He was on duty one-third of the time he was on picket. At the reserve posts, crude shelters were built and usually the men could have fires for warmth. In order to reach his post the picket often had to travel 5 and even more miles and then commence his 2-hour watch.

It was on these extended picket lines that the best opportunities for swapping souvenirs took place. Often an informal truce between the combatants was agreed to and then the exchanges began. During the winter of 1862-1863 pickets on both sides at Fredericksburg sent small boats and even rafts across the Rappahannock River carrying tobacco from the Confederates in exchange for coffee and salt from the Federals. Newspapers also were desirable items of exchange.

It should be pointed out that in all theaters of the War these exchanges took place. Violations of the informal truces were about zero. The enlisted men of both sides would not permit their officers to violate a truce, even if the officers had been so inclined. It is a remarkable tribute to the sense of fair play among the enlisted personnel of both sides.

Belt buckles were in demand — especially in the early months of the War. In the Fall of 1861, Federal pickets exchanged various articles with Confederate pickets and among these articles swapped were C.S. caps with AVC letters (Alabama Volunteer Cadets). At these truces the pickets laid down their arms, went up to each other, shook hands, talked and swapped articles. Then they returned to their lines and picked up their muskets, ready for combat again.

Near Cedar Mountain, Virginia, pickets of the 111th Pennsylvania Infantry found their Confederate counterparts to be quite friendly. When the officers were at a safe distance the trading would begin. These veteran enemies would steal out of their rifle pits, quietly wade into midstream of the river separating them and complete their "deals" like two schoolboys. And not a shot would be heard until they were safely back in their own lines.

At Batchelder's Creek, North Carolina, the dog mascot of the 23rd Massachusetts Infantry, by the name of Chapple, strayed into the Confederate lines and was gone for several weeks. One day word came in from the Confederates that a dog with the name of Chapple on the collar was in their possession and they were willing to exchange the dog for some tobacco. The exchange was made to the mutual satisfaction of Federals and Confederates, alike.

News and jokes were exchanged as well as items. On Folly Island, South Carolina, the Confederate pickets would tell the Yankee pickets about any battle news which the Yankees had not heard. On one occasion a Confederate picket remarked to the Federals that General Beauregard had such an exalted opinion of the Yankees on Folly Island that he was coming over to visit them and give each Federal "a farm six feet by two."

At Bermuda Hundred, in June 1864, soldiers of both sides established a temporary truce. While the truce was underway, the Confederates would say: "if we-uns are ordered to fire, we'll fire high at first so you-uns can get to cover." When their officers were about to break the truce the Confederate enlisted men would say: "Get into your ditches, Yanks, our folks are going to shell your camps."

In another exchange the opponents would permit their adversaries certain privileges. At Wapping Heights, men of the 144th New York Infantry got permission from their enemies to fish in a stream which separated the opposing forces. After fishing, the Federals would meet with the Confederates and exchange coffee for Richmond papers.

On the Bermuda Hundred front during the winter of 1864-65 the weather was very cold. At Christmas time a Confederate called to a soldier in the 2nd Pennsylvania Heavy Artillery to lend him an axe to cut some wood as he and his fellow soldiers were nearly frozen. The axe was thrown over into the Confederate line. A short time later it was returned in good order.

The winter continued to be a very cold one. On New Year's Day, 1865, fuel was scarce on both sides along the Petersburg front. The only fuel left was in No Man's Land between the opposing forces. A truce was established and squads of men of both armies marched toward each other, armed only with axes to cut down the timber. When the two sides met they shook hands, exchanged articles, and questioned each other about the war. Then they all went to work cutting up the trees. After dividing the wood they carried it back to their respective lines.

During the siege of Chattanooga, a Federal soldier got permission to retrieve a horse which had run into the Confederate lines. Permission was granted; he got his horse. As he rode back to his lines, three Confederate horses which had been feeding on the same ground ran into the Federal lines. These horses were caught and promptly driven back to their Confederate owners.

3. Items made for souvenir collectors: During the war, soldiers made souvenirs with their own hands, usually either to pass away long periods of inactivity in camp or, if prisoners of war, to be used to trade for food.

In the first category was Spencer Tuthill of the 20th New York State Militia. Tuthill was a fine mechanic and an artist in carving. He showed his ingenuity in carving beef bones; his work was well-nigh perfect. On one occasion he carved the figure of a woman on the outside of a finger ring; it was perfectly formed and extended all the way around the ring. While the men of another New York regiment, 149th Infantry, were at Brooks Station, Virginia, in April 1863, they became very proficient in the manufacture of pipes, rings, and small ornaments from the root of a shrub known as "Laurel" which grew plentifully in the camp area. The men also made many ornaments from bones; these were beautifully inlaid with colored sealing wax. Many friends of the regiment's rank and file received treasured souvenirs sent home by the men who spent many hours on these carvings.

Federal prisoners at Camp Ford, Tyler, Texas, displayed great skill in their work. A captured Federal naval officer made primitive but workable turning lathes. He was assisted by an army lieutenant. These lathes, in turn, were used to turn out checkers and chessmen — which were then finished off by a jack knife. These game pieces were attractive enough to find ready buyers among both prisoners and guards.

At Point Lookout, Confederate prisoners made various items, not only to pass the time away but also as a source of revenue. They made rings, brooches, watch chains, and a great number of other items from bone and Gutta Percha. They sold many of their items to their captors, 2nd New Hampshire Infantry, as well as other prison guard units. Some of the items made were amazing! One Confederate prisoner made a clock which kept excellent time. The front and back were made from the sides of a tin canteen. Another soldier built a stationary steam engine, perfect in all its parts. A young Alabamian, using only such materials as could be found in the prison, made a perfect locomotive which actually pulled a miniature train of cars around the circular track, made specially for this train. So unique and perfect was this train that a Federal officer purchased it and sent it home to his children, paying the soldier well for it.

"MERRIMAC" GAVEL: During and after the War soldiers and civilians alike delighted in making useful items from famous military and naval objects and historic sites — Bricks from Libby Prison, pieces of stockade from Andersonville, pieces of wood from the Marshall house in Alexandria, etc. Just as famous ships like the U.S.S. CONSTITUTION of the war of 1812, so it was with famous vessels of 1861-65. Many people wanted a piece of a particular man-of-war. When ships were sold for scrap after the War enterprising individuals would cut up the wood and metal into small sections and sell them to ex-servicemen and patriotic organizations.

The object shown here is a wooden gavel, 8½" long to the end of the handle with an old brass plate affixed to the block of wood, reading:

Piece of the Rebel Ram
"VIRGINIA"
Formerly The
USS MERRIMAC

SOUVENIRS: The snuff box is still filled with snuff. Marked on front of the box is C. Parker's 1860 Patent.

The copy of a U.S. belt buckle is "made from mud taken from the creek at Petersburg, Virginia". This unique souvenir came from the old GAR Post in Brattleboro, Vermont. An accompanying photograph shows the reverse of this mud "buckle."

Marius B. Peladeau

SOUVENIRS: Each of the three items in this grouping is of interest to the Civil War collector. The handmade camp mirror is marked U.S. The brass covered tin box was used to hold ink pen tips and is embossed with pen tip on the cover. The hard rubber pipe is decorated with medallion of George Washington. It was dug up at Fredericksburg, Virginia from the camp site of the Army of the Potomac, winter of 1862-63. The pipe stem is broken off.

Marius B. Peladeau

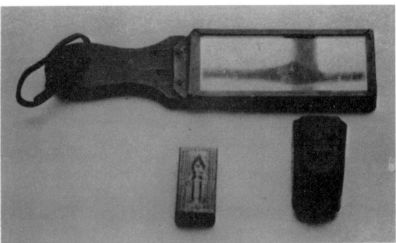

ANDERSONVILLE RELICS: This grouping of relics of Andersonville prison came from Post 55, the Stanton Post of the GAR in Los Angeles, California. Among the relics here is a thin piece of the Andersonville stockade and a large piece of wood from the "Dead Line."

Bill and Sue Coleman

SPENCER CARBINE (C.S. USED): Shown here is one of the 94,196 Spencer carbines bought by the U.S. during the War. This specimen — Serial Number 25565 — was captured from one of Kilpatrick's cavalrymen near Union, South Carolina during Sherman's campaign around Columbia. Carved on the left side of the butt is:

A. Jones S.C.

The Spencer, patented in 1860, was one of the first successful breech-loading carbines. Its use on the battlefield was often the turning point of the fire fight.

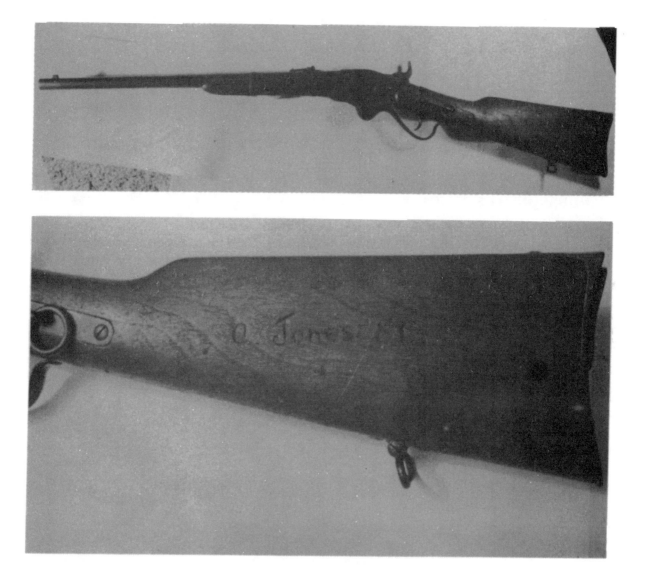

SPY COMPANY (no picture): Both sides had their "spy companies", units composed of daring volunteers who risked their lives again and again in getting information behind the enemy's lines.

In February 1863, Colonel George H. Sharpe, 120th New York Infantry was appointed to Hooker's staff to head up the intelligence gathering efforts of the Army of the Potomac. And in the Shenandoah Valley the name of Major Henry Young became a household word. Opposing the Federals were such men as McNeill, Gilmor, and the legendary, elusive, Mosby.

One of the most famous units was the "Jessie Scouts," which originally served under Fremont in the West who named them in honor of his wife. These scouts were transferred to Sigel in the Shenandoah Valley and performed especially effectively at Second Bull Run. A man named Captain Grenewald of York, Pennsylvania was chief of the Jessie Scouts in West Virginia, and of the "Grey Eagle Scouts" in the Valley under Milroy. In July 1863, the captain and some of his men succeeded at Falling Waters, Virginia, in destroying a pontoon bridge, and capturing part of Lee's wagon train in retreat from Gettysburg.

Long after the Jessie Scouts had left the Shenandoah Valley their name became a general term used by civilians and soldiers alike to be attached to the Federal scouts who wore gray uniforms and risked their lives behind Confederate lines. Little is known of their accomplishments (and their fatal mistakes) since they left no written record.

The Confederates, too, had their daring scouts. And we know of one of these "spy companies." This unit was raised in Fayetteville, Arkansas. It was organized as a cavalry unit, armed with shotguns. While serving under its commander, Captain A. V. Reiff, it provided information which saved the Confederates from defeat at Oak Hill.

Life for these scouts who wore the uniform of their adversary was hazardous in the extreme. Discovery meant death. For example, shortly before Gettysburg, a spy was hanged by General Kilpatrick. Men of the 151st New York Infantry had seen this spy in their camp a few days before, disguised as a peddler. In a false bottom of the peddler's tin cup were found plans of the camp.

STENCILS, IDENTIFICATION DISCS AND BADGES: This grouping emphasizes some of the means by which soldiers could identify their property and themselves. The top two items comprise a stencil kit and stencil belonging to Captain Augustine W. Clough, Co. "H" 13th Maine Infantry. The stencil kit consists of the inkwell and a japanned tin container, the stencil is 7" by 1¾".

The second stencil is lead-backed, 4½" by 1¾" and belonged to E. A. Healey, Co. "C" 48th Massachusetts Infantry. This regiment served in the siege of Port Hudson.

The third stencil belonged to A. J. Eggleston, Battery "M" 2nd Pennsylvania Artillery. He enlisted July 28, 1862 and was discharged for disability January 22, 1865. The stencil measures 3½" by 1¼".

The fourth stencil is only 2½" by 1¼" in size. It belonged to M. L. Plummer, Co. "C" 19th Maine Infantry. He enlisted August 25, 1862 and was discharged June 7, 1865. His regiment helped repel Pickett's charge at Gettysburg.

The brass identification disc (left side, top) was worn by Thomas A. Davis, Co. "D" 41st Massachusetts Infantry. This has the Lincoln motif with the words "War of 1861, Abraham Lincoln President, U.S." encircling the President's profile view.

Beneath this disc is a shield-shaped identification badge with embossed eagle and crossed flags over:

> Sergt. J. H. Beckman
> Co. E 91st Ind. Vol.

The disc on the right side of the photograph belonged to "Wm K. Hastings, Co. H. 62 P.V." The motif on the disc is a shield surrounded by "the Union and the Constitution, War of 1861." Directly underneath the shield is "age 19 years," Hastings' age at the time of his enlistment. He was killed at Cold Harbor, June 3, 1864.

The inscribed Maltese cross (5th Army Corps) belonged to George Larkin, Co. "B" 191st Pennsylvania Infantry.

Gary Wolfer
(Photographed by Glenn Riegel,
Andy D'Angelo Photography, Reading, Pa.)

STENCIL: This brass stencil looks as if it had been recovered from a battlefield or camp site. (In fact, a substantial number of the stencils now existing were from camps, routes of march or battle sites.) This stencil was the property of Private Charles W. McGregor. He was born August 20, 1835 and enlisted August 14, 1862, at Madison Barracks, Sacketts Harbor, New York. McGregor was discharged June 24, 1865 at Harpers Ferry, West Virginia. He died April 23, 1913 at the New York State Soldiers and Sailors Home.

Robert G. Borrell, Sr.

STENCIL (Civilian): Although most stencils found in camp sites or on battlefields are military, some also appear which were used by tradesmen and sutlers who followed the armies. Presumably, the one shown here falls into that category. It is quite large for a stencil being 7⅝″ by 2¾″ and is made of thin, stamped brass. It reads:

Louis Postinick
947
Wall St. Mk. Brlyn. N.Y.

The stencil was recovered from the battlefield site of Nashville, Tennessee.

STENCIL: Navy stencil, made of brass, measures 2½" by 1½". The stencil has the sailor's name

O. F. Read

and U.S.N. cut into the brass.

James Stamatelos

STENCIL INK BOTTLE: Here is the type of ink used by the soldier in stenciling his equipment and clothing. Of special interest are the directions printed on the label. The bottle itself is small, 1¾" tall and ¾" in diameter. The original cork is still in the bottle which is dark glass. The original blue label reads: S. M. Spencer's Stencil Indelible Ink.

Directions are to stir ink thoroughly; put a single drop on a bit of glass; work into the brush; lay the stencil on the article with one cloth thickness between the stencil and table, free from starch, sizing, or grease; brush stencil briskly until ink shows through; heat with flat iron or expose to sun; wash in hot soap suds; . . . follow directions.

STIRRUP, C.S.: Among the rare Confederate stirrups are a few with State identification, e.g. TEXAS, etc. Shown here is one used by a North Carolinian. The stirrup is similar in appearance to the "normal" metal stirrup, measuring 5¼" from top to bottom with a width at the bottom of 4¼". Cut out in the bottom of the stirrup is: N. Car:

The stirrup was dug up on a battlefield or camp site but whose location is unknown to the author.

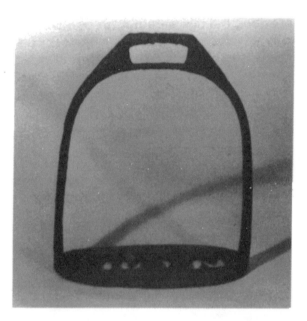

STOCKS: Two leather stocks which were used early in the war are shown here. The wider of the two is of plain leather and issued to enlisted men. The other stock is of fine Russian leather for use by officers. Both buckles have 1855 patent dates.

Marius B. Peladeau

Stocks were issued to soldiers to force them to hold up their heads, and to keep their necks warm. In lieu of stocks the officers were permitted, by regulation, to wear neckties provided the ties were not "to be visible at the opening of the collar." (One may well ask why an officer would wear a tie if it could not be seen!) As for the enlisted men, they solved the problem of discomfort in wearing the "dog collars" by simply throwing them away. After a few weeks' service the stocks were no longer around, thus becoming rare items for the collector.

CAMP STOVE: This stove is probably of Civil War vintage, although stoves of similar design have appeared in post-Civil War times. The stove shown here is oil-burning, 9⅜" high and has a cast iron base. The 4" wick is surrounded by a sheet iron enclosure that acts as a heater. The mica window permitted the use of the stove to see if the wick was lit. Markings:

Union
C.O. & C.G. Co.
Gardiner, Mass. USA

Alan R. McBrayer

SWAMP ANGEL (Parrott Cannon): The Confederates had their "Whistling Dick" of Vicksburg fame (a rifled 18-pounder) while the Federals had their "Swamp Angel" on Morris Island. Both cannon were gaining their reputations in 1863. The "Swamp Angel" an 8-inch Parrott, fired incendiary shells at ranges up to 4½ miles. But it blew up on its 36th round of firing. (See pp. 188-189 of Volume II of the *Encyclopedia* for more details on the "Swamp Angel.")

The gun was put into position later and today can be seen in Cadwallader Park, Trenton, New Jersey. The photographs here were kindly taken in 1974 for "Dewy" Albert — the leading authority on U.S. military buttons until his recent death.

Although the "Swamp Angel" did not function very long, the Parrott cannon proved its worth. For example, a 300-pounder Parrott, weighing 26,000 pounds, threw shells weighing 250 pounds each. In shelling Fort Sumter, one of these huge guns threw 15,000 pounds of metal in one day. A Confederate officer in Fort Sumter (Captain John Johnson) commented on the effect of the projectiles on the Fort. One of the Parrott's shots cracked a massive pier entirely through and partially destroyed it. A series of hits destroyed one entire casemate arch, bringing down the Terreplein with gun, carriage, etc. These arches, built of the best gray brick laid in cement, were 22 inches thick, while on the axis they were 21 feet long.

ARTILLERY OFFICER'S PRESENTATION SWORD: Handsome artillery sword presented by his men to a newly-promoted officer of a heavy artillery regiment. Made by F. Jahn (?) of Philadelphia. The sword is engraved:

Presented to
Lieut. O. J. Smith
by
the members of
Co. E, 2d C.V.A.

The sword was presented in November 1863. Smith was promoted from First Sergeant to Second Lieutenant in the 2nd Connecticut Heavy Artillery. This unit was one of the heavy artillery regiments which Grant assigned to the Army of the Potomac to serve as infantry. It served under Grant at Spotsylvania, Cold Harbor, and Petersburg and then served under Sheridan in the 1864 Shenandoah Valley campaign. Beginning as a private at Bull Run, July 21, 1861, Orlow J. Smith enlisted in the heavy artillery regiment as a first sergeant, July 21, 1862. He was promoted through the various commissioned ranks to a captaincy by the end of the War.

NONCOMMISSIONED OFFICER'S PRESENTATION SWORD: While presentation swords for commissioned officers are relatively common, a presentation NCO sword is very rare. Shown here is a regulation type, 31½" blade marked Ames, and dated 1862. Its interest lies in the inscription:

Sgt. Wm. Doyle

Co. A

9th Ct. Inf.

Reportedly, Doyle was presented with this sword when he was promoted to sergeant. He enlisted from New Haven, Connecticut on September 10, 1861 and was appointed corporal. On January 6, 1864 he re-enlisted as a "veteran" and was promoted to Sergeant July 20, 1864. The 9th Connecticut Infantry served in the Department of the Gulf 1862-1864, and fought under Sheridan in the Shenandoah Valley campaign in the fall of 1864.

CAVALRY SABER (C.S.): This saber was Confederate used and very possibly Confederate assembled. The blade was probably shipped to the South where the remaining parts of the saber were manufactured and the saber assembled. The blade has the logo of J. E. Bleckmann, one of the smaller Solingen, Germany manufacturers at the time of the Civil War (See Vol. II, p. 176 of the *Encyclopedia*). The saber is 40¾" long overall, with a 34¾" curved blade. Markings on the blade are limited to the Bleckmann logo; the scabbard throat has the Roman numeral VIIII. With the throat removed one can see the numeral 28 and a small s. All metal parts of the hilt and pommel are brass and rather crude, showing considerable filing for shaping. The iron scabbard is a wrap-around type brazed at the seam. There are two iron rings on the scabbard and a rather large drag that also indicates considerable filing for shaping.

William F. Marshall

SABER (C.S.) CAVALRY

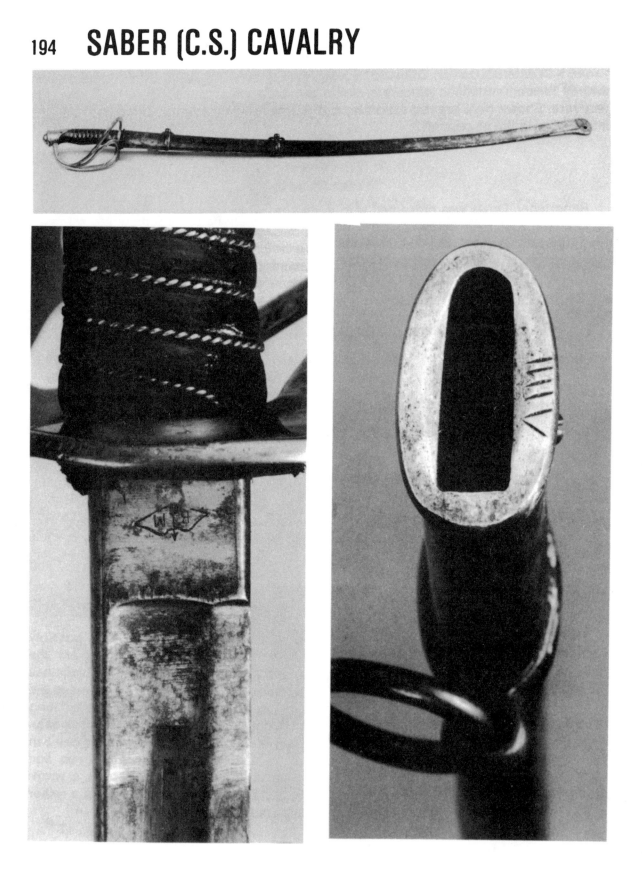

TELEGRAPH SENDING KEY: It is well known that both sides used the telegraph extensively from 1861 to 1865. This kit has the sending key along with other essentials of a sending apparatus — all mounted on a small platform of wood. In faint markings on the platform is the following:

> Ft. Kearney
> U.S.
> 1862
> No. 5

TELESCOPE: This telescope was carried by Captain William Newell, Co. "H" 2nd United States Sharpshooters. (Company "H" was from Vermont.) Newell came from Dorset, Vermont. He enlisted as a sergeant, but was commissioned December 1, 1862 as a Second Lieutenant and then Captain on May 18, 1864. He was discharged for wounds on June 21, 1864.

Marius B. Peladeau

TOBACCO AND SMOKING ACCESSORIES: Tobacco was in great demand by the soldiers of whom a substantial proportion were pipe smokers. Pipes varied from exquisitely carved presentation pieces to the very inexpensive and short-term types like the clay pipes sold by sutlers. The finest specimen of carved pipes the writer has encountered is the presentation pipe pictured on page 200 of Vol. II of this *Encyclopedia* series. The proud owner, Captain John F. Vinal, is shown in the accompanying photograph courtesy of Robert L. Kotchian. Vinal was commissioned Captain of Company "A" 3rd Massachusetts Cavalry, August 23, 1862. He was promoted Major February 1, 1863 and Lieutenant Colonel on September 2, 1864. He resigned August 15, 1865.

Expensive pipes were available only to a few men. Most of the rank and file used the types of clay pipes shown here. But the disproportionately large number of clay pipes in collections can lead to questionable conclusions. Only clay pipes survived decades of exposure to the elements in camp sites and battlefields. The beautiful wooden pipes obviously did not. So we must assume that the proportion of clay pipes to the total used is difficult to establish. This is equally true in the case of glass containers, e.g. bottles, found in camp sites and battlefields. Wood, cardboard and metal containers did not fare as well as those made of glass.

GOVERNMENT TOBACCO RATION: Just before the end of the War the Federal Government decided to assist the enlisted men in the Army to obtain tobacco directly from the Subsistance Department. Thus the outrageous prices demanded by sutlers would be circumvented. Now the Government department charged with feeding the troops would also furnish tobacco at cost prices to the men up to 16 ounces per month for each soldier. The cost of this tobacco would be deducted from the soldier's pay, exactly in the same way his clothing accounts were handled. In a General Order (No. 52) dated March 30, 1865, the War Department announced the new policy. But Lee's surrender a week later made the order obsolete before implementation.

SMOKING KIT: Although similar in design to a smoking kit described on page 166 of Volume IV of the *Encyclopedia*, this kit differs essentially in size and composition. The one shown here is of brass, 5⅛" long and 1¾" wide.

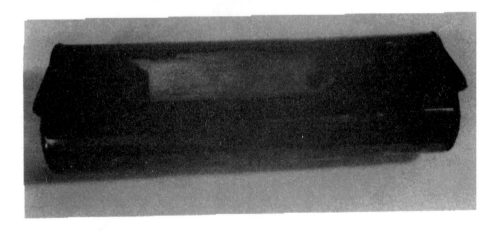

CIGAR CASE: Made of heavy tin for use in the field. Holds four cigars. It is 7" long, 2½" wide and ⅝" in depth. The hinged lid is 5½" long. No markings.

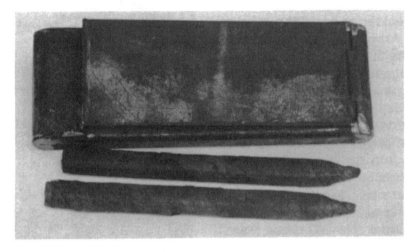

CIGAR CASE: Illustrated here is a photograph of a cigar case and its owner — Lieutenant Robert L. Orr of the 1st Pennsylvania Artillery Regiment.

Kendall B. Mattern

TOBACCO AND SNUFF BOXES: Three interesting boxes — all used during the War — and all of different material. The oval box is of tin 3⅛" long and 2⅛" wide. The top lid is stamped:

USE
P. Lorillard
Century
Fine Cut Chewing
tobacco

The larger rectangular box is of heavy pewter, 3¼" long and 2⅛" wide. The top lid is decorated with a factory building and smoke stack motif, while the bottom of the box is stamped:

DIXON & SON

This is the name of the famed maker of powder flasks. The smaller box is of tortoise shell 2¼" long and 1½" wide. This belonged to a New England family and reportedly was also used in the Revolutionary War.

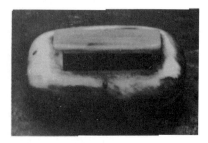

TOBACCO PIPES: Shown here are three pipes used during the War. These three are chosen mainly to illustrate the wide diversity in Civil War pipes both in design and quality. The largest pipe is a handsome, carved specimen very similar to a pipe illustrated on page 199 of Vol. II of this *Encyclopedia* series. The smallest pipe is of hard rubber in the shape of a horse's hoof and was found at Vicksburg in the Confederate lines. The third pipe is of red clay and came from a C.S. camp near Charleston, South Carolina.

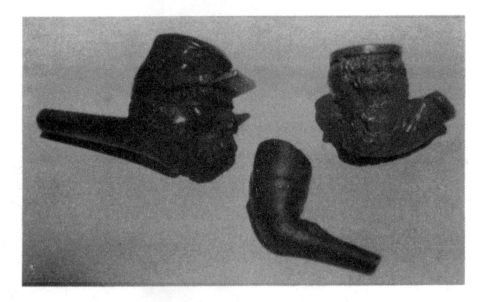

CASED PIPE: In its original, beat-up velvet-lined leather covered case is this Civil War Meerschaum pipe. On both of the brass ferrules are brass, applied eagles. The eagle on the bowl is larger than the one on the stem, but both are finely cast in relief. The pipe was well loved; it is nearly smoked through and the stem nearly worn out by being held between the teeth. A New York City label is inside the case. The pipe came from Maine.

Marius B. Peladeau

PIPE (Hand carved): Much of the leisure time in camp was passed by the soldiers in carving out various items for their own use. One of these items was the tobacco pipe. In general, the carving was pretty good. The example shown here has a hand holding the pipe with a leaf-like pattern overflowing at the top of the bowl. Carved in relief around the bowl is the following identification:

T. Adams, Co. H
3d N.H.V.

The bowl is 2″ in diameter and the overall length of the pipe is 9″.

James Stamatelos

PIPE: This beautiful carved pipe is marked in the velvet of the case:

William Birnbaum
Manufacturer
67 Nassau St. N.Y.
St. John & Maiden Lane

The carved head strongly resembles Phil Kearny. The silver band is engraved with the initials A.P.P. This was Alfred A. Patterson, a seaman by vocation who enlisted age 25 in Co. "L" 28th Maine Infantry on January 2, 1864. He was killed before Petersburg June 18, 1864.

Marius B. Peladeau

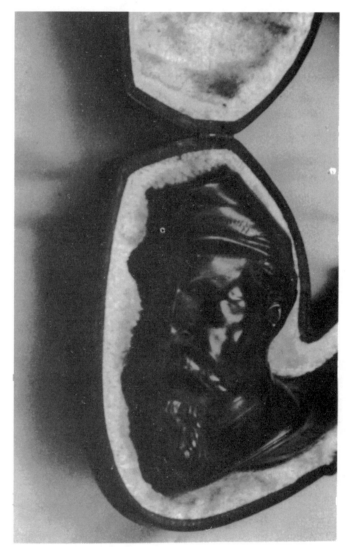

PIPES RECOVERED FROM CAMP SITES AND BATTLEFIELDS:

Left Row (top to bottom): Newmarket, Antietam, Antietam, South Carolina, Port Hudson.

Middle Row (top to bottom): Winchester, September 19, 1864, South Carolina, Vicksburg, Vicksburg, Vicksburg, Vicksburg.

Right Row (top to bottom): Vicksburg, Seige of Savannah, Vicksburg, Seige of Savannah, Atlanta, Fort Ethan Allen, District of Columbia.

Tall Pipe — Port Hudson, Marked: W. O. Bullock
                                        PA. C.S.

TOILET KIT: This "Brooks Patent" toilet kit consists of a tin cylinder 8½" long and 1½" in diameter. The attached oilcloth wrap is waterproofed and measures 8¾" by 11½". Contents include a razor, comb, shaving brush, toothbrush, jackknife, scissors, court plaster, pen, paper, etc. It was carried by Private Gilbert W. Greene, who enlisted at age 18 in Co. "F" 15th Massachusetts Infantry and later served as First Sergeant Co. "C" 4th Massachusetts Cavalry.

James Stamatelos

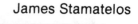

SHAVING KIT: This kit consists of a sailor's handmade razor box (wood) measuring 1¾" wide, 11½" long, and 1" deep, with a swivel lid. On the lid are carved sailing ships. The sailor's initials D. N. are carved on the handle. The kit contains an original razor and shaving brush.

James Stamatelos

RAZOR: This razor has a white bone handle engraved:

Sergt J. Archer
4th N.J. Inf

This razor is 9½″ long when open and 6″ long when closed. It was manufactured by Frederick Renolds, Sheffield, England.

Edmund Girard

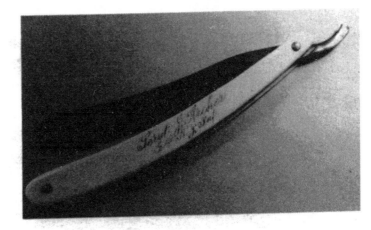

RAZOR STROP: This type of strop was in common use during the War. The overall length is 13¾″ while the strop itself is 9¾″ exclusive of handle. In addition to the patriotic motif (Eagle with E. PLURIBUS UNUM) there is much lettering on both sides of the strop, consisting mainly of warning about imitations and directions for use. The maker was Joseph Emerson of Charlestown, Massachusetts.

SHAVING MIRROR: This type of mirror was widely used throughout the War. Many were imported and sold over here by sutlers and town merchants. The specimen shown here is tin and was made in Paris.

A. Collin MacDonald

RAZORS: Shown here are two unusual razors. The U.S. Navy razor was made by Joseph Allen & Sons, Sheffield, England. The U.S. Cavalry razor was made by Wostenholm & Son.

Marius B. Peladeau

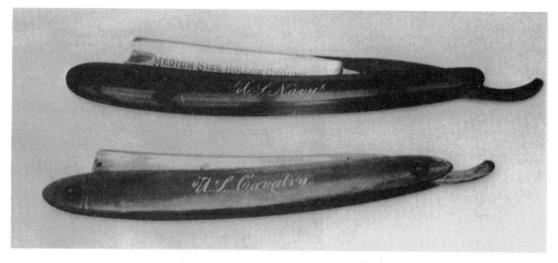

RAZOR (Identified): An identified soldiers' razor is shown here. It is 10¼" in length when open and 6½" when closed. The handle is inscribed:

Co. C 1st Vt Cav

This razor was manufactured by B. Wade and Butcher of Sheffield, England.

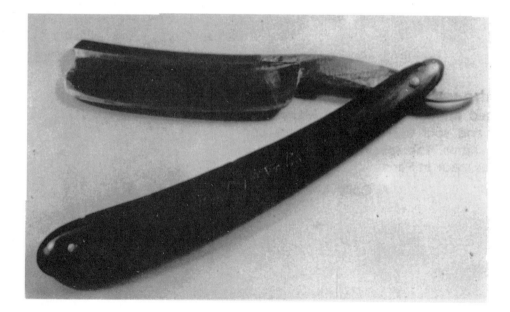

LICE COMB: The comb shown here has been identified as a "lice comb." It is of bone, 3½" long and 1½" wide. The comb was recovered at Harrison's Landing, Virginia.

Bill and Sue Coleman

For a long time these small combs were an enigma to me (and possibly other collectors as well). We now know that lice combs were usually made of metal, e.g. brass, and were used not only in the field but at permanent installations like prison camps where lice tended to flourish. Much confusion has resulted from the fact that mustache combs were small also, and resembled lice combs in appearance. However, mustache combs were *generally* made of hard rubber.

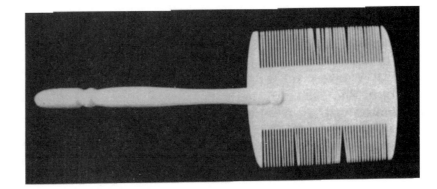

MUSTACHE COMB: This little comb is of ivory — with handle it is 4" long. The comb proper is 1¾" long and 1½" wide.

MUSTACHE COMBS: (Left) The size of the teeth on this comb would indicate that it was to be used on the moustache. It is well made of hard rubber, 3⅞" long and 2⅛" wide at each end. On the front of the comb are the words:

Fine
Peerless
Combs

(Middle) A fine comb made for the officer or soldier who sported a moustache and who intended to keep it in well-groomed shape. The comb is of hard rubber, 2¾" long, 1 9/16" wide and marked:

I. R. Comb Co.
Goodyear 1851

(Right) Most moustache combs were made of hard rubber. However the comb shown here is of hard maple. It is 2¾" long and just 1¼" wide from top of the comb to the bottom of its teeth. All teeth are still there; none are broken or missing.

COMB CASE: Comb cases probably saw only limited use by troops in the field. But this one certainly did; it came from the effects of Dan J. Weaver, sutler of the 3rd Maryland Infantry. The case is 7" tall and 7" wide. It is decorated with an American eagle and shield and the lettering COMBCASE. The 3rd Maryland Infantry served in the 12th Army Corps 1861-1865.

MIRROR (Presentation Scrimshaw): Presentation mirrors are very rare. But a presentation *Scrimshaw* mirror of the Civil War is at least little short of a miracle in the writer's opinion. The term Scrimshaw applies to carved or engraved articles but for Americans is usually restricted to whalebone or ivory items made by American whalers. The engraving on this "one of a kind" item is clearly shown on the accompanying photographs. It was presented to a R. D. Cox by the men of Battery "C" 1st U.S. Artillery.

Robert G. Borrell, Sr.

TOMPION: Here is another example of the Civil War soldier's ingenuity in coming up with workable substitutes for equipment items. In this case it is a tompion made from a carved piece of wood capped with a cartridge case. The total length is 2⅛". Picked up on the Wilderness battlefield.

Bill and Sue Coleman

BROADAXE (C.S.): The broadaxe shown here is of very special interest. It was used by C.S. engineers and is so marked. The axe itself, has a blade 11″ in length and a 37″ hickory handle. One side of the axe head is flat (for hewing), the other side is beveled (for splitting or chopping). The flat side has the following stamped markings:

(Note: The first "A" in "ALA" has been almost entirely obliterated, and it could possibly read 4th LA.)

Nashville
Plow Works
C.S. Eng.s 1862
4th ALA

The beveled side is stamped: 72.

Don Kent

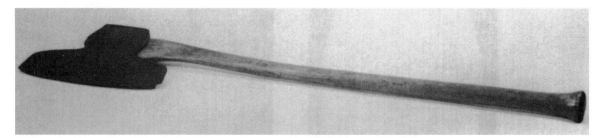

TOOLS: Shown here are examples of tools extensively in use throughout the War. The long chisel, 6½", came from the C.S. arsenal at Augusta, Georgia. The shorter chisel, 6¼", originally had a wooden handle. It was used in making wagon wheels and came from Shiloh. The other three tools in this grouping were used by farriers (blacksmiths) on the field. The thin-handled hammer is marked U.S. — is 10" long and came from Grierson's camp at La Grange, Tennessee. The nail snippers, 5¼" long, came from a North Carolina cavalry camp. The other farrier's item was found in a cavalry camp site of the Atlanta campaign.

TOOLS (C.S.): Confederate-marked tools are extremely rare. Shown here are two tools, both with a Confederate association. The wooden mallet is marked CSN and may well have seen service on some Confederate war vessel. It was found in an antique shop in Manistee, Michigan. Manistee was a busy lumber port in the latter half of the 19th Century. The monkey wrench is identical to one which was found when the C.S. IRONSIDES at the C.S. Navy Museum, Columbus, Georgia, was raised. This particular monkey wrench was found in an antique shop in Columbus, Georgia. The Columbus Iron Works built blockade runners and even issued their own C.S. currency.

Larry Jarvinen

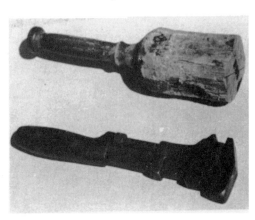

HATCHET (C.S.): Found in a C.S. fort on Cowpaster River, Virginia. This fort, established to guard a railroad bridge, was burned by a U.S. cavalry unit. The hatchet was found in some rocks at the fort. The hatchet has a 4″ cutting blade; the hammer side is 2″ long. The handle is a replacement.

J. L. Downey

HATCHET: A hatchet has been found on the Chancellorsville battlefield with the markings:

Tho's T. Potson
Sheffield
2

This hatchet was very probably imported by the Confederacy since the North had many excellent manufacturers of edged tools.

Kendall B. Mattern

TRUNK: This officer's trunk was used by Assistant Sergeon J. A. Richey, 83rd Pennsylvania Infantry. He enlisted November 6, 1863 and was discharged on surgeon's certificate of disability on October 24, 1864. Of special interest is the Adams Express Company label for transmitting the trunk to Philadelphia from Fortress Monroe.

Kendall B. Mattern

UTILITY BOX (U.S. Navy): This canvas-covered utility box came from the U.S.S. *MIAMI.* The box has a metal latch and measures 8″×12″ and is 3″ deep. It is stenciled USS *MIAMI* as shown in the photograph.

Martin J. Fowler

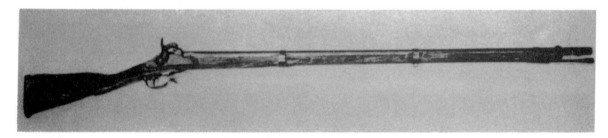

VIRGINIA MILITARY INSTITUTE MUSKET: This model 1851 cadet Springfield musket was recently recovered from the Maury River, southeast of Lexington, Virginia. It was one of 300 cadet Springfields ordered to be sent to the VMI in 1850 by President Zachary Taylor. The cadets had impressed the President with their marching skills during a visit to Richmond. He rewarded the young soldiers with the newly designed cadet muskets.

When General David Hunter's troops closed upon Lexington in June of 1864, the muskets, along with other items, were loaded onto barges to be floated by canal to Lynchburg. Seven miles below Lexington Federal Cavalry came upon the flotilla. The cadets threw the muskets into the river to avoid capture.

Keith Gibson
VMI Museum

WALLET: This Confederate wallet is of brown leather, 7¼" by 3¼" when closed and 7¼" by 6½" when open. A 1-inch leather strap keeps the wallet closed. Carried by:

Solomon Dunham (?)
Hancock, Virginia

Samuel B. Padgett

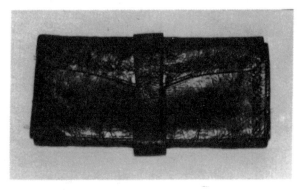

WALLET AND MISCELLANY: The leather wallet shown here, including the carved object, stencil and jackknife were carried by Daniel N. Neal of New Sharon, Maine. He enlisted as private in Co. "E" 15th Maine Infantry on December 11, 1861. He was 19 years old and a farmer by vocation. He was mustered out January 19, 1865. The knife is marked Jos. Rogers & Sons and has stag handles. The stencil is marked D. N. Neal.

Marius B. Peladeau

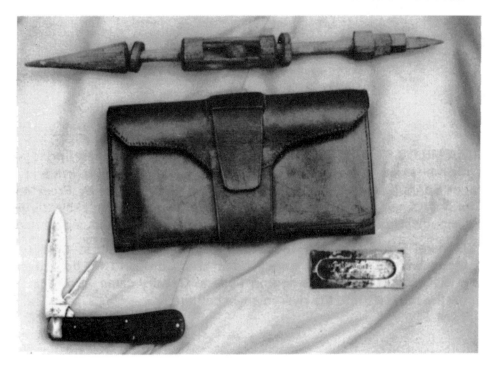

WATCH CHAIN: This unique chain of ivory, or possibly bone, is 9¼″ long overall. The heart-shaped ornament at the end has as its center the word WAR in script letters. This watch chain was dug up at Fredericksburg.

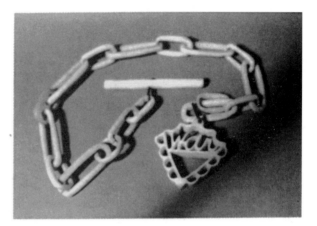

WATCH FOB: Although watch chains were worn most often with the watches of the Civil War period, it is known that watch fobs also were worn. Shown here is a watch fob worn by Private T. Williams of the 1st Maine Infantry. His initial W is on one side and the badge of the 24th Army Corps on the other. Since the 1st Maine Infantry was not in the 24th Corps then it follows that Private Williams was transferred to a regiment that *was* in the 24th Corps or he belonged to another regiment in the first place. The black leather fob strap is 3½″ long and carries a brass fob tip only ¾″ long.

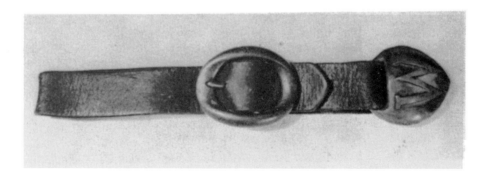

WATCH: This silver hunting cased watch and chain were carried by Sergeant E. S. Gould, Co. "H" 5th New Hampshire Infantry and is so inscribed on the font cover. The watch case is 2″ in diameter and the chain, also of silver, is 15″ long. Marked on inside the case.

Made for H. P. Hendrick
Nashua, N.H.
by Paul Breton, Geneva
#47669

Sergeant Emery S. Gould enlisted at age 25 from Winchester, N.H. on October 23, 1861 and was discharged for disability on February 5, 1863.

James Stamatelos

WEIGHING SCALES. Two examples of scales are shown here. One from the Western Theater of War (Shiloh), the other from the Eastern Theater (Coggins Point, Virginia). The Shiloh scales have lost their hooks; the "body" of the scales is 6″ long. These scales were probably used by a sutler to weigh his wares. In fact, the scales shown here are very similar to those we used to see in local grocery stores fifty years ago. On one side of the face of the scales are numbers 0 to 24, that is 0, 4, 8, 12, 16, 20, 24). At the top of the scales is a spread eagle and the words:

Warranted
Ballance

"Ballance" is an archaic spelling of "Balance".

The other scales shown here are about the same size as the "Shiloh" scales and generally similar in design and appearance. However, these scales are marked:

Foster's Improved Spring Balance
Warranted

They were dug in the Confederate Commissary Depot established in Prince George County after Wade Hampton's cattle raid of over 2,000 cattle at Coggin's Point, Virginia. This Commissary Depot was set up to slaughter and weigh this "captured" beef for General Lee's hungry army.

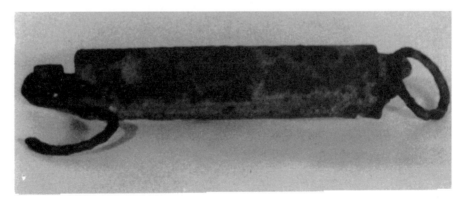

WHISTLE: Probably made by a soldier to pass the long hours in winter camp, this whistle has four holes in it. It is made of hard wood, 3½" long and 2½" wide. Carved on the bottom of the whistle is:

C (?)

WILLARD'S HOTEL MENU: During the War Washington was "the heartbeat of the nation" and Willard's Hotel was a central meeting place in the city. As the most famous of all the city's hotels it was frequented by political leaders, business men, contractors for military and naval supplies, among others. In addition, those officers and men who could afford to pay the prices would gather there as a welcome change from the drab conditions in camp.

Shown here is a menu of July 5, 1862, both front and back of the menu are shown. Although "Bobby Lee" had just defeated McClellan's attempt to take Richmond, good food was the order of the day!

Michael Hammerson

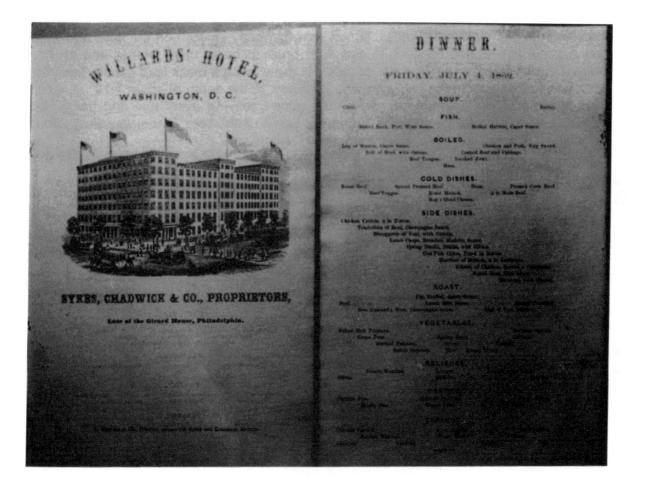

WOODCUT: During the War both the troops at the front and the folks at home eagerly awaited the latest issues of Frank Leslie's and Harper's illustrated weeklies. These weeklies owed much of their popularity to their illustrated material furnished by "artists at the front." This illustrated material was made available by wood cuts, such as the one shown in the accompanying photograph. Wood cuts were used in wood engraving for the newspapers' illustrations. A block of box-wood, or several pieces screwed or tongued together, was used. It was usually necessary to link several pieces together since the wood was cut across the grain and large pieces were not easily procured. These wood blocks, about one inch in thickness, at first were perfectly smooth on the face; and were then rubbed with a little flake-white and Bath brick to make them whitish and slightly rough. On this prepared surface the design was drawn with a black lead pencil. Then the block was turned over to the engraver who cut away, to the depth of about 1/20" all those parts which had not been blackened by the pencil, leaving every line and dot of the drawing projected, thus serving as a "stamp" or type to print from. In this way illustrations for newspapers and "weeklies" were prepared.

Elisha Noyce, *The Boy's Book of*
Industrial Information 1859. pp. 134-5

The specimen shown here is 3½" by 6" in size. It is in 3 sections. Marked on the back: 727

Kendall B. Mattern

WRITING KIT: This kit is of neo-classical design and made of gutta percha. It is inlaid with pewter scroll work. It measures 5½″ by 3½″. The kit has a pink silk lining and consists of a small notebook with lined paper and a pencil holder.

Markings: Brevete S.G.D.G.

Alan R. McBrayer

INKWELL AND PEN. The inkwell is made of LIGNUM VITAE, an extremely hard wood, and is designed to resemble a miniature barrel. This was a popular style during the Civil War period. The pen is also of the same material. Dimensions of the inkwell are 2⅛″ tall with a diameter of 1⅜″. The pen is 5½″ long.

Alan R. McBrayer

WRITING EQUIPMENT

INK WELL: This ink well was taken from the Adjutant General's Office of the Confederate forces in Fairfax Court House, Virginia, July 17, 1861.

Kendall B. Mattern

INK BOTTLES: Ink containers like this one have been recovered in large numbers from the Civil War sites. This example is of interest in that it has the original paper label still on the bottle. The bottle is octagonal in shape, of a bluish-tinted glass, 2½″ tall and 2⅜″ in diameter at the base.

Shown beside the bottle is one identical in size and shape except that this one is made of colorless glass instead of the bluish-tint. This second bottle was found in the C.S. lines at Fredericksburg, Virginia, on October 20, 1964. Collectors will recognize at once this type of ink bottle which has been found in substantial numbers on Civil War sites.

WRITING PEN: Letter writing and diary keeping were very extensively indulged in throughout the War by both sides. A much appreciated gift to the man going off to war was the "metallic pen." That many of these pens were carried is attested to by the specimens, either complete or in fragments, which have been found on battlefields and camp sites. The one shown here is 5¾" long. The box is 7½" long, 2½" wide and 1" deep. The box is marked:

Bestor's Golden Metallic Pen
S. J. Bestor
Original Inventor
and sole managing agent for their
manufacturing and sale
Hartford, Conn.

Bill and Sue Coleman

NOTE PAPER AND ENVELOPE: This little note is illustrative of a common method of exchanging ideas informally while at the front. The commander of the 54th Massachusetts Infantry on Morris Island, South Carolina, was Colonel E. N. Hallowell. Troubled with diarrhea, this officer received fruit from one of his lieutenants and thanked him in the note shown here. First Lieutenant Charles M. Duren rose from the ranks to become a commissioned officer in the 54th Massachusetts Infantry (a black regiment). Lieutenant Duren was discharged for disability on May 15, 1865. The notepaper is 7" by 4½". The initials are embossed.

PATRIOTIC ENVELOPE (Zouave Regiment): This is an example of the type of envelopes used by soldiers when sending mail. It was sent by a member of Company "F" 9th New York Infantry, famous in the War as "Hawkins Zouaves." Many regiments had their own envelopes, purchased from sutlers and sent home with pride.

Martin J. Fowler

ZOUAVE MANUAL: This is the cover of *The Zouave Drill* manual written by Colonel Elmer E. Ellsworth, the first Northerner killed in the War. The manual consists of four pages and was printed in Philadelphia 1861. The manual also contains a short biography of the youthful Ellsworth who fell at the Marshall House in Alexandria, Virginia, pulling down a Confederate Flag.

Martin J. Fowler

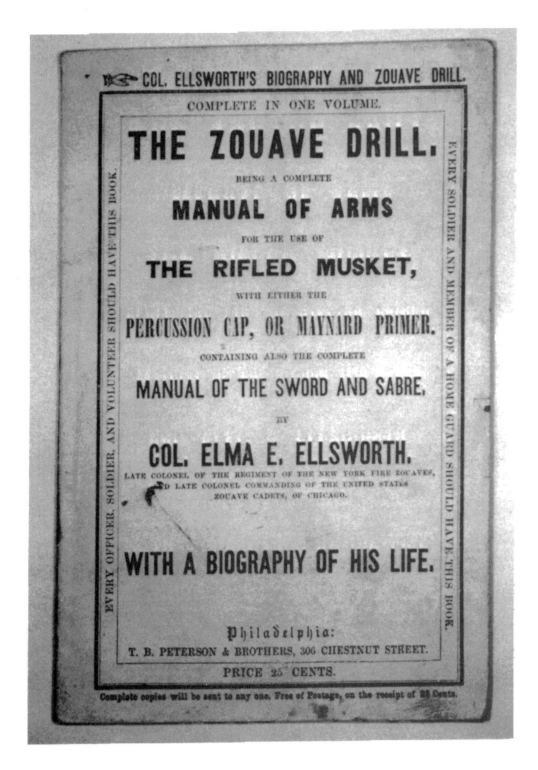

COL. ELLSWORTH'S BIOGRAPHY AND ZOUAVE DRILL.

COMPLETE IN ONE VOLUME.

THE ZOUAVE DRILL.

BEING A COMPLETE

MANUAL OF ARMS

FOR THE USE OF

THE RIFLED MUSKET,

WITH EITHER THE

PERCUSSION CAP, OR MAYNARD PRIMER.

CONTAINING ALSO THE COMPLETE

MANUAL OF THE SWORD AND SABRE,

BY

COL. ELMA E. ELLSWORTH.

LATE COLONEL OF THE REGIMENT OF THE NEW YORK FIRE ZOUAVES,
AND LATE COLONEL COMMANDING OF THE UNITED STATES
ZOUAVE CADETS, OF CHICAGO.

WITH A BIOGRAPHY OF HIS LIFE.

Philadelphia:
T. B. PETERSON & BROTHERS, 306 CHESTNUT STREET.

PRICE 25 CENTS.

Complete copies will be sent to any one, Free of Postage, on the receipt of 25 Cents.

EVERY OFFICER, SOLDIER, AND VOLUNTEER SHOULD HAVE THIS BOOK.

EVERY SOLDIER AND MEMBER OF A HOME GUARD SHOULD HAVE THIS BOOK.

BIBLIOGRAPHY

(ANONYMOUS)
  The Bivouac, Vol. I, Boston, 1883

BARTLETT, A. W.
  History of the Twelfth Regiment New Hampshire Volunteers, Concord, N.H. 1897

BOYLE, JOHN RICHARDS
  Soldiers True (111th Pennsylvania Infantry), New York, 1903

BRAINARD, MARY G. G.
  Campaigns of the One Hundred and Forty-Sixth Regiment New York State Volunteers, New York, 1915

CADWELL, CHARLES K.
  The Old Sixth Regiment (6th Connecticut Infantry), New Haven, 1875

COLLINS, GEORGE C.
  Memoirs of the 149th Regt. N.Y. Vol. Inf. Syracuse, N.Y. 1891

CROWNINGSHIELD, B. W.
  A History of the First Regiment of Massachusetts Cavalry Volunteers, Boston, 1891

DICKENS, CHARLES (ED.)
  All the Year Round, No. 160, (May 17, 1862), London, 1862

FLOYD, FREDERICK CLARK
  History of the Fortieth (Mozart) Regiment New York Volunteers, Boston, 1909

FORCE, MANNING F.
  "Personal Recollections of the Vicksburg Campaign" in *Sketches of War History* (Ohio Commandery, Order of the Loyal Legion of the U.S.), Vol. I, Cincinnati, Ohio, 1888

GERRISH, THEODORE AND JOHN S. HUTCHINSON
  The Blue and The Gray, Portland, Maine, 1883

HANABURGH, D. H.
  History of the One Hundred and Twenty-Eighth . . . New York Volunteers, Poughkeepsie, N.Y. 1894

HAYNES, MARTIN A.
  History of the Second Regiment New Hampshire Volunteers, Manchester, N.H. 1865

KING, W. C. AND W. P. DERBY
  Camp-Fire Sketches and Battlefield Echoes, Springfield, Mass. 1888

LINCOLN, WILLIAM S.
  Life with the Thirty-Fourth Mass. Infantry, Worcester, Mass. 1872

MARK, PENROSE G.
Red, White and Blue Badge (93rd Pennsylvania Infantry), (N.P.) 1911

McKEE, JAMES HARVEY
In War Times, (history of the 144th New York Infantry), (N.P.) 1903

NOYCE, ELISHA
The Boy's Book of Industrial Information, New York, 1859

PAGE, CHARLES A.
Letters of a War Correspondent (James R. Gilmore, editor), Boston, 1899

PARKER, THOMAS H.
History of the 51st Regiment of Pennsylvania Volunteers, Philadelphia, 1869

PROWELL, GEORGE R.
History of the Eighty-seventh Regiment Pennsylvania Volunteers, York, Pa. 1901

STANYAN, JOHN M.
History of the 8th N.H. Volunteers, Concord, N.H. 1892

TILNEY, ROBERT
My Life in the Army, Philadelphia, 1912

TOURGEE, ALBION W.
The Story of a Thousand (History of the 105th Ohio Infantry), Buffalo, N.Y. 1896

VAIL, ENOS BALLARD
Reminiscences of a Boy in the Civil War, Brooklyn, N.Y. 1915

VALENTINE, HERBERT E.
Story of Co. F 23rd Massachusetts Volunteers, Boston, 1896

WALKLEY, STEPHEN
History of the Seventh Connecticut Volunteer Infantry . . . 1861-1865, Southington, Conn. 1905

WARD, GEORGE W.
History of the Second Pennsylvania Veteran Heavy Artillery (revised), Philadelphia, 1904

WARE, E. F.
The Lyon Campaign in Missouri, (1st Iowa Infantry) Topeka, Kansas 1907

WILLSON, ARABELLA M.
Disaster, Struggle, Triumph (126th New York Infantry), Albany, N.Y. 1870

WOODWARD, E. M.
History of the Third Pennsylvania Reserve, Trenton, N.J. 1883

INDEX

TO VOLUMES I - V

C

Q

R

S

T